The Exodus & Beyond

Book II of UNLOCKING THE DREAM VISION

The Exodus & Beyond

Book II of UNLOCKING THE DREAM VISION

By R.J. VON-BRUENING

The Exodus & Beyond
Book II of Unlocking the Dream Vision
Copyright © 2021 by R.J. von-Bruening. All rights reserved.

Scripture quotations are taken from the Holy Bible, King James Version, Cambridge, 1769. Used by permission. All rights reserved.

Book design; Copyright © 2021 by R.J. von-Bruening. All rights reserved.
Cover design by R.J. von-Bruening
Illustrations by R.J. von-Bruening
Interior design by R.J. von-Bruening.

ISBN-13: 978-1-7329096-4-9

1. World History
2. Religion

Table of Contents

Introduction

To all those who seek the knowledge hidden within the mysterious esoteric symbolism, I bid you welcome to the second book of UNLOCKING THE DREAM VISION. Within the following pages we will discover the hidden secrets and the forgotten history of the great Exodus out of Egypt, in the process, we will also go far beyond what is traditionally believed or found in the biblical story.

It should be noted that it is necessary and highly recommended that you have read the first book UNLOCKING THE DREAM VISION: The secret history of creation. The following information can only be properly understood if you are aware of the secret history of creation that is hidden within the esoteric symbolism.

In this part of our journey, we will explore in detail the mysterious twin brothers that continued the great Exodus after the deaths of Moses and Aaron that we first encountered in the Dream Vision of Enoch and revealed in the verse:

'And I saw till they left off crying for that sheep and crossed that stream of water, and there arose the two sheep as leaders in the place of those which had led them and fallen asleep [lit. 'had fallen asleep and led them'].'
(Book of Enoch, 89:39)

As we will discover, these few unassuming lines from the Dream Vision found deep within the Book of Enoch will reveal an astounding series of events that will completely change our understanding of the great Exodus out of Egypt. It will also answer the great mystery of why all the different ancient cultures worldwide all have the same architecture style, gods, iconography, mythology, and the same polytheistic religious structure built around the complete devotion and sacrifice to the gods in a way never imagined before.

1

Chapter 1

Understanding the Esoteric Timeline

Before we can begin our journey into the Exodus, we must first fully understand the esoteric timeline we first discovered in "Unlocking the Dream Vision, The secret history of creation." During this process, we will expand upon and reconcile this highly radical timeline with the accepted traditional historical timeline we are all familiar with.

Our starting point is to understand that the accepted historical timeline was initially conceived of and imposed by the learned fathers of the early Catholic Church. This change enabled the Catholic Church to take the 36,525-year long history of ancient Egypt and fit it into their biblical interpretation that the world was only six thousand years old. To overcome this little dating 'problem,' the learned fathers of the early Catholic Church adopted the inspired solution from the Christian scholar Eusebius (260-265 to 339-340 AD); whereby he proposed that "*The year I take to be a lunar one, consisting, that is, of 30 days: what we now call a month the Egyptians used formerly to a year...*" This allowed Eusebius to take 36,525 years of Egyptian history as recorded by Egyptian historian Manetho and realign it with the Catholic Church's interpretation that the world was only six thousand years old, by simply dividing it by 13. Furthermore, this little sleight-of-hand has been going on ever since. [1]

While this gives us a basic idea of how this change was instituted by the Catholic Church, it is slightly more complicated in actual practice. Because if we take the accepted historical timeline and multiply it by thirteen, we will rapidly discover that it only appears to work for some dates and not for others. This anomaly occurs due to Eusebius basing his timeline around four critical historical events with an esoteric understanding of the Exodus. By examining each of these four events, we will begin to understand how the fathers of the early Catholic Church put this into practice and, more importantly, how this esoteric timeline is connected to the accepted historical timeline.

The first of these four events was the great Exodus out of Egypt by the Israelites. The second was when Enoch was taken away from the generations of the Earth and the destruction of King Solomon's Temple that followed shortly afterward. The third event is the crucifixion of Jesus Christ. With the fourth being the reign of Justinian I from 527 to 565 AD with his revival of Roman Law. The final piece of the puzzle, the esoteric knowledge of the Exodus, will be explored further as we examine the other events.

To understand how the learned fathers of the early Catholic Church changed the timeline, we must first start with the accepted historical timeline for the destruction of King Solomon's Temple and the Babylonian captivity of the Israelites, which is believed to have occurred at about 587 BC or 586 BC. However, as we discovered in our journey through the Dream Vision of Enoch, the event of Enoch being taken away from the generations of the Earth and the destruction of King Solomon's Temple occurred at approximately 14,415 BC. Additionally, we also discovered that the great Exodus out of Egypt occurred almost 18,000 years earlier around 32,000 BC. Now, if we take these two radical dates and divide them by thirteen and compare them to the accepted timeline, we will discover that they still do not work out correctly. The reason why this does not work is because we still lack a small but highly critical piece of esoteric knowledge about the great Exodus out of Egypt that is not known or even suspected by the general public.

This missing piece of knowledge is a radically different interpretation of the Israelites' 40-year journey through the wilderness after they refused to cross Jordan into the promised Land of Canaan. This radically different esoteric interpretation is that the forty years of the Israelites wandering the wilderness recorded in the biblical story in reality represents forty generations. That might seem like quite a leap for many, but as we have already learned from our journey through the Dream Vison of Enoch, the biblical story has been edited with numerous books completely removed or radically changed to fit different political or religious viewpoints over the centuries. Additionally, we have also learned that such a small change could significantly impact our overall understanding of the entire story. In this particular case, it will allow us to begin

4

reconciling this radical esoteric timeline with the more accepted historical timeline.

Our next step in understanding this esoteric interpretation that "*the forty years of the Israelites wandering in the wilderness*" represents forty generations is to figure out how long each generation lived. To answer this question, we need only to return to the biblical story of Abraham and his descendants that is contained within the Book of Genesis. Within the story of Abraham, we discover that Abraham and his descendants are said to have lived approximately one-hundred-and-forty years. This small, but critical piece of information will allow us to start learning how the Christian scholar Eusebius came to his "*inspired solution.*"

Our next set of steps is to return to the esoteric dates of 32,000 BC for the Exodus and 14,415 BC for when Enoch was taken away from the generations of the Earth and the destruction of King Solomon's Temple. If we take our new found esoteric knowledge that the journey of the Israelites wandering through the wilderness was forty generations; with each generation being hundred-and-forty-years long and multiply them together, we will get a total of 5,600 years (40x140= 5,600). The next step in this process is to take this number and subtract it from the esoteric start date of the great Exodus out of Egypt at 32,000 BC, which will give us a date of 26,400 BC (32,000-5,600= 26,400). The next step is to then subtract the date of Enoch when taken away and the destruction of King Solomon's Temple at 14,414 BC from 26,400, this then gives us 11,985 years (26,400-14,415= 11,985).

This number of 11,985 is the all-important number that we take and divide by thirteen, which then gives us 922 years (11,985/13= 922). This 922, is the number that allowed Eusebius to create his inspired solution. To understand what Eusebius did next, all we must do is take 922 and add it to the accepted historical date of destruction of the King Solomon's Temple of 587 BC. This then gives us a date of 1509 BC (578+922= 1,509). The final step is to then add the forty years of wandering the wilderness in the traditional Exodus story in the Bible, which then provides us with a date of 1549 BC (1,509+40= 1,549).

This date of 1549 BC is the generally accepted historical date given for the end of the Second Intermediate Period and the beginning of the New Kingdom in Egypt with the 18th Dynasty that began with the Hyksos' expulsion. This is also remarkably close to the accepted time of the rule of Amenhotep IV, better known as Akhenaten, the heretic Pharaoh. The date of 1549 BC is also about the same time that modern scholars place the Mycenaean civilization at its height. It is also the time that King Cecrops I of Greece either builds or rebuilds Athens, following the great flood of Deucalion, which, according to mythology, helped

5

bring an end to the Silver age in Greece. King Cecrops I became the first of several Kings of Athens whose life is considered part of Greek mythology.

The next step in this process is to realize that the early learned fathers of the Catholic Church were fully aware that approximately 14,415 years had passed since the destruction of the First Temple until their own time, which was around sixteen-hundred-years ago by our modern calendar. This is the next critical piece of information that allows us to understand how Eusebius reconstructed the esoteric timeline to fit into the Catholic Church's belief that the Earth is only six-thousand-years old. If we divide 14,415 by 13, it gives us the number 1,109 (14,415/13= 1,109). If take this number and add it to the traditional historical date of 587 BC for the destruction of the First Temple, we end up with 522 AD. Remarkably, this date is within five years of the modern accepted historical date of the first year of Emperor Justinian I's rule, believed to have been between 527 AD to 565 AD. What makes this timeframe so important is that Emperor Justinian sought to revive the Roman Empire's imperial greatness and reconquered much of the lost western half of the Roman Empire during this time period.

Historians typically view Justinian's rule as a distinct epoch in the history of the late Roman Empire and the beginning of Byzantine civilization. His reign was marked by the ambitious, but ultimately only partly realized "*renovatio imperii*" or "*restoration of the Empire*." Justinian was unsuccessful in his grand ambitions to return the Roman Empire to its former glory. However, he was successful in Byzantine culture's great blossoming, and he also launched a significant building program that yielded such masterpieces as the Church of Hagia Sophia in modern-day Istanbul, Turkey. [2]

Although Justinian is usually best known for his grand building projects trying to realize his dream of restoring the Roman Empire. He actually left a much more incredible legacy that still impacts our modern world to this day. This aspect of his legacy was that he began the uniform rewriting and codifying of all Roman law. This effort resulted in the excellent legal work known as the "*Corpus Juris Civilis*," or "*Body of Civil Law*" which still provides the foundation of civil law for many modern states. More significantly, it provided the fundamental legal framework that was to become the basis for creating the earliest kingdoms in Europe that would later grow into the many different peoples, cultures, and nation-states of modern-day Europe. [3]

This piece of information allows us to understand that the estimated 'rebirth' of the last major religion of the Lord-God faction that we explored during our first journey through the Dream Vision of Enoch, must also be closely related to Justinian's rule and the rebirth of Roman Law. It also allows us to realize that

Justinian's reign is the real cut-off point between the ancient and modern world and when this new historical timeline created by Eusebius was instituted by the Catholic Church. It is also the point in history whereby the learned fathers of the early Catholic Church quietly hid from the world the long forgotten ten-thousand-year history of a great Dark Age that befell humanity that occurred after the terrible destruction of the Heaven and the horrors of the final battles that are remembered as the End Times or End of Days that led to the great transformation.

The final piece of this dating puzzle is the death of Jesus Christ. The dating of this all-important event was handled quite differently from the rest of the timeline. In that, it was simply placed five-hundred years before the rule of Justinian. The reason for this appears to have directly related to the Millennialism and Apocalyptic thought that consumed much of western Christianity during this time. At the time countless Christian philosophers held many debates that furiously argued over when Jesus Christ was actually born and when the world would end, with these debates continuing to this very day.

These debates led large numbers of early Christians, both literate and illiterate to accept the idea that the apocalypse would occur around the year of 1000 AD. Which according to the newly accepted timeline presented by the early Catholic Church during Justinian's reign would be 1,000 years after the crucifixion of their savior, Jesus Christ. It appears that Justinian and the early Catholic Church merely placed themselves at the midpoint of this Apocalyptic and Millennialism idea of when the apocalypse would happen. The primary reason this was done was to simply keep the peace within European society. It was, in many ways, a simple political solution for a highly emotional subject that allowed the Catholic Church to acknowledge the Millennialism groups while also keeping the idea of the apocalypse far enough into the future that it would not present any real political problems or potential issues for the Church or Justinian's rule.

It is from these debates and Eusebius' *'inspired solution'* that we see the beginning of the trend that the Catholic Church and western civilization in general continues to this very day, which is to always place earlier historical events and civilizations with some multiple of five hundred years before the Catholic Church's arrival in any given area of the world. For example, the ancient Meso-American civilizations are all dated from 500, 1,000, 1,500, 2,000 years before the arrival of the Europeans and the priests of the Catholic Church. This same practice also holds true for the civilizations of the far East, like China or India. Although at present, one may have doubts about such a claim.

Nevertheless, as we proceed through the rest of our journey, it will become apparent that no other conclusion can be made.

All of this allows us to realize that the significant events within the accepted historical timeline are very simply divided by thirteen and then either added or subtracted from either the Exodus or the destruction of King Solomon's Temple to give us the historical dates we all know of. Additionally, and to help add another layer of confusion, the original accepted start date for ancient Egypt is directly based upon this interpretation of the date for the death of Jesus Christ. This is also another example that the early learned fathers of the Catholic Church were very much aware of the esoteric timeline.

To understand how the accepted starting date of 3,100 BC for Egypt is based upon the accepted idea that Jesus Christ lived approximately 2,000 years ago, we must remember our esoteric knowledge that the Great Flood of Noah occurred at roughly 72,000 BC. We must then subtract the esoteric time of the Exodus from this number, which will give us 40,000 years (72,000-32,000= 40,000). The next step is to take this number and then divide it by thirteen, which will give us 3,077 years (40,000/13=3,077). We then only need to add this number to the accepted historical date for the death of Jesus Christ, which is 33 A.D., this will then give us a date of 3,110 BC (3,077+33=3,110). This date of 3,110 BC is only ten years from the modern-day accepted historical date for Upper and Lower Egypt's unification by the Pharaoh Menes which is typically placed sometime between 3,200 to 3,000 BC.

With this final piece of the puzzle, we can now understand how the learned fathers of the early Catholic Church were able to use the "*inspired solution*" from Eusebius to fit almost 72,000 years of human history into a 6,000-year timeline. Additionally, with us now being aware of this historical sleight-of-hand and how it was accomplished, we can also easily understand how it has been slightly modified over the centuries into the historical timeline we know of today.

This allows us to place the accepted historical timeline over the esoteric one. By doing this, we get a much clearer picture of how long ago many great historical events actually occurred and why so much information is missing. In order for simplicity, we will use the accepted timeline of ancient Egypt for this example, since much of the accepted historical timeline is built around it. Please note that these dates are only an approximation, due to the great uncertainty of the dating for both the traditionally accepted historical timeline and the esoteric one.

Within the historical timeline, the Proto-dynastic period of Egypt is traditionally placed at 3,200 to 2,665 BC and includes the First and Second Dynasties. In the esoteric timeline these would be the years between 72,000 to

65,000 BC. Additionally, it is common for all the events that occurred before Great Flood to be included in the traditional timeline. Which, unfortunately, just adds to the confusion of this ancient time.

The next great period of Egypt is the Old Kingdom, which is traditionally believed to have been between the years 2,664 to 2,155 BC under the rule the Third to Sixth Dynasties. Within the esoteric timeline, these are the years between 65,000 to 50,000 BC. It is during the Old Kingdom that scholars believe that the Great Pyramid was built. However, as we know from our journey through the Dream Vision of Enoch, the Great Pyramid was actually built long before the Great Flood and related to the Fall of the Watchers and the Lord-of-Light. But we also learned that as soon as the aftermath of the Great Deluge had subsided and the Earth had been reconquered, the other two large pyramids were built upon the Giza Plateau as great political statement. [4,5]

As the Old Kingdom came to an end, primarily because of political upheaval and civil war, it gave birth to the time known as the First Intermediate Period. Which is believed to have occurred between 2,154 to 2,052 BC with the Seventh to the Tenth Dynasties ruling at this time. In the esoteric timeline, these are the years between 50,000 to 47,000 BC.

After the great internal upheaval of the First Intermediate Period, the Middle Kingdom was born. It was a time that was marked by great growth, both economically and with Egypt's population, under the Eleventh, Twelfth, and part of the Thirteenth Dynasties. This time is normally placed between 2,052 to 1,786 BC. In the esoteric timeline, these are the years between 47,000 to 39,000 BC. Towards the end of the Middle Kingdom, population growth appears to have out striped food production that led to great suffering and internal strife for the Egyptian people. It is also during this time that the Egyptians began to allow foreign tribes to begin settling in the eastern part of the Nile delta. As we will explore later, the settlement of these tribes helps bring about the Second Intermediate Period of Egyptian history between 1,786 to 1554 BC. with the thirteenth to seventh dynasties and the rule of the Hyksos.

Within the esoteric timeline, the Second Intermediate Period are the critical years between 39,000 to 32,000 BC. It is during these years that the story of Abraham, the destruction of the cities of the plains, and earliest settlement of the first Hebrews in Egypt occur. As we will discover, it is towards the end of this time of foreign rule of Egypt that the event remembered as the Hyksos expulsion, which is also remembered as the great Exodus out of Egypt in the Bible begins at around 32,000 BC.

It is during the last years of the Second Intermediate Period that the Eighteenth Dynasty arises and establishes the New Kingdom historically believed to be the years between 1,554 to 1,075 BC under the rule of the Eighteenth to Twentieth Dynasties. Within the esoteric timeline these are the years between 32,000 to 26,400 BC. As we explore the Exodus in the following chapters, we will discover this is the time period of the legendary divine twin brothers who continued upon the great journey out of Egypt once Moses and Aaron had passed from this Earth. It is also during this time that the mysterious 'Sea People' fall upon Egypt.

The Third Intermediate Period is believed to have occurred between the years of 1,075 to 664 BC, with the Twenty-first to Twenty-fifth Dynasties ruling Egypt. Within the esoteric timeline these are the years between 26,400 to 14,415 BC when a great Dark Age fell upon humanity. It was an age that lasted until Enoch was taken away from the generations of the Earth shortly before the destruction of King Solomon's Temple and Citadel.

The final phases of Egyptian history are the Late Period between 664 to 332 BC with the twenty-sixth to thirty-first dynasties. In the esoteric timeline, these would be the years between 14,415 to around 12,600 BC. Soon after, began the time known as Ptolemaic Egypt with it normally being believed to have occurred between 332 to 30 BC. This was followed by Roman Egypt, typically placed at 30 BC to 476 AD. Within the esoteric timeline, these last phases of Egyptian history, which once again placed the Egyptians under foreign rule, occurred during 12,600 to 10,775 BC. These are the final years before the great destruction we explored during journey through the Dream Vision of Enoch covered in 'Unlocking the Dream Vision: The secret history of creation.

As we journey through the Exodus and beyond, we will gain a much better understanding of the crucial events that occurred during years between the great Exodus at approximately 32,000 BC to the destruction of King Solomon's Temple and Citadel sometime around 14,415 BC and the great Dark Age that fell upon humanity during these years. To begin our journey, we must first answer the critical questions concerning the identity of the people we known as the Hebrews.

Chapter 2

Historical evidence of the Exodus

Our journey into the Exodus begins with the two biggest questions concerning the great Exodus out of Egypt by the ancient Hebrews, as recorded in the Bible. With the first being who were the people that came to be known as the Hebrews or Israelites? While the second question simply being is there any historical evidence from other sources that support the biblical story of the Exodus?

Although many would say that there is no historical evidence for the Exodus as it is recorded in the Bible. It has been well known by historians for hundreds of years that the early Hebrews in Egypt spoken of in the Bible were the ancient people known as the "*Hyksos*." This is not an Egyptian name, but it comes from the Greek word "*Huksōs,*" that is derived from the ancient Egyptian expression "*hekau khasut*." This term is believed by scholars to mean "*rulers of foreign lands*." The Jewish historian Josephus gives the word *Huksōs* or Hyksos the meaning of "*Shepherd Kings*" or "*Captive shepherds.*" [1]

According to Josephus in his work "*Contra Apion*" or "*Against Apion*" from the first-century AD, he debates the similarities between the traditional Jewish account of the Exodus with the two Exodus-like events that the Egyptian historian Manetho describes. However, there has been significant debate over how Josephus and the works of Apion interpret Manetho and what Manetho himself may have recounted. Among historians, there is little doubt that

Josephus identifies the Hebrew Exodus of the Bible with the first Exodus that is mentioned by Manetho. In this first Exodus, Manetho speaks of how 480,000 Hyksos or "*Shepherd Kings*" as Josephus refers to them, left Egypt for the city of Jerusalem. Josephus provides us with the earliest recorded use of this term Hyksos from the Egyptian phrase "*Hekw-Shasu*" which is primarily a Hellenized form of the ancient Egyptian phrase of "*hekau khasut.*" [2,3,4]

Additionally, Josephus and Apion both recount a second Exodus that is mentioned by Manetho in his lost work, "*Aigyptiaca*." They speak of a legendary figure of ancient Egypt known as "*Osarseph*," whom Apion claims is equated with Moses of the Bible. The story claims that he was a renegade Egyptian priest who leads an army of "*lepers and leprous priests*" against a Pharaoh named "*Amenophis,*" and drove him out of the country after this Osarseph formed an alliance with the Hyksos. The word "*Amenophis*" is the Greek version of the Egyptian word "*Amenhotep*," which means "*Amun is pleased*." It was an ancient Egyptian phrase that was associated with the first Pharaohs of the 18th Dynasty and was not the name of any particular Pharaoh. Historians and scholars also do not interpret the references of "*lepers and leprous priests*" in the story as literally referring to the disease. Instead, it is a symbolic reference to a strange or unwelcome belief system by a foreign people. [5,6]

After the renegade Osarseph and his followers had driven out Amenophis, they are said to have ravaged Egypt by taking her treasures of gold and silver and committing many sacrileges against Egypt's traditional gods and temples. Soon after these events, Pharaoh returns with a large army and expels them from Egyptian lands forever. Towards the end of the story, Apion claims that the renegade priest Osarseph changed his name to Moses and then led his remaining "80,000 *lepers and leprous priests*" into the wilderness towards the city of Jerusalem. [7]

Unfortunately, there is no additional historical evidence to support Apion's claim that this heretical priest Osarseph changed his name to Moses. While at the same time, there does not appear to be any evidence disproving it. Additionally, Josephus makes no mention of this claim in his work "*Against Apion*." If it were a false claim, one would think that Josephus would have pointed it out and used it in his arguments against Apion. However, as we will shortly discover, there might be more truth to this claim than scholars have been initially led to believe. Although the second Exodus that both Josephus and Apion refer to appears to be a closer match to the Exodus story contained within the Bible, most scholars claim that the first Exodus could be the actual event recorded in the Bible.

There are many scholars and historians that agree that both Exodus stories as presented by Josephus and Apion are somehow related to the biblical story. However, these same scholars and historians tend to dismiss the idea that these accounts from Josephus about the Hyksos are directly related to the biblical story of the Exodus. The few who do believe that Josephus' and Apion's reports are a historical account of the Exodus story of the Bible from an Egyptian point of view tend to support the Josephus interpretation, with the first Exodus being the event that is eventually recorded in Bible many centuries after the event. Nevertheless, as we will now begin to learn, Josephus and Apion were correct to connect these stories of the Hyksos being expelled from Egypt with the biblical Exodus out of Egypt. Also, in the process, we will learn that the event remembered in the Bible as the great Exodus out of Egypt by the Hebrews is the secret to understanding one of the greatest mysteries of the ancient world and why there was a worldwide collapse of the Bronze-Age civilizations. However, to understand this and so much more, we must first take a much closer look at the people the ancient Egyptians called the "*Hekw-Shasu.*"

Scholars claim that the phrase "*Hekw-Shasu*" means "*Shepherd King.*" However, if we look at the actual words that make up this phrase, "*Hekw*" and "*Shasu.*" We will quickly discover the first of many purposeful deceptions of just who these people were. The word "*Hekw*" is not Egyptian but is a later Greek form of the Egyptian word "*Habiru.*" It is believed by scholars that the word "*Habiru*" means "wanderer" and that the word "*hekau*" referred to by Josephus is a corrupted Greek version of the Egyptian word "*Habiru.*" It is sometimes written as "*Hapiru,*" or more accurately as "*Apiru,*" which means "*dusty or dirty.*" This appears to have been a common term used throughout the Fertile Crescent for people who were variously described as bandits, outlaws, raiders, and sometimes mercenaries. It is the original form of the word that becomes the modern word "*Hebrew.*" Unlike the word "*Hekw,*" the word "*Shasu*" is an ancient Egyptian word that refers to a group of Semitic-speaking cattle and sheep nomads that the ancient Egyptians had dealings with from time-to-time during the Middle Kingdom. This seems to imply that the word "*Shasu*" could be a corrupted Greek version of the older Egyptian word "*khasut.*" [8,9,10,11,12,13,14,15]

We will take a much closer look at who these "*Shasu*" were in just a moment. But even with this small piece of information. It allows us to understand the true meaning of this ancient phase, "*Hekw-Shasu,*" does not mean "*Shepherd King*" or "*rulers of foreign lands*" But it is a term that is something much closer to meaning "*dirty wandering cattle nomads [shepherds]*" or "*dusty cattle nomads [shepherds] that wander.*" This allows us to understand that this phrase started out as more of a general description of a type of nomadic people that herded cattle and sheep than any single group like the Hyksos. It is only when the Hyksos take over Egypt that this term becomes known as a derogatory phrase that is meant as an insult by referring to them as "*Shepherd Kings*" or "*Captive shepherds.*" With the ancient Egyptians implying that the only thing these people were kings of where their dirty herds of cattle and sheep.

Many may find it surprising that we know quite a bit about these "*dirty wandering cattle nomads*," which were commonly known as the "*Shasu*" to the ancient Egyptians and the people of the Fertile Crescent. Although the exact origins of these "*Shasu*" are unknown, we do know they were primarily composed of numerous small nomadic tribes that lived in and around the eastern parts of the Fertile Crescent. Thousands of years ago and for some unknown reason, the great majority of these small nomadic tribes in the eastern parts of the Fertile Crescent, primarily located in the lands that make up most of modern-day Iraq, western Iran, and the many valleys of the Zagros Mountains, began uniting with one another. It is possible that this grouping together of smaller tribes into larger groups was to help provide for the mutual defense of their people from the various powerful city-states, kingdoms, and empires that also occupied the lands in which they lived. It is also highly probable that intermarriage between the different tribes was also a major factor in uniting the different tribes into a larger community. Nevertheless, no matter how it occurred, this uniting together of numerous smaller tribes into a much larger tribal grouping created an entirely new type of nomadic community. [16,17,18]

One of the primary factors that made this nomadic group so vastly different from any other tribal group that had come before was its large size due to this uniting together of numerous smaller tribes into one larger tribal group made up of hundreds, if not thousands of members. This uniting into such a large group created a new set of unique problems that small individual tribes made up of a few dozen or so individuals usually did not have to contend with as they scratched a living from the lands they occupied. One of the most significant changes that occurred was that they were forced to become a "*semi-nomadic people*" instead of a purely nomadic people as they had been for thousands of years. This momentous change came about simply because it is challenging to keep a large group of people on the move all the time. Additionally, it becomes very complicated to feed so many mouths while always on the move. This small change may not seem that significant at first, but in time it had a considerable impact on how these people lived and how they dealt with other groups.

At first, the greatest change was the cessation of their need to constantly move from place to place, looking for food and resources. Once the smaller tribes had united into one large group, they would instead move until they came to a rather

14

lush area. They would then temporarily settle in that area and live there until they had depleted all the natural resources and polluted it with their waste. This quickly became a constantly repeating pattern of existence for these people. Once they had settled a lush area, they would begin striping the land of all its animals and edible plants for themselves and their livestock. This would naturally produce huge amounts of human and animal waste, which would pollute the local water sources, making them undrinkable for man or beast. Once they had stripped the land and polluted the water, they would then pack everything up and move on to the next area and then repeat this pattern. The amount of time they stayed in any one place was directly related to the amount of food and water available in that given area. This highly destructive form of living off the land would tend to leave the area as a wasteland for many years once they had left. This destruction of the local resources and polluting the water sources was one of the primary reasons why other people tended not to like these people or want them in their lands. [19,20]

The next unique thing that happened is what makes these people so very different from all the other tribes of the ancient world that had come before them. This major change was that they created and maintained an advanced military arm to protect their people and their temporary settlements. This change adds a great amount of weight to the idea these people may have originally united together to help provide for their common defense against greater powers. This military arm was vastly different from any of the other ancient tribal people or civilizations that existed up to this point in time. What made them so unique was that this force was truly a professional army of soldiers made-up of swordsmen, spearmen, archers, and stone-throwers. Additionally, they are also the first people known to have used the horse and the chariot. This gave them a great military advantage that allowed them to stand against much larger powers and civilizations. They also created the first heavy mounted cavalry. Remarkably, they had also developed siege warfare to a high level. They are also the first people to develop advanced bronze and iron weapons, which gave them an important advantage over other tribes and civilizations. Not only did they have a highly professional, well-equipped army, but this army had the full support from the rest of the community without question. Their military advantages of the horse and chariot, advanced bronze, and iron weapons, combined with siege warfare made them a dangerous foe to the city-states of the ancient world. This was especially true when they fought against the typical part-time warrior farmers that almost all the city-states called upon to protect or fight for the various civilizations of the Fertile Crescent. [21,22]

This professional military arm also allowed these tribes to pillage, plunder, and rob just about any group that came into conflict with them. This was especially true when they ran out of food or other resources, they would take it by force. The ancient Egyptians viewed these *Shasu* as little more than *"Brigands,"* which is nothing more than a gang of people that lives by pillaging. Over time they became the basis of the ever-famous highway robbers of travelers remembered in countless ancient tales. [23]

Politically, they were organized by clans under a single tribal chieftain, which they commonly called "King." This King was advised by and would have to get the approval from a council of tribal elders that came from each tribe or large clans that made up the larger group. These tribes also had a highly developed and potent religious priesthood. This priesthood was an entirely separate class from the rest of the tribal group that only answered to the gods. This religious class maintained and controlled all the religious aspects of the community without question. The priesthood was always closely associated with the king and the professional army he commanded. For they were the ones that gave the king the right to rule over the tribes and were the real political power of the larger group. [24,25,26]

It is unknown exactly which 'god' these *Shasu* originally worshiped before they entered Egypt, but the Egyptians said the Hyksos worshipped a god called *"Hadad."* This god Hadad of the Hyksos is believed to be the same god that was known as *"Adad"* to the Babylonians and Assyrians. The god Adad was a powerful weather, water, and fertility god of the Babylonian and Assyrian pantheons. Scholars believe that numerous Semitic-speaking nomadic tribes of the Fertile Crescent had adopted the god Adad and several other gods from both the Babylonians and Assyrian pantheons as their own once they came into contact and traded with these major civilizations. Scholars and biblical historians have also linked this god Hadad of the Hyksos and the god Adad of the Babylonians with the god of the Hebrews known by his later name as YHWH or *Yahweh.* [27,28,29,30,31,32,33]

The primary reason for this connection between the Babylonian god Adad, the Hyksos god Hadad, and the God of the Bible is because they are very similar to one another with all having a common twofold aspect to them. This god was believed to be both the giver and destroyer of life. The Babylonians said that the god Adad brought his rains, which caused the land to bear grain and be fruitful, hence his title *"Lord of Abundance."* His mighty storms, terrible hurricanes, and great floods were thought to be evidence of his vengeful anger against his enemies, when he brought darkness, want, and a cruel death to all that opposed him. He often became a god of war when he unleashed his wrath upon his enemies. Both Adad and Hadad, like the God of the Bible, was believed to a highly jealous god that would punish any human or god or that stood against him or disobeyed his divine commands. When the Hyksos went into battle, he became known as "*Yehweh Sabaoth*" or "*The God Armies*." [34,35]

As you are undoubtedly aware, the name "Yehweh" is very similar to the later traditional name of the God of the ancient Israelites known as "*Yahweh,*" who is described in the Bible as being a jealous, vengeful, and often wrathful God. As with the Bible, in both the Babylonian and Assyrian pantheons, this god became associated with divination and justice. It was common for him to be addressed as the "*lord of prayers and divination.*" He was also invoked to preside over haruspices, the ancient ceremony where a religious official interpreted the omens by inspecting the entrails of sacrificial animals or as a witness in legal cases. This god was also commonly invoked in curses and magical spells that were designed for protection. [36]

Surprisingly, this god that the Babylonians called Adad is unlike the other great gods of the ancient world because he does not appear to have an actual 'cult center' peculiar to just himself located in one holy area. However, there is ample evidence that he was worshiped in Mesopotamia's most important ancient cities and towns. Including the cities of Babylon and Ashur, the capital of Assyria, with there being several sanctuaries and a few temples built for him in both areas. Nevertheless, what makes him so different from other gods is that although there were many places for the worship for Adad and they were located at important religious sites, not one of them was the actual 'center' of the belief, nor were they built just for the worship of Adad. [37]

An example of this can be found in ancient Babylonia at an early center of his cult, a temple known as the "*House of Great Storms*" at Karkar. This temple was located within an ancient fortress located on the Orontes River in western Syria. Within this temple, the god Adad was the head of the local pantheon, but the temple was not built only for the worship of Adad. This temple was a place to worship all the gods of the Babylonian pantheon, in which the god Adad just happened to be the leader of this particular temple. This is one of the aspects that make this god Adad a bit different than the other gods. Because he was commonly believed to be one of the most important gods within the Babylonian and Assyrian pantheons. However, at the same time, he was only a minor deity, while he was commonly believed to be critically important for the world's very existence. Although he was believed to an important god, he was not generally included with the highest-ranking gods, nor was he the leader of the gods. [38]

Although there is still significant debate over the issue by scholars and biblical historians, we can see that it is very difficult to deny that the God of the

Bible and the ancient Babylonian god Adad, who later becomes the god Hadad of the Hyksos, are the same. If it was not for the Hyksos slowly moving into and then settling in the far eastern parts of the Nile Delta, starting at some time during the Twelfth Dynasty of Egypt, this cult of Adad might have died out.

Returning to the immigration and settlement of these tribal people that eventually become known as the Hyksos to the Egyptians. The first phase of this immigration does not appear to have been violent or against the Egyptians' wishes. By the end of the Thirteenth Dynasty, the Hyksos, had grown in number and established an independent realm in the eastern Nile Delta centered in and around the city of Avaris. This independent realm slowly led to the formation of the Fourteenth Dynasty under the Hyksos in Lower Egypt that coexisted with the Thirteenth Dynasty of Upper Egypt. The establishment of the Fourteenth Dynasty by the Hyksos marks the beginning of the time known as the Second Intermediate Period of Egyptian history. [39,40,41]

Soon after the establishment of the Fourteenth Dynasty, the Hyksos invaded the rest of the eastern Nile Delta, where they also took over their fellow brother tribesmen living in the area, thereby creating the Fifteenth Dynasty of the Hyksos. They also invaded the territory of the Thirteenth Dynasty, which helped cause its collapse, that left a political power vacuum in Upper Egypt, which may have led to the rise of the Sixteenth Dynasty, based in Thebes. The Hyksos eventually invaded and conquered both Lower and Upper Egypt, albeit for only a short time and ruling from Thebes. After leaving Thebes or being thrown out by the local Egyptians, the Seventeenth Dynasty of the Egyptians retook control of Thebes. This new Dynasty reigned for a short time in peaceful coexistence with the Hyksos Kings of Lower Egypt, possibly being their vassals. [42,43]

What makes these events so important is how the Hyksos took over the area of the eastern Nile Delta and then the rest of Egypt. The way they initially took over the eastern Nile Delta and then the rest of Egypt is so unique to these people that it can be used to trace their movements long after the Egyptians forced them out of Egypt. The takeover by the Hyksos begins as soon as they entered a new land, they would start to settle in the area with the largest number of tribal people that were similar too themselves. In the case of ancient Egypt, they settled in the eastern part of the Nile Delta known as the Land of Goshen centered around the city of Avaris. Historians, Egyptian records, and biblical tradition all agree that this was an area where earlier waves of tribal people had been allowed to settle by the Egyptians. Once they had settled in the Land of Goshen and had taken over the city of Avaris, they began to take over the other existing tribes around this central area. This process involved the killing of the local tribal chieftain and his family. The Hyksos would then install their own chieftain as the leader of this tribe. They would also begin intermarrying with the primary clans of the tribe they took over to help cement their control. [44]

Once they had consolidated their political power and established their control over the local tribes in this central area, the Hyksos then begin one of the most unique types of invasion and settlement ever seen in human history. It would begin by them slowly invading the nearest surrounding villages and communities located around the city of Avaris. This appears to have been done by simply walking their army into the village or town and then killing its leader, his family, and anyone else that held any political power within that community. The Hyksos would then install their people into those positions of power. What makes this Hyksos invasion so unique is that once they were in control of the local population, they would not change the day to day life of the local people. These new rulers would more-or-less leave everything intact, allowing the local people to keep using their customs, laws, and traditions that they had always known. This same pattern of leaving society intact for the common people is seen over and over as the Hyksos slowly take over Lower Egypt. [45]

During this takeover of Lower Egypt, we also see another pattern that is unique to the Hyksos, which is how they dealt with the local population once their army had arrived at the gates. If the Hyksos were welcomed or the locals quickly surrendered without a fight, the Hyksos would either require the local leaders to swear oaths of loyalty to the Hyksos King or if they refused, they would simply be killed and replaced. If the local leaders swore loyalty to their new rulers, then the Hyksos would remove a few of the family members of the local leaders back to the city of Avaris, to help ensure that the locals would honor their oaths. They would also settle a small group of their people in the village help keep an eye of their new subjects. Once these events played out, life would quickly return to normal for the average person of the lower classes. The only real change that the commoner would notice is that their new Hyksos rulers would require the community's "cult center," and its priest to be relocated to the central area of settlement. This would have the effect of requiring the local population to go to the main site of the Hyksos' settlement so they could give their offerings and prayers to their gods. [46]

If the population put up a fight, then the results would be vastly different. If the Hyksos had to conquer the village, they would always kill the rulers of the community along with anybody who took part in the fighting. Afterward, the Hyksos would usually uproot all the remaining people of the community and move them all back to their central area of settlement, abandoning the site. If, by chance, the entire community took part in fighting them, then the Hyksos would show no mercy and would slaughter the whole community, leaving the bodies of men, women, and children where they fell. They would also loot and then destroy the buildings of the settlement, abandoning the site forever. [47]

If the village was in a critical area or provided a vital service or resource, once the Hyksos had conquered it and killed the elites. They would remove approximately half of any remaining population back to the Hyksos' central area while settling an equal number of their people in that community while replacing the elites. This unique form of invasion and settlement leaves distinct evidence that appears as if some communities and even regions were quickly depopulated for no apparent reason. This depopulation has the appearance as if the people had abandoned their villages in a short amount of time leaving everything behind. While at the same time, other communities were completely destroyed, with only the dead occupying the burnt-out ruins. However, there were other areas where life continued the same way it always had because the local population had peacefully surrendered to the Hyksos. These areas may have survived, but they tended to exist at a much lower level of advancement or economic activity once the Hyksos had taken control. This unique pattern of invasion and settlement is something we will see again and again as we go deeper into the Exodus story. [48]

The next important aspect of this type of invasion is that it took place over a surprisingly long period of time. It was a prolonged form of invasion and settlement. According to historical accounts, this process took a couple of generations for the Hyksos to fully take over Lower Egypt in this manner. Based on the historical and archaeological evidence we have; it appears that the Hyksos were only invading and taking over a village or small community approximately once or twice every year. [49]

After the Hyksos had taken over, they would begin reorganizing the local society in a unique way. This would start by breaking the people into three general but distinct groups or classes. The first was the elite rulers of the tribe or village, normally made-up of the warrior class of the Hyksos. The second was the priesthood of the Hyksos that was always separate from the other levels of society. While everyone else was part of the lower class that were broken up into smaller groups, normally based on occupation. They also began the practice of only allowing the son or sons of the lower classes to enter the same profession as their father. As we go deeper into the Exodus story, we will see that this establishing of this simple class structure is seen several times. [50,51]

The next important change that the Hyksos forced upon the communities they took over was the moving the religious cult center and the priest of each community back to the Hyksos' city of Avaris. This would allow them to control all the different cult centers of the different communities. Once they had relocated all the local religious cult centers into one area, they would slowly begin to change the belief system and eventually impose their own, but not in the way most would think. What is truly remarkable, is they did not alter the original religious belief, traditions, or rituals of the local people. However, they did reorganize the local pantheon of gods into a new order. This always involved taking the local male fertility god, who was normally a minor god, and elevating him to being the Supreme god of the local pantheon. They would then place the traditional Earth Mother or Mother Goddess alongside this new Supreme god as his consort or wife. They would also take the local "Lord of the waters" and place him as the "King of the gods" alongside the local Messenger god. They would also reorganize the local mythology about the different gods and goddesses so they all appeared to be under the control of this new Supreme god or one of the other two major gods, both of which were always in the service of the Supreme god. In Egypt, this minor male fertility god was the god "*Amun*," more commonly known as "*Amun-Ra*," the god of the sun, air, and the harvest. [52]

Amun-Ra, was one of the most powerful and popular gods of the ancient Egyptian pantheon and was the patron god of the city of Thebes. He was worshipped as one part of the "*Theban Triad*" of gods that included Amun-Ra, Mut, the Mother Goddess and Khonsu, the god of the moon and time that was very similar in aspect to the Babylonian god Adad. Although Amun-Ra is now customarily thought of as the Supreme leader of the Egyptian pantheon, he started as only a minor fertility god and remained in that position until the time of the New Kingdom. It is during the time of the Hyksos ruling Egypt that this minor male fertility god was elevated to the status of being the Supreme King above all the Egyptian gods. By the beginning of the Eighteenth Dynasty of the New Kingdom, Amun-Ra had become the most powerful god in Egypt and his worship bordered on monotheism. By this time, the other ancient Egypt gods were considered as only mere aspects of Amun-Ra and his will. During this time, his name was changed from Amun to Amun-Ra, with his priesthood becoming the most powerful in Egypt until the coming of Christianity. [53]

Although the Hyksos were able to accomplish much during the hundred or so years of the Second Intermediate Period, in the end, they were unable to complete their total takeover of Egypt. The primary reason was because the Seventeenth Dynasty collapsed abruptly. Soon afterward, Pharaoh Ahmose I, who founded the Eighteenth Dynasty that ushered in the New Kingdom, began the long process of retaking all of Egypt back from these *Hekw-Shasu*. It took almost one-hundred years for the Egyptians to finally expel the Hyksos from their rightful lands. [54]

It is during this time of the Hyksos' expulsion from Egypt that the great Exodus recorded in the Bible occurs. According to Manetho, this expulsion of the Hyksos consisted of two separate expulsions that were many years apart from one another. The first expulsion of the 480,000 Hyksos that Josephus recorded, occurred once the Egyptians had retaken control of Upper and Lower Egypt. These 480,000 people consisted primarily of the lower classes of the Hyksos and their servants. It is what the ancient Egyptians did next that is by far more important to understanding the story of the great Exodus out of Egypt that is contained within the Bible. [55]

Although the Egyptians had expelled all the lower classes of the Hyksos, they did not expel the elites of the ruling class of the Hyksos during this first expulsion. The Hyksos elite were to suffer a vastly different fate at the hands of the Egyptians and were enslaved by them. One of the primary reasons for this enslavement was to simply humiliate the elites of the Hyksos as much as possible. It is during this enslavement of the Hyksos elite that the meaning of the term *Hekw-Shasu* changes from something like "wandering cattle nomads" to the much more derogatory meaning of "*Shepherd Kings*" or "*Captive shepherds*" that Josephus refers too, and who were viewed by the Egyptians as nothing but dirty little kings that only ruled over their equally dirty herds of cattle and sheep. [56,57]

By being aware of this critical piece of information that the Egyptians enslaved the elites of the Hyksos begins to answer the mystery of the biblical account of the enslavement of the Hebrews. Which according to the biblical story, the Hebrews were enslaved by the Egyptians and forced into hard labor for untold generations. However, we can now understand that this biblical story of the Hebrews' enslavement is speaking of the enslavement of the Hyksos elites once the Egyptians had retaken their homeland. With understanding that it was the elite classes of the Hyksos that were enslaved by the Egyptians, we can easily understand that their enslavement would have been vastly different from the common people of the lower classes of society. Since they were from the elite class, it is safe to assume that their enslavement would not have normally consisted of hard labor, but it is much more likely they were turned into everyday household slaves that had to wait on and serve their new Egyptian masters. As with the slavery itself, this was done to humiliate the Hyksos elites as much as possible.

This humiliation of being enslaved as a household servant was also done to deny the Hyksos elite a place in the Afterlife. This was because within ancient Egyptian society, a simple household slave was so unimportant and of such a low social standing that the Egyptians would not give them the honor of allowing their name to be written down, thereby denying them the chance of an Afterlife because nobody would remember them. To the Egyptians and many other cultures of the time, this was viewed as one of the greatest insults that any person could suffer or be subjected to, especially a group of elites. The very thought of not being remembered was a fate worse than death itself. This punishment is but one example of the lengths the ancient Egyptians went too so they could humiliate these "*Shepherd Kings*" as much as possible. This is also the reason why there is are no Egyptian records of the enslavement of the Hebrews that is spoken of in the Bible. It was because the Egyptians would not allow the Hyksos elite the honor of having their names written down so they could be remembered. [58]

In addition to taking the Hyksos elite as slaves, the Egyptians also took several technical and military innovations from the Hyksos. The Egyptians copied their chariots as they copied their composite bows and advanced bronze and iron weapons. The Egyptians also copied their advanced fortification and siege techniques and weaponry. The Egyptians also took the Hyksos livestock and crops. This helped to introduce new foods to feed the ever-growing population of Egypt during the Eighteenth Dynasty. All these cultural advances that were taken from the Hyksos would become a decisive factor in Egypt's later success in building a vast empire that controlled much of the Middle East during the time of the New Kingdom. It also shows us that the Hyksos were much more advanced than a simple tribal people. [59]

Many may find it somewhat surprising that it appears that the Egyptians allowed the Hyksos elite to continue practicing their religion. Although the Egyptians allowed them to practice their religion, their worship, and their priest could only be authorized and happen under the ever-watchful eye of Pharaoh and his priests. This 'ever-watchful-eye' would need to be an individual that world be completely loyal to or directly controlled by Pharaoh, but they would also need to be acceptable to the Hyksos. This person would ideally be an individual from the most important Hyksos tribe or clan that was raised and trained from a young age by the Egyptians. Once this person had come of age, he would try to "reeducate" the Hyksos in order to show them the errors of their ways. This would also have the added effect of humiliating the Hyksos elites even more by taking over and changing their religious beliefs, much as they had done to the Egyptians. This allows us to understand the events that led up to the second Exodus mentioned by Manetho, where a renegade heretical Egyptian priest called Osarseph led "*80,000 lepers and leprous priests*" to rebel against Egypt to escape their enslavement under mighty Pharaoh. This also allows us to understand that it is second Exodus of the Hyksos elites under the command of a renegade priest that is recorded in the Bible and not the first expulsion of 480,000 Hyksos. Additionally, this also allows us to understand that the claim made by Apion that this heretical Egyptian priest *Osarseph* changed his name to Moses may be valid. [60,61,62]

If we take this information and combined it with the traditional biblical story along with our existing esoteric knowledge of the Dream Vision of Enoch. It will allow us to reconstruct a much more realistic chain of events that is remembered in the Bible as the great Exodus of the Israelites out of Egypt.

Chapter 3

The Exodus out of Egypt

As with the biblical story, our starting point is the beginning of the Eighteenth Dynasty and the Hyksos expulsion by the Egyptians. Once the Egyptians had reestablished their control of Upper and Lower Egypt, they summarily expelled all the people of the lower classes of the many tribes that made up the Hyksos. At the same time, they enslaved all the elites of each of the tribes, including the Hyksos priesthood.

This is the event that becomes known as the first expulsion of the Hyksos and is the first Exodus that Josephus and Apion both recount in their works. What became of these 480,000 people is unknown. They seem to have simply disappeared into the sands of time without leaving any trace behind. As for the Hyksos elites that had been enslaved, they began a prolonged and humiliating enslavement as the lowest class of people in ancient Egyptian society, a slave that served as a common household servant. A person of such low standing, they would not be remembered because their names would not be written down, and therefore be denied an Afterlife.

As we discovered in the last chapter, the man that is remembered as Moses in the Bible may have been the child of a high-ranking Hyksos who was a slave in service to Pharaoh's house or court. At some point in his early life, he was noticed as a young man of talent and was picked out for greater things, either by Pharaoh or a ranking member of his court. He would have been taken into

Pharaoh's house and raised, educated, and trained as an Egyptian. According to the biblical story this task was undertaken by Pharaoh's daughter. Over time he would be groomed as an "approved" adviser to the head priest of the Hyksos, entirely loyal to and under the control of Pharaoh, but also acceptable to the Hyksos. At some point in his young adult life, he has a change of heart and wishes to help his fellow enslaved Hyksos. The biblical account is rather vague on the details, but Moses kills an Egyptian he saw abusing a fellow Hyksos. It is this crime of murder that forces Moses to leave Egypt and enter the wilderness to escape Egyptian justice.

With our better understanding of the events surrounding this enslavement, and because of something we will learn about much later in this story. We can speculate with confidence that it probable that the event of Moses murdering an Egyptian on behalf of a slave is a highly sanitized version of a small uprising in the court of Pharaoh that was led by Moses. An uprising that was quickly crushed by the forces of Pharaoh, but in the process, it resulted in the death of at least one Egyptian. This would have forced the young Moses to flee into the wilderness to escape a painful, humiliating, and public death. He would have been viewed as a traitor by the Egyptians with it being equally possible that the enslaved Hyksos would also view him as some type of traitor. This would have left him with nowhere to hide in Egypt.

In such a scenario, it would make the Egyptians, as with all governments of history, launch a new program of oppression against their Hyksos slaves. According to both the biblical account and the Dream Vision of Enoch, the Egyptians began a program of "*destroying their little ones*" by "*cast(ing) their young into a river of much water.*" Although this sounds horrible to our modern sensibilities, it was a common approach in the ancient world when a major power began wiping out a people, especially one that had started any type of uprising or rebellion. They would begin by punishing the enslaved adults by taking their children and selling them into slavery to a foreign buyer. If the child was an infant or was too young to be sold into slavery, primarily because nobody would buy it, it would be killed. It would also not be uncommon for the Egyptians to torment the parents by forcing them to witness this killing, which in this case was by drowning them in the waters of the Nile.

While these events were occurring, Moses is said to have encountered a 'God,' who claimed to be the God of Abraham, Isaac, and Jacob, and who manifested itself in the form of a burning bush. Moses is instructed by this God of Abraham to return to Egypt and free His people from Pharaoh's bondage; upon his arrival, both the biblical account and the Dream Vision say that he first met with Aaron, who then met with the elders of the tribes and who spoke on his behalf.

26

"And Moses and Aaron *went and gathered together all the elders of children of Israel: And Aaron spake [spoke] all the words which the LORD had spoken unto Moses, and did the signs in the sight of the people. And the people believed: and when they heard that the LORD had visited the children of Israel, and the he had looked upon their affliction, then they bowed their heads and worshipped.*"
(Exodus, 4:29-31)

After meeting with the tribal elders, Moses and Aaron then meet with Pharaoh whereby the famous words of *"Let my people go"* are uttered. What is truly remarkable in this entire situation is that Moses was able to be included in a meeting of the elders of Israel and then was able to meet with Pharaoh thereafter. The key to understanding how something like could have happened is Aaron. With the most straightforward explanation being that Aaron must have been the High-priest of the Hyksos. This would explain how a man believed to a criminal and possibly viewed as a traitor by both the Egyptians and the enslaved Hyksos was able to stand before the elders of the tribes and receive an audience with Pharaoh without being arrested. Only a man of such standing who had total control of the entire community could call such meetings or provide protection to Moses from the Egyptians.

By realizing that Aaron was the High-priest of the Hyksos, an enslaved people that must have always been a threat to the Egyptians. It is no real surprise that the meeting with Pharaoh went poorly and why Pharaoh is presented as having such a dismissive attitude towards Moses, Aaron, and their people. It also helps to explain why Pharaoh responded so harshly to their request to release the Hyksos from their bondage, by commanding his taskmasters to increase their burdens. This new oppression helps make the elites of the Hyksos begin turning against Moses and Aaron. These events in turn lead to the famous Ten Plagues of Egypt.

Within our journey through the Dream Vision of Enoch, we explored the events surrounding this great Exodus out of Egypt and how it was related to the radioactive traces of Potassium-40 found in Icelandic marine sediment samples and ice cores that were dated to approximately 32,000 BC. We also explored how this was evidence that some type of wide spread nuclear event had occurred. However, we did not have the opportunity to explore the actual events of the Ten Plagues or what type of nuclear event would have been needed to produce the Ten Plagues of Egypt as they are recorded in the Bible. [1]

Based upon the radioactive evidence, it is blatantly obvious that there was a massively destructive event of a nuclear nature that occurred 34,000 years ago.

Additionally, the Dream Vision of Enoch refers to the Egyptians as being "*blinded,*" which we speculated could be the result from the brilliant flash of light that is created when a nuclear weapon is detonated. We also have the detailed biblical account of the Ten Plagues that paints a fascinating picture that is eerily similar to the effects of deadly radioactive contamination of the ecosystem. For us to continue with this line of speculation, we need to take a much closer look at the Ten Plagues of ancient Egypt as they are recorded in the Bible. [2]

Returning to the biblical account starting in chapter seven of the Book of Exodus, verses 14-25; we are told of the first Plague, a Plague of Blood that poisoned the Nile river and then all the waters of Egypt. It has been speculated by many people that an earthquake or volcanic event may have caused this poisoning of the Nile. The most common idea is that an earthquake caused a massive amount of deadly gases that could have been trapped under the Nile river basin to be released into the waters. Such an event would kill every living creature in the river, thereby contaminating the Nile and turning the waters red as their corpses began to decompose. Unfortunately, there is no actual evidence to support this hypothesis, nor does it explain the radioactive evidence or the other Plagues.

By taking the radioactive evidence into account and the reference from the Dream Vision of the Egyptians being "*blinded,*" we can speculate that the Plague of Blood may have been caused by the detonation of a nuclear weapon. What is truly remarkable is not only could a nuclear blast create the Plague of Blood as it is described, but the aftereffects of such a blast can also explain the other nine Plagues as well. All we must do is perform a little thought experiment where we imagine what would happen if we were to detonate a nuclear weapon over the Nile somewhere upstream of Egypt.

An ideal spot would be where the Nile River was flowing in a relatively straight line over roughly flat ground for a dozen or so miles. Looking at a map of the Nile river, we will find that just south of Upper Egypt, in the Nubian Desert just before the 3rd Cataract of the Nile, would be an ideal location. It would also be ideal if the weapon was detonated at just the right height over the river so the fireball would come close too, but not come into direct contact with the river's surface. If this was to happen, it would produce numerous unique effects upon the river and its ecosystem.

The first thing that would happen right after the weapon detonated is that the water would absorb the bulk of the radiation, and the water would become superheated. The combination of the massive heat from the blast and the radiation it creates would both help to superheat the water. Microseconds later the shock-wave of the blast would hit the water with such force it would turn the fish and other wildlife in the river into a boiling bloody goo for miles in both directions of the blast. This would contaminate the river and turn the water a nasty blood red color that would soon reek of death. This is eerily similar to what is described as the first Plague of Blood and the poisoning of the Nile. The story also says that it took seven days for the river to clear and become usable again. This short amount of time for the contamination to be flushed into the Mediterranean Sea, supports the idea that it was a relatively localized event that only effected a dozen or so miles of the river.

Chapter eight of the Book of Exodus describes the next three Plagues that befell Egypt. The first was of frogs, the second was of lice, and the third was flies. These Plagues would be the natural by-product of the Nile river being contaminated, which would have simply drove these creatures away from it. Chapter nine provides us with the next three Plagues to befall Egypt, all of which help support the idea that a nuclear device may have been used.

The fifth Plague was a pestilence or "*Murrain*," which is an antiquated term for a plague or epidemic that affected domestic animals and crop blight. This Murrain that falls across the land results in the death of the Egyptian livestock. Interestingly, the Bible says that the Hebrew cattle and sheep were unaffected by this pestilence. This Murrain that strikes the Egyptian's livestock, but not the Hebrew's, fits the profile of what happens due to localized radioactive contamination. The most likely reason the Hebrew's herds were unaffected by this Murrain was that they were located just outside the radiation plume and were not exposed to the contamination or came into contact with the contaminated waters of the Nile. The sixth great Plague that fell upon the Egyptians was one of "*boils breaking upon man and beast*." The Plague of boils is the first clear description of what we now know of as radiation poisoning. Where the skin begins to blister either from direct radiation poisoning or from being exposed to any fallout or holding contaminated items.

The seventh Plague is one of "*hail being mingled with fire*." This Plague has been traditionally misinterpreted with the general idea that the hail itself was on fire and burning with a flame. However, this idea is incorrect and based on a modern misunderstanding of the ancient archaic meaning of the word "*mingled*." To our ancient ancestors, "mingled" meant "*to prepare by mixing*" and not the modern definition of "*to bring or mix together two substances, usually without fundamental loss of identity.*" [3,4]

That might not seem like an important difference between the two, but it significantly impacts our understanding of this Plague. Because in our modern mind, "*mingled*" is merely mixing two or more substances together that do not undergo any chemical reactions. For example, if we mix sugar and salt together, it is still just sugar and salt that are mixed and it does not undergo any chemical reactions on their own, thereby turning into a new substance. However, to our ancient ancestors this sugar and salt mixture would not be viewed simply as a mixture of sugar and salt. To them, it would be an entirely new substance that was both sugar and salt with the properties of both, but they would not have identified it as being either sugar or salt while at the same time thinking it was like both. They would think of the sugar and salt as being *"mingled"* together and creating an entirely new substance that had the properties of both salt and sugar.

Once again, that might seem strange to our modern way of thinking. But what it means is that the description given in the Bible of *"hail being mingled with fire"* is describing something that is neither "hail" nor "fire," but it is a substance that had properties of both hail and fire at the same time. Which, if we think about this for a moment, is a rather good description of highly radioactive fallout, debris, and other contamination that was mixed within storm clouds that would have been pushed north by the winds. In its journey, this radioactive material would have been pushed higher into the atmosphere. Where it would slowly become coated in water ice, turning it into hail, which then fell to the ground over Egypt.

This hail would look like regular run-of-the-mill hail, at first, but for anybody that was caught out in it or tried to pick any of it up, they would quickly receive radiation burns. The victim's exposed skin would feel as if it was on fire, with their skin turning red and blistering very quickly, looking much like a second-degree burn. If an individual picked some of this material up and held for any amount of time, the effects would worsen with it causing additional destruction of the skin itself. If it was held for too long, it would cause what would look like third-degree burns with the flesh turning black that would have quickly rotten off the bone. Such an event would be a genuinely gruesome sight and would have been unimaginably terrifying for the ancient Egyptians. To them it would have been a *"hail mingled with fire,"* because it looked like normal hail, but it would have burned like the flame of a fire for any that touched it.

Chapter ten of the Book of Exodus describes two of the final three Plagues to strike Egypt, one of Locusts that was then followed by three days of darkness. Both of which are easily explained by the aftereffects of the detonation of a nuclear weapon. The locusts would be driven by the original blast, with them trying to move away from it and the contamination in the same manner as the Plagues of frogs, lice, and flies. This would have naturally driven any Locusts or other insects straight up the Nile River Valley, right into the heart of Egypt.

30

The three days of darkness is much like the hail mingled with fire. It is just the remaining debris, fallout, and other contamination from the blast that create a black rain slowly drifting over Egypt that blocked out the sun.

Chapters eleven and twelve of the Book of Exodus give us the final and possibly the most horrible of all the Ten Plagues of Egypt; the death of the firstborn. Although radiation is not selective enough to kill only the firstborn, it would lay waste to the very young, especially infants. A more likely scenario would have been that the radiation would have killed many young Egyptian children, hitting newborns the hardest. With the most probable reason for the story of the firstborn was simply so their God would not look like a horrible merciless killer of innocent children. The story was simply changed, so only the firstborn died. Although this is still horrible, it is also highly symbolic, for the firstborn were traditionally the inheritors of the family's titles, lands, and wealth. So, symbolically, this represents a direct and devastating attack on the very fabric of Egyptian society.

After the deaths of the firstborn, in chapter eleven of the Book of Exodus, we discover that the Hebrews or, as we now know, the Hyksos elites, *"borrowed jewels"* from the Egyptians. It also presents Moses as being beloved by all, including the servants of Pharaoh. As with the death of the firstborn, this appears to be nothing more than the biblical writers presenting the ransacking of Egypt's many golden and silver treasures in a positive light. Remarkably, this is very close to what Apion claimed Manetho had spoken of in his second Exodus. That a renegade priest named *Osarseph* led an army of 80,000 Hyksos that ravaged the land of Egypt by taking the treasures of Egypt and committing many sacrileges against the traditional gods and temples before leaving for the wilderness in an Exodus out of Egypt. This is the critical connection that allows us to reconstruct the entire story leading up to the Exodus in a much more realistic chain of events that are rooted more in history and less in religious tradition and interpretation.

Once again, our starting point is when the Egyptians had retaken political and military control of Upper and Lower Egypt at the beginning of the Eighteenth Dynasty. During and after they had regained control, they rounded up all the Hyksos. They first forcibly expelled all the common people that made up the lower classes. This is the first Exodus of the 480,000 shepherd kings that is mentioned by Manetho and who Josephus mistakenly connects to the biblical Exodus. After expelling the commoners, the Egyptians then enslaved the Hyksos elite as common house slaves and servants. Although the Hyksos elites were turned into slaves, the Egyptians left the Hyksos's overall religious structure in place. The reason this was done was because the real political and social power of the Hyksos laid with the priesthood. This would have been the easiest way for the Egyptians to control such a large group of people who were always a threat. It the Egyptians could control the priesthood, then they would directly control the political system of the Hyksos, thereby controlling the entire community.

This small insight allows us to understand for the first time, on how the man remembered as Moses could have entered Pharaoh's household and how he came to have such influence and standing among the elites of the tribes. He must have been the son of a high-ranking member of the Hyksos leadership or priesthood who was a house slave to Pharaoh. He would have been handpicked at a young age, possibly by the Pharaoh himself, to be raised, trained, and educated by Pharaoh's court to be an adviser or possibly even a priest for the Hyksos. He would be one of their own, but he would be loyal to Pharaoh. This would mean that the story of the baby Moses being placed within an ark and set upon the waters of the Nile who was later found by Pharaoh's daughter was written to hide this connection.

Although it is highly probable that Moses was trained as an Egyptian priest, it is difficult to believe that the Hyksos would have accepted him as one of their own. It seems more likely that he would have filled the role of being Pharaoh's "official" religious adviser to the Hyksos' Head-priest. This would help to explain how Moses came to know Aaron. In this role as Head-priest, Aaron would have naturally had dealings either with Pharaoh or the representatives of Pharaoh. Strangely, according to the Bible, Aaron did not become the Head-priest of the tribes of Israel until after leaving Egypt.

To help us understand this, we need to remember the tribal structure of the Hyksos and their enslavement. Before the events of the Ten Plagues and the Exodus, it is likely that Aaron was viewed more as a shaman by the Hyksos than a priest in the traditional sense. For a shaman is normally thought of as being a man of unquestionable knowledge and mystical power. For he is the one that was chosen by the gods and speaks with them on the tribe's behalf. Although he speaks to the gods, he also a man that provides hope, faith, leadership, and advice for his people in times of trouble. He is also the keeper of the history of the people. He was a man whose power and standing came directly from the gods and whose word could not be questioned by the people, including the Chief or King of the tribes. To his people, he was much more than a simple priest or religious leader that followed some religious belief, and was in many ways the very heart and soul of the tribe.

It was this type of man that Pharaoh's religious adviser would have dealt with. A man that would have had the knowledge that would have allowed the man remembered as Moses to learn who he was, a Hyksos, and not an Egyptian.

It would have also been where the young Moses would have begun learning of the god of the Hyksos known as Hadad. It was this knowledge that led this young priestly adviser from Pharaoh's court to organize an uprising, which was quickly crushed by the Egyptians. An event that is remembered in the Bible this event is as Moses killing an Egyptian and who is then forced into a self-imposed exile in the wilderness for fear of punishment from Pharaoh.

During this exile, Moses encounters the God of the Hyksos, Hadad, who manifests itself as a burning bush and instructs him to return to Egypt to free His people. Upon Moses's return, we are told in both the biblical account and the Dream Vision of Enoch that he first meets Aaron, the shaman and religious leader of Hyksos' tribes. Soon after, they both meet with Pharaoh and demand the release of their people. Pharaoh, naturally, flatly refuses to release the enslaved Hyksos or Hebrews. Pharaoh's refusal to free the slaves is the event that brings upon the Egyptians the ten terrorizing Plagues by the God of the Hebrews.

These Plagues would have caused chaos, confusion, and weaken the Egyptian state's power and control, regardless if they were natural or artificial. Pharaoh would have been forced to retreat to his capital in the city of Thebes in order to deal with the ongoing disaster. This would have allowed the Hebrews under the leadership of Moses and Aaron to begin an uprising. During this time, they looted Egypt of many of her treasures and then began an Exodus out of Egypt. While Pharaoh was trying to gain some control over the disaster of the Plagues, he would have received news that the enslaved Hyksos had risen-up, looted and ransacked the countryside, and had left to the east. Pharaoh would have then ordered his remaining forces after the escaping slaves to punish them for their crimes and kill this Moses and Aaron, who caused all these problems in the first place.

These events bring us to the actual Exodus out of Egypt when 80,000 Hyksos under the joint leadership of Moses and Aaron, leave the city of Avaris and the Land of Goshen on the eastern part of the Nile delta. Soon after, this then brings us to the most famous and controversial part of the entire Exodus story, the crossing of the Red Sea. Numerous biblical scholars and historians have claimed and argued over the years that this is a "typo" and that it was, in reality, the "Reed Sea" that these Hyksos or Hebrews crossed. There are some significant problems with this claim, with the first and most damning one being the simple fact that not one of these biblical experts has ever presented any evidence showing that it is a "typo" as they claim. What is even more damning, is that the earliest known versions of the Exodus story in ancient Hebrew, all clearly state that it is the *"Red Sea"* they crossed. Thereby destroying the scholarly claim of it being a typo. [5,6,7,8]

The second major problem with this idea is that we know precisely where the "Reed Sea" was and what type of land it was. The "Reed Sea" that the biblical scholars speak of was a long narrow strip of marshy wetlands covered in reeds that stretched from the Red Sea's northernmost point up to the Mediterranean Sea. This "Reed Sea" was destroyed in the 1860s when the Suez Canal was built through the Isthmus of Suez. This once marshy reed-covered strip of land was not some problematic area to get through but was crisscrossed by numerous roads built and maintained by the Egyptians because these roads where their main trade route to the east. [9,10]

So, the very idea that this "Reed Sea" was the location of the Red Sea crossing is obviously being made by individuals that either have no knowledge of the area or they are betting on the simple fact that the average person, especially the typical American, has not actually read the biblical story or will take the time to look at a map. It is also evident that the scholars are also betting on the fact that the average person has next to no knowledge of ancient texts or where to get the information in the first place. This should make us very skeptical of anything they claim because a simple reading of the biblical story and looking at Google Earth or another detailed map of the area with a little research would allow someone to quickly see the scholars and historians are pushing a highly misleading and blatantly false interpretation of the Exodus story.

Because if we follow the biblical story of the Hebrews' journey out of Egypt while using a map of the area, we will notice that it takes them to the southernmost point of the Sinai Peninsula by the Straits of Tiran in the northeastern part of the Red Sea. These are the Straits that lead into the Gulf of Aqaba in the northeastern part of the Red Sea. Additionally, and possibly more important, if we also look at the entire Red Sea basin on a detailed map showing the seafloor. We will discover that this site is the only possible area of the entire Red Sea basin that the ancient Hebrews could have crossed. This is because almost the entire Red Sea basin is shaped like a canyon that has sheer drop-offs that extend almost straight down for hundreds of feet, approximately 600 to 1,200 feet (183 to 366 meters) from the edge of the current shoreline. In comparison, the Straits of Tiran are much shallower with a gentle slope that a person could easily walk upon if the water was removed. [11]

If we look closely at the Straits of Tiran, we will see that today the Straits have two primary channels. The one on the east side of the Straits and closest to Saudi Arabia, is approximately 70 meters deep (229 ft.) and a few kilometers across (1.8 miles). The second channel to the west is 205 meters deep (672 ft.)

and is about 15 kilometers wide (9.3 miles). There are also a few small islands that lay between the two channels. [12]

This is important because if we recall from our esoteric knowledge and based on the radioactive evidence, the Exodus occurred approximately 34,000 years ago. This is the time when the Earth was in the middle of the last great Ice Age that made the planet a vastly different world, than the one we see today. One of the most striking features that impacted the entire globe was that sea levels were much lower than today. With it estimated that the world's oceans were, on average, about 125 meters (410 ft.) lower than today. If we could go back to this ancient time, we would find that the Red Sea was a much smaller body of water than it is today. It would have been a long narrow sea that was lined with narrow beaches that ran to sheer cliffs hundreds of feet high on both sides of the Sea for much of its length. Not only would the entire Red Sea look entirely different, but the Straits of Tiran would have also been an entirely different landscape than what we see today. If we strip away 125 meters of water and account for 34,000 years of erosion. We end up with only one shallow channel that may have been approximately 800 to 900 meters (2,625 to 2,953 ft.) wide with less than a hundred feet of water (30.5m). It would also not be out of the question that this channel may have been even shallower with it being less than 50 feet (15.25m) deep at times due to tidal changes and storms. [13]

By realizing how shallow the waters were at this ancient time in the Straits of Tiran. It makes it easy to understand and imagine that if a large enough storm was to develop in the right place in the Red Sea basin. It could suck up vast amounts of water and empty the Straits of Tiran, which would have allowed the ancient Hebrews to cross on relatively dry ground to the other side. Then a short time later, as the Egyptians entered the now empty Straits pursuing their former slaves, the storm would have naturally moved away while dropping all the water that it sucked up and emptied the Strait. This would create a massive storm surge that would have been forced back violently into the Straits, which would have easily wiped out the Egyptians as recorded in the Bible. This allows us to realize that this could have been a completely natural event. However, it would have been viewed as a great miracle by those who saw it happen, especially after the recent events of the Plagues.

The only problem with this entire scenario would be the timing of getting the Hebrews there at the right moment to cross as the water was sucked out of the Straits by a massive storm. However, we are told in the Exodus story that the Hebrews had camped for a short period before the parting of the Red Sea. We are also told in both the biblical account and the Dream Vision of Enoch, that the Lord-God of the Hebrews impeded the forces of Pharaoh for a short time before allowing them to enter the crossing in pursuit. Both accounts indicate that some sort of "timing" was involved, which could be explained by a massive storm and having to wait for it to form and move. The biblical account of the parting of the Red Sea also adds significant weight to the idea that unusually large storm may have been responsible for this greatest of miracles.

"And Moses stretched out his hand over the sea; and the LORD caused the sea to go back by a strong east wind all that night, and made the sea dry land, and the waters were divided."
(Exodus, 14:21)

After crossing the Red Sea, the Bible says the Hebrews then journey to the Mountain of God, Mount Horeb, also more commonly known as Mount Sinai. The location of Mount Sinai as described in the Bible remains a hotly disputed topic. But if we consider that the ancient Hebrews crossed the Red Sea through the Straits of Tiran and then closely follow the directions given in the Book of Exodus. They will lead us to the 8,000+ ft. tall (2,580 m) "Mount Jabal al-Lawz" in western Saudi Arabia located at 28° 39' 15.73" North, by 35° 18' 16.35" East.
[14]

This is a highly unusual mountain that numerous people over the years have suspected is the real Mount Sinai of biblical tradition. One of the most striking features of this mountain is that the entire top part of the mountain is covered in black rock, but it is not from volcanic activity. The top of this mountain is strangely covered with countless pieces of burnt granite, which is a clear indication that at some ancient point in time the entire top of the mountain was subjected to extreme heat close to the melting point of granite, which is 1,215-1,260 C (2,219-2,300 F). This burnt granite appears to be evidence of the events described in the Bible of when the God of Abraham, Isaac, and Jacob descended from the sky and sat upon His Holy mountain, as described in the Book of Exodus. [15,16,17,18]

"And it came to pass on the third day in the morning, that there were thunders and lightnings, and a thick cloud upon the mount, and the voice of the trumpet exceeding loud' so that all the people that was in the camp trembled. And Moses brought forth the people out of the camp to meet with God; and they stood at the nether part of the mount. And mount Sinai was altogether on a smoke, because the LORD descended upon it in fire: and the smoke thereof ascended as the smoke of a furnace, and the whole mount quaked greatly."
(Exodus, 19:16-18)

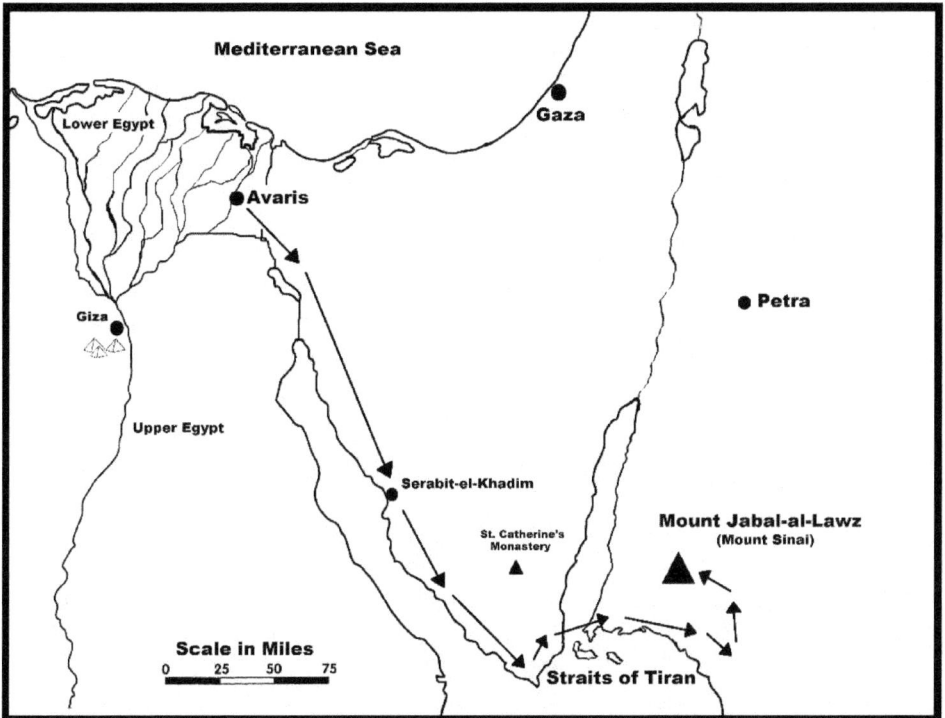

Exodus route of the Israelites to Mt. Jabal al-Laws.

In addition to the burnt granite, below the mountain on the plain that the ancient Hebrews would have camped upon, there is a central large stone that has numerous pictographs of cattle carved into it. Which seems to support the famous "*Golden Calf*" story of Bible when the Hebrews turned their backs upon their God. Close to this large alter-like stone is another site that has twelve stone pillars built around another large stone that looks like an altar. Which according to Exodus chapters twenty and twenty-four, Moses set up an altar "*at the foot of the mountain*" after writing down God's Laws in the Book of the Covenant. The altar was for burnt sacrifices and peace offerings of sheep and cattle and was to be constructed without steps, and without cut or chiseled stone. Next to this altar, Moses was commanded to construct twelve stone pillars that symbolized the twelve tribes of Israel. These sites, along with others around the base of the mountain, help support the idea that Mount Jabal al-Lawz is the real Mount Sinai of the biblical story. [19]

Remarkably, the government of Saudi Arabia has forbidden visitation to the sites of the possible altar and pillars and claim the entire site is historically

37

insignificant. They have not offered any explanation on why access to the site is forbidden nor why outside experts have not been permitted to examine the sites even with supervision. The Saudi government has also blocked off all paths to the sites with fences and warning signs. They have also built a police station in front of the site with the area being patrolled. The patrols are known to approach those who get close to the fences and to follow those anywhere in the vicinity. Although this is not proof, the current actions of the Sandi government restricting access to sites are highly suspicions that this site is much more important than they would like the public to believe. [20,21,22,23]

According to the Bible, it is at this point in their journey that the Hyksos elite began calling themselves the *"Israelites"* which roughly translates to meaning *"men who saw God."* What is not widely known is that the word "Israel" is not one word describing a people or nation. In Jewish and Christian texts of the Greco-Egyptian area during the Second Temple period of Judaism, it was understood to mean *"a man seeing God"* from the Hebrew words *"'yš -r'h - 'el,"* or in English, *"Is-ra-el."* The first word *"'yš"* or "Is" translates to meaning "man" when it is singular, but if combined with another word, as in this case, it becomes plural, meaning "men." The second word, *"r'h"* or "ra," does not translate directly into English. It is generally interpreted as meaning "to see" or "can see," with other translations interpreting as it being closer to "who see." The third word in this phrase is *"el,"* it is an ancient term that refers to God or gods depending on its usage. This then provides us the meaning of the word *"'yšr'h'el"* or "Israel." Which depending on the interpretation of the word *"r'h"* or "ra," a direct translation into English would be something like *"men to see God,"* *"men can see God,"* or even *"men who saw God.* This allows us to easily understand why the next generations referred to themselves as the *"children of Israel,"* or more appropriately, the *"children of the men who saw God."* [24]

After the events surrounding the Mountain of God, the Israelites then begin their long journey into the wilderness to the promised "Land of Canaan." Remarkably, the Biblical text does not say where this promised Land of Canaan was actually located. There are numerous vague references in the biblical text that place its location in reference to unknown rivers and cities whose locations have been forgotten or have yet to be found. However, the truth is, the Bible does not say where the Land of Canaan was located at. Nevertheless, there are a few critical clues to its location contained within the Book of Numbers when the Israelites departed from Mount Sinai and in the story of the Spies that Moses sent into the Land of Canaan once they had arrived at its borders.

According to the Book of Numbers, after spending two years, two months, and twenty days the Israelites left their encampment at the base of the Mountain of God. We are told they first embarked upon a three-day journey, which took them to the edge of the vast wilderness they called Paran. This would have placed them at the edge of the northwestern desert of modern-day Saudi Arabia. The Bible then implies that from this point, they journeyed straight to the promised Land of Canaan.

The traditional interpretation is that from this point, the Israelites then began a journey northward towards the area of what is today the modern-day nation of Israel and the city of Jerusalem. This traditional interpretation makes absolutely no sense. This is because the Egyptians were still entirely in control of this area, and it would have been impossible for these "*Shepherd Kings*" to return to any area under Egyptian control. This is the critical clue that allows us to realize that the traditional interpretation is wrong. However, although the traditional interpretation is wrong, it provides us the next critical clue and that there were only two possible directions the ancient Israelites could have taken, with one being south with the other being east.

If we follow the incomplete information given in the Book of Numbers and the Bible in general, there is no information or references that the Israelites traveled south along the Red Sea. This leaves only one possible direction for the Israelites to have journeyed, eastward into the vast wilderness of what we call the Saudi Arabia peninsula. The Bible also implies that the Israelites went directly to the Land of Canaan once they had left the edge of the wilderness of Paran. They would have traveled eastward from Mount Jabal al-Lawz across northern Saudi Arabia to the area that lays approximately between the border of modern-day Kuwait and Saudi Arabia on the west coast of the Persia Gulf. However, 34,000 years ago, the entire Persia Gulf of today was one broad and long valley with one large river that eventually flowed into what is now the Gulf of Oman and then into the Arabia Sea. Additionally, this location would have been an area where the mighty rivers of the Euphrates and Tigris with any other ancient rivers merged as then flowed down into this grand valley.

In the Book of Numbers, we are told that once the Israelites had arrived at the borders, Moses chose men from each tribe to go into this Land Canaan as spies to see what type of land it was and what type of people lived there. Upon their return after forty days of searching the land, these spies describe where they went and what they saw. Our next clue to the location of the Land of Canaan comes from the group of spies that goes to the south of the land where they find that the "*people were strong and lived in great walled cities*," and more importantly, they "*saw the children of Anak*." A people who have been traditionally believed to be giants or very close to being giants. Then the spies describe to Moses that:

"The Amalekites dwell in the land of the south: and the Hittites, and the Jebusites, and the Amorites, dwell in the mountains: and the Canaanites dwell by the seas and by the coast of Jordan."
(Numbers 13:29)

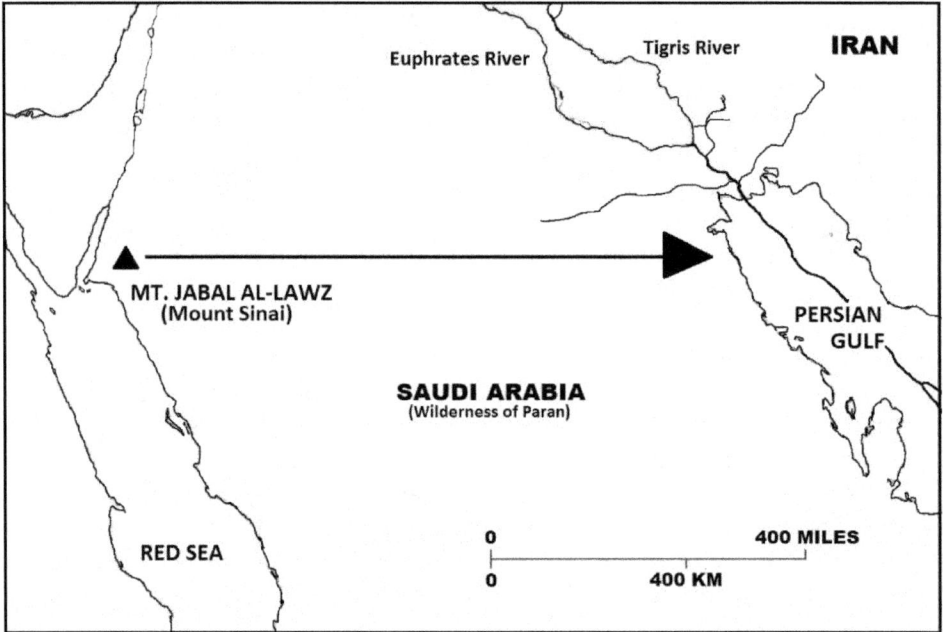

Map of the Israelites journey to the Land of Canaan.

This description in no way matches the traditional interpretation that the ancient Land of Canaan is the area of the modern-day nation of Israel. One of the essential clues in the above verse is that the "*Canaanites dwell by the seas and by the coast of Jordan,*" which implies that "Jordan" is not a river as traditionally believed, but is a land that is next to a large body of water. By realizing that the main body of the Israelites were in the area of the northern part of the valley that is today the Persia Gulf. The description that is given in the Book of Numbers beings to make more sense and appears to be describing the southwestern lands of the modern-day nation of Iran. Especially when we remember that 34,000 years ago, the Persia Gulf was a long broad valley that had a massive river system running its length that was fed by the Tigris and Euphrates rivers. It is also believed that there may have been at least one large lake with numerous smaller bodies of water fed by this large river in this long

40

valley. However, before we can explore this idea in more depth, we first need to examine the next part of the story of the spies sent into the Land of Canaan and the events that took place after they had returned and reported what they saw.

Once the spies had reported back to Moses and the Israelites, the people began to "*murmur*" and refuse to go into the Land of Canaan and fight the strong people that lived there. For this transgression and their refusal to follow the commands of their Lord, the Israelites are punished by having to wander the wilderness for forty years until "*that generation who transgressed against their Lord had passed from this Earth.*" We are then vaguely told of the Israelites wanderings through the wilderness until that first generation had passed from the Earth and their children and their children's children were the ones that followed Moses. The Bible also tells us that during this time, the Israelites had grown to massive numbers that were far larger than the original group of 80,000 Hyksos that Manetho claimed had left Egypt. After forty years of wandering, these children of Israel eventually return to enter the promised Land of Canaan. However, unlike before, we are provided with more information about the location of these children of Israel and their eventual crossing Jordan into the promised Land of Canaan.

After forty years of wandering through the wilderness, the Bible states that these children of Israel come to and camped upon the "*plains of Moab, by Jordan near Jericho.*" In order for us to figure out where these "*plains of Moab, by Jordan near Jericho*" were and the real location of the Land of Canaan was actually located we need to return to the Book of Numbers and the few additional clues it contains.

Our first clue to their location can be found in chapter thirty-one of the Book of Numbers where the Israelites are commanded by their Lord-God to conquer a people called the Midianites. The Book of Numbers provides a surprisingly detailed account of the Midianites' destruction at the hands of the Israelites. It also gives us a view into the world of the tribes of the children of Israel and how they more-or-less operated as pillagers, raiders, looters, and bandits as they moved around the wilderness in their wanderings.

In this chapter, we are told that the Israelites' army killed all the men of the Midianites on the battlefield and then took all the remaining men, women, and children as captives. Along with "*all their cattle, their flocks, and all their goods.*" We are then told that all these captives, except those few female children and young women who had not "*known man by lying with him,*" were all then brutally murdered in cold blood. Then the remaining virgin women and female children were taken by the different male members of the various tribes as wives. This is an example of how the Israelites numbers were able to grow, they simply just conquered other people and took their young female virgins as wives after they had killed every man, woman, and child. Although this type of behavior may seem harsh or even brutal, it was a common practice in the ancient world to kill every single person of a conquered people, except for the young female virgins, who then became wives of the conquers.

Once the Midianites had been destroyed, their bounty and women spilt up among the various tribes of the children of Israel. The Bible then says the children of Israel began to prepare to enter the Land of Canaan with them staging this invasion on the "*plains of Moab, by Jordan near Jericho.*" This is our next clue that the ancient Land of Canaan are not the lands in and around the modern-day nation of Israel.

To understand how this very short phase is the key to realizing that the entire traditional interpretation that this verse is describing the area around the river Jordan in modern-day Israel is incorrect. We must first understand the origin and ancient meaning of the words "*Jordan*" and "*Jericho*." Additionally, we must also understand that the word "near" was added when the Bible was translated into English in the 1600s and not contained within the original text. Which then changes the phase to "*the plains of Moab, by Jordan Jericho.*" The next step is to understand the origin and the ancient Hebrew meaning of the words Jordan and Jericho. The origin of the word "*Jordan*" is believed to be derived from the Hebrew word "*yarden,*" which means "*to flow down*" or "*descend.*" In modern terms, it simply means a place where water flows down. The origin of the word "*Jericho*" is unknown, but it is believed to be possibly from or is related to the Hebrew words "*yareach,*" which means "moon," and the word "*reyach,*" which means "*fragrant.*" [25]

With our understanding of the mystical esoteric symbolism and the secret history of creation that it holds, we can quickly recognize the symbolism of the "*moon,*" with its traditional relationship to the Mother Goddess. If we add the additional possible meaning of "*fragrant*" to "*moon,*" we can easily realize that it must be referring to a temple or holy site connected to the Earth Mother or Mother Goddess. When we combined this with the ancient meaning of the word "*Jericho*" meaning to "*to flow down,*" we can recognize the esoteric meaning that this is a description of a Temple dedicated to the Mother Goddess near a river flowing down through a valley, in the land of Jordan that located next to the plains of Moab.

This understanding allows us to realize for the first time that this part of the story is not speaking of a "city" named "Jericho" as is so commonly believed but it is really speaking of a Temple dedicated to the Moon or Mother Goddess that is in the land of Jordan by a river that flows by it, or Jericho. As with all

42

Temple complexes, this Temple would have been supported by a near-by city, which according to the Bible was the first city the Israelites conquered once they had entered the Land of Canaan, commonly known as Jericho.

When we combine this information with our knowledge that the Persian Gulf did not exist at this ancient time, we can easily see on any map of the area that just to the west of this long shallow valley, there was and still is to this day a broad plain as described in the Biblical text. Today it is a vast sandy plain that makes up the eastern part of Saudi Arabia, but 34,000 years ago, it would have been a lush grassland.

Our next major clue comes from the description given in the Book of Numbers when Moses is shown the borders of the Land of Canaan by his Lord, shortly before his death.

"And the LORD spake [spoke] unto Moses, saying, Command the children of Israel, and say unto them, When ye come into the land of Canaan; (this is the land that shall fall unto you for an inheritance, even the land of Canaan with the coasts thereof:) Then your south quarter shall be from the wilderness of Zin along by the coast of Edom, and your south border shall be the outmost coast of the salt sea eastward: And your border shall turn from the south to the ascent of Akrabbim, and pass on to Zin: and the going forth thereof shall be from the south to Kadeshbarnea, and shall go on to Hazaraddar, and pass on to Azmon: And the border shall fetch a compass from Azmon unto the river of Egypt, and the goings out of it shall be at the Sea. And as for the western border, ye shall even have the great Sea for a border: this shall be your west border. And this shall be your north border: from the great Sea ye shall point out for you mount Hor: From mount Hor ye shall point out your border unto the entrance of Hamath; and the goings forth of the border shall be to Zedad: And the border shall go on to Ziphron, and the goings out of it shall be at Hazarenan: this shall be your north border. And ye shall point out your east border from Hazarenan to Shepham: And the coast shall go down from Shepham to Riblah, on the east side of Ain; and the border shall descend, and shall reach unto the side of the Sea of Chinnereth eastward: And the border shall go down to Jordan, and the goings out of it shall be at the salt sea: this shall be your land with the coasts thereof round about. And Moses commanded the children of Israel, saying, This is the land which ye shall inherit by lot, which the LORD commanded to give unto the nine tribes, and to the half-tribe: For the tribe of the children of Reuben according to the house of their fathers, and the tribe of the children of Gad according to the

house of their fathers, have received their inheritance; and half the tribe of Manasseh have received their inheritance:"
(Numbers, 34: 1 -14)

Although both Jews and Christians traditionally believe that this is describing the area between the Mediterranean Sea, the Dead Sea, the northern part of the Red Sea, and the small river Jordon in the modern-day nation of Israel. However, as we have just read, the area between the Black Sea, the Caspian Sea, with the northern mountain range between these two areas, including the strip of land following the Zagros Mountains southward towards the Arabia Sea, in what is the modern-day nation of Iran, is a much better fit to what is described in the Bible. We are also provided with additional information on the day Moses dies. Before his death, he is commanded by his Lord to:

"Get thee up into this mountain Abarim, unto mount Nebo, which is in the land of Moab, that is over against Jericho; and behold the land of Canaan which I give unto the children of Israel of possession:"
(Deuteronomy 32:49)

By understanding that the plains of Moab were located on the western side of the broad valley that is today the Persian Gulf. We can realize that there is only one large mountain on the western side of the Persia Gulf that matches this description of Mount Nebo in the Bible. Which is the 9,957 ft. (3,035m) tall Mount Jebel-Shams that is located in the southeastern part of the Arabian Peninsula south of the Strait of Hormuz in the modern-day nation of Oman. It is the highest peak in the grouping of mountains known as the Hajar range that overlook the Gulf of Oman with the southern parts of Iran being visible across the Persian Gulf. But, thirty-four thousand years ago, instead of looking across the waters of the Persian Gulf Moses would have seen a great river that had whipped around the Strait of Hormuz slightly to the north and then run down into what is today the Gulf of Oman, thus forming a large delta area that emptied into the Arabian Sea. Given the geographical layout of this part of the Persia Gulf, this river would have flowed down the rather steep slopes before it flattened out forming the delta region as it emptied into the Arabian Sea. [26]

When we put all these clues together, we can realize that thirty-four thousand years ago, this entire area would have been a lush land with abundant plant life, wildlife, and fresh water. An abundant and beautiful land that must have seemed like the perfect place to build a temple dedicated to the Earth Mother and life itself. A place that was by the plains of Moab, in the land of Jordan were the waters flow down, or as the Bible records it, the *"plains of Moab, by Jordan [near] Jericho."* With also realizing that Mount Jebel-Shams in the modern-day nation of Oman, may be the Mount Nebo that Moses was commanded to stand upon. We can understand for the first time in modern-history that the ancient Israelites were camped just west and northwest of the Strait of Hormuz and later crossed into the Land of Canaan in this general area.

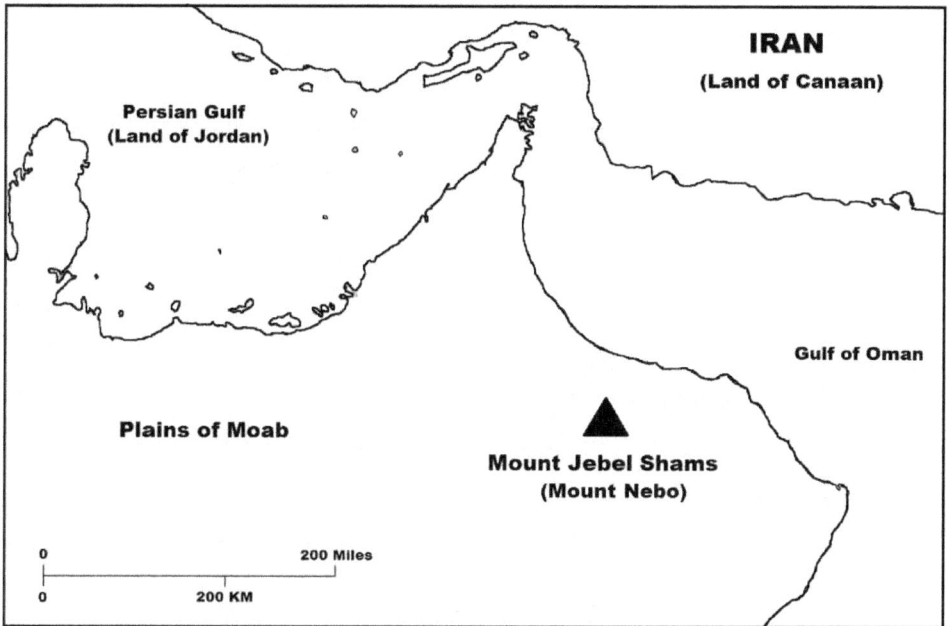

The Plains of Moab.

This understanding then allows us to say with some confidence that the ancient Land of Canaan was actually located in the area that is today the Islamic nation of Iran and not the lands of the modern-day nation of Israel 1,187 miles (1,910 km) to the west. This is the esoteric knowledge of the true location of the ancient Land of Canaan. However, this esoteric interpretation may be a bit difficult for many to accept at this moment. We will explore why this knowledge was lost and why the modern-day nation of Israel became known as the Land of Canaan.

Chapter 4

Invasion and Settlement

Although the esoteric idea that the modern-day nation of Iran could be the true location of the ancient Land of Canaan may seem strange. It will in time, explain several the mysteries of the ancient world. Our starting point for this part of our journey is just before the Bronze Age collapse and the numerous tribes we know that moved into the area the Iranian Plateau, also known as the Persian Plateau and the countless valleys of the Zagros Mountains.

We know very little about the ancient tribes that settled in the areas between the Black Sea and the Caspian Sea, in what is now the far northwestern part of Iran and the southern parts of the modern-day nation of Azerbaijan. We do not know where they may have originally come from or the language they spoke. Historians have proposed numerous different theories about where these people came from and who they were. With many believing that they came from the lands of southern Russia around the northern parts of the Caspian Sea. However, the truth is, nobody has any idea or evidence where these people came from. Historically, they literally just seem to show up out of nowhere. [1]

Historically, scholars call these mysterious people that settled on the Iranian Plateau and in the valleys of the Zagros Mountains the *"Proto-Indo-Europeans."* Although we do not know where these people came from, we know that once these people arrived on the Iranian Plateau, they quickly displaced, subdued, or oppressed the people that were already living there. As with not knowing where these people originally came from, we also do not know what language these people spoke, nor do we know what racial or ethnic group they belong to. However, it is suspected that they were made up of numerous different ethnic groups and tribes that lived all around the Fertile Crescent and were not actually "one people." We also know that once they had settled the Iranian Plateau and the valleys of the Zagros Mountains, their numbers quickly grew. Over the centuries they slowly moved outward into the surrounding areas and in the process, they become the people we known as the "*Indo-European people.*" [2,3]

Since these Proto-Indo-European and later Indo-European people are not made up of one single people, culture, or racial group, scholars identify them through the common language they are believed to have spoken and the common linguistic terms they used. This Proto-Indo-European language is believed to be the mother tongue of almost all modern-day languages. It has been one of the primary methods historians have used to trace the Indo-Europeans' movements through the ages. Since there is little to no archeological evidence of these people, almost everything we know about them comes from the languages, cultures, and mythologies that came from later daughter cultures that were descended from them. It is also important to remember that we are speaking of a large diverse group of people made up of many different tribes, cultures, customs, and languages that we identify through the common language they spoke. This common tongue is known as the Proto-Indo-European language and then later as the Indo-European language group as they began to spread out from the Iranian Plateau. [4,5]

Although the origin of these ancient people who invaded and settled the Iranian Plateau is a complete mystery to modern scholars. We can begin understanding with our newly found esoteric knowledge that these mysterious Proto-Indo-European people that seem to appear out of nowhere on the Iranian Plateau, just before the Bronze Age Collapse, are the ancient Israelites of the Bible with their arrival and settlement of the Land of Canaan. This idea may seem outrageously radical at the moment, but as we learned with our journey through the Dream Vision of Enoch as a whole. It only takes one or two small pieces of information to radically change our entire understanding of the story.

Our first step in understanding this, is to take this radical idea that the ancient Israelites spoken of in the Bible are the people we know historically as the Proto-Indo-European people and combine it with our esoteric knowledge from the Dream Vision that the Exodus continued after the tribes had crossed "*steam of water*" under the leadership of the legendary divine twin brothers.

"Then that sheep, their leader which had become a man, withdrew from them and fell asleep, and all the sheep sought it and cried over it with a great crying. And I saw till they left off crying for that sheep and crossed that stream of water, and there arose the two sheep as leaders in the place of those which had led them and fallen asleep [lit. 'had fallen asleep and led them']." (Book of Enoch, 89: 38,39)

As we will discover, this radical idea along with the above verses from the Dream Vision of Enoch will allow us to understand the hidden esoteric story of the great Exodus out of Egypt by the Israelites contained within the Bible. It will also allow us to trace their movements through history and around the world, in a way never imagined before.

Our next step starts during the wanderings of the Israelites through the wilderness. During this time, the Bible tells us that the twelve tribes of Israel conquered an unknown number of other tribes and people they encountered during their wanderings. The Bible also details how the armies of the tribes of Israel would kill every man, woman, and child, except the virgin women, of every people they came into conflict with during their time in the wilderness. This helped to vastly increase their numbers, but it also introduces new words, customs, and cultural elements into the culture of the tribes.

Over time this influx of new words and their need to communicate with each other would naturally lead to these different tribes to create an entirely new language or common tongue. It is this common tongue that these people created to speak with each other that becomes the language we call Proto-Indo-European, the mother tongue of almost all languages today. However, at the same time, each tribe would keep speaking their original language among themselves before they joined with the other tribes. This new common language of the tribes would naturally influence the original tribal languages transforming them into almost entirely new languages as they wandered around the wilderness. This is a critical clue that the wandering in the wilderness and the later second part of the Exodus had to have occurred over a much more extended time than the forty years recorded in the biblical story. Because it usually takes many generations for multiple languages to fuse and transform into a new one.

The Bible tells us that once the first generation that rebelled against their Lord had passed away, and their numbers had grown large, the children of Israel returned to enter into the ancient Land of Canaan by force. The Bible also tells us that after the tribes conquered the Land of Canaan, the tribes of Judah and Benjamin, together with the tribe of Levi, settled in this Land of Canaan. According to the Book of Joshua, once this initial settlement was complete, the

49

other tribes continued with the Exodus to the lands each tribe had inherited by the casting of lots. Which according to the Dream Vision of Enoch and from our esoteric knowledge, occurred under the leadership of the legendary divine twin brothers.

By understanding where the ancient Land of Canaan was located and that the Israelites of the Bible are actually the Proto-Indo-European tribes that settled these ancient lands. We can begin understanding that the later immigration, invasion, and settlement of the Indo-European people are the other tribes of Israel moving to their inherited lands under the leadership of the twin brothers. As we continue deeper into this esoteric idea, we will learn that these twin brothers of myth and legend are the next step to understanding how the Israelites moving to their inherited lands and the immigration of the Indo-European speaking people of history are the same people. We will also discover how this second phase of the Exodus is directly connected to the Bronze Age collapse of civilization and how it becomes the political, social, and religious foundations that will become the civilizations of the Classical Ancient World.

For many, even with our esoteric symbolic knowledge of the Dream Vision of Enoch, this revelation may be slightly hard to believe that the Israelites of the Exodus and the Proto-Indo-European speaking people of history are the same people. As radical as this idea may be too many, as we go farther into the story, we will discover that if we combined this idea with the legends and mythology of the twin brothers, we can trace their movements across the world and that they match the immigration of the Indo-European people. Not only can we trace their movements, but we also learn how they assimilated the existing local pantheon of gods into their own—thereby transforming both into a new religious system that incorporated elements of both. During this process, we will also be able to reconstruct some of the original religious belief that these children of Israel brought with them. We will also learn the secrets of what happened to the tribes that settled the Land of Canaan.

For us to understand how these different and conflicting ideas fit together and how they are connected to events that unfold in the Land of Canaan. We must start with this second phase of the Exodus under the leadership of the divine twin brothers' leadership as each tribe moved to their individual lots of land.

By realizing that the ancient Israelites of the Exodus are the Proto-Indo-European people that later become the Indo-European people. We can easily understand from history that the first lands that these Indo-European people or Israelites entered was the Indus Valley to the south. History remembers these people as the Indo-European *"Aryan"* speaking tribes that appear to have come in several waves into the Indus Valley that occurred over centuries. Strictly speaking, "Aryan" is purely a linguistic term, like "Proto-Indo-European" and "Indo-European," and does not refer to "one people" or one "racial group." It is used to help identify the different waves of tribes that came through the Hindu Kush that washed deeper and deeper into the Indus Valley and the Punjab, eventually reaching the upper Ganges River that all spoke an Indo-European language we call "Aryan." Scholars and historians believed this Aryan language is the original language that gave birth to the Sanskrit language. There is also the additional twist to the story that the first wave of tribes to arrive in the Indus Valley were not the Aryan speaking Indo-Europeans, but they were the tribes that had been displaced and then pushed out of the Land of Canaan as the Israelites settled it. [6]

Historically, these Aryan speaking people's movement into the Indus Valley has been viewed as an invasion. However, we now know that it was not always a violent invasion, but it was more of a slow settlement with fits of violence that eventually led to a complete political takeover of the Indus Valley. Remarkably, this settlement of the Indo-European people in the Indus Valley follows the same pattern we saw in Egypt with the Hyksos.

As the Aryan speaking tribes first moved into the Indus Valley's pastoral lands, they first encountered local tribes that were very similar to themselves that were already established in the area and on the adjoining lands. Once the Aryan numbers had grown large enough from this first settlement, they started taking over the local tribes, just as they had done before in Egypt. As with Egypt, these Aryan speaking tribes would normally only remove the tribe's or small village's leadership and replace them with their own. They would then begin assimilating the rest of the people into their tribe while allowing the local people to keep their religious beliefs, customs, culture, and language. The only real change that occurred for the commoner was that their religious leaders and places of worship were relocated to the central area where the ruling class of the Aryans had settled. Although this settlement is similar to what occurred in Egypt, the archaeological evidence shows us that unlike Egypt, the existing Bronze Age Indus Valley civilization, known as the Harappan, appears to have already been in a slow state of collapse when the Aryan speaking tribes first began to arrive in the Indus Valley. [7]

It is unknown why the Harappan civilization of the Indus Valley was collapsing at this point. It is possible that the earlier waves of refugees from the settlement of the Land of Canaan to the north had put incredible stress upon the existing civilization. It is equally possible that it was due to natural changes in rain fall or changes with the Indus river that the Harappans depended upon. Nevertheless, it also just as equally possible that some other factor like prolonged warfare or disease was behind its collapse. Ultimately, in the end, it matters little why the Harappan civilization was collapsing because it quickly crumbled once the Aryan speaking tribes began their migration deeper into the Indus Valley. There is also little doubt that much violence marked the coming of these first tribes, for these Aryan speaking tribes were nomadic warriors armed with horses, chariots, with a mixture of advanced bronze and iron weapons. There is also ample evidence that once the Aryans had taken over, the native people lived side-by-side peacefully with the new arrivals, keeping their own beliefs, customs, and practices alive. Although there are many examples of the locals and the Aryans living peacefully, archaeologists have found puzzling evidence that many other villages and city-states of the Indus valley were either abruptly abandoned or completely destroyed. While the archaeologists may find this type of evidence puzzling, we can quickly recognize that it is the same pattern we first encountered in Egypt with the Hyksos. We will also see a similar pattern unfold once these Aryans had gained a solid foothold in the Indus Valley and began to reorganize the local pantheon of gods. [8]

As we saw in Egypt, as these Aryan speaking Indo-European people begin their settlement of the Indus Valley, we see the same common feature that is unique to these people and how they settled an area as they moved onto new lands. As we have already started to learn, when these Indo-European tribes began moving into a new land, as with Egypt, they did not arrive as one large group, but they came slowly in small groups, most likely as individual clans. This first step was obviously to gather intelligence on the area and the people who lived there. Just as they had with the Land of Canaan, this information would then allow the tribes to pick the most promising area with a few small tribes that were similar too them in order to establish a solid foothold and base of operations. Once this was accomplished, a second wave would then begin entering the area and surrounding lands.

This stage of settlement appears to be a time of much violence in the Indus valley as the Aryan tribes began to take over the surrounding tribes and small villages. Once they had taken over enough villages and small communities that allowed them to established a solid foothold with a central base of operations, they begin to challenge the city-states that made up the Harappan civilization for their political and military control of the surrounding lands. As the city-states were being conquered or destroyed, a third wave would begin to arrive. This would consist of all the remaining tribes, with their women, children and livestock which would then help establish control of the surrounding lands that the original tribes had first settled.

After they had established themselves and their political power was secure, the Indo-European or Israelite tribe that was to inherit the land would take control. Once they were firmly in control, the other tribes would then begin moving on to the next area, where they would repeat this same process. Once the main body of the tribes had moved on, the remaining tribe that had inherited the land would begin their unique process of fusion and assimilation of the native population. This assimilation took the form of them replacing any of the remaining elites of the local area with their own, normally through intermarrying with them, while also rearranging the local pantheon of gods. As they rearranged the pantheon, they took great care to slowly change it and the existing belief system so that it was acceptable to the lower classes that made most of the population. To understand how they accomplished this social and religious change, we must take a much more in-depth look at how the local population of the Indus Valley was taken over by the Aryans during this settlement.

As we saw in Egypt with the Hyksos, once the Aryan tribes had gained a solid foothold, they would begin slowly taking over the surrounding tribes, villages, and small communities that were closest to their primary area of settlement once their numbers had grown large enough. This population growth of the Aryans is from a combination of taking over surrounding communities and the arrival of fellow tribesmen coming into the area. Once their numbers had grown large enough and they had taken over enough land, they would begin challenging the city-states spread throughout the Indus Valley. What happened to each of these different communities was directly dependent on whether the people resisted these Aryan speaking tribes or not.

If the city-states welcomed them and the elites of that community swore allegiance to the leadership of the Aryans. Then next to nothing would happen to them or the local people. The only real change would be that several family members of the ruling elites would be relocated to the central area of settlement. This was done to ensure their loyalty and that they would honor their oaths to their new Aryan rulers. They Aryans would also settle a large clan in the area that would also help in ensuring the local elites and the population would follow the wishes of their new Aryan overlords. The only other change that would occur was that the local religious cult center and its priest would also be relocated back to the central area of settlement of the Aryan rulers.

If the community resisted the Aryans but quickly surrendered without much of a fight. Then the Aryan tribes would usually kill all the elites, who would then be replaced with loyal Aryans. They would then remove approximately half the native population back to the central area of settlement. These people would then be replaced with an equal number of people either from the Aryan tribes or tribes loyal to them. Remarkably, in both situations, very little if anything would change for the common people that made up the lower classes of the community. Their religious beliefs, customs, and practices would be left intact by their new rulers, with only the local cult center of the community and its priest being relocated to the main settlement of the Aryans.

If the elites of the community resisted and the common people of the lower classes did not. For example, if a city-state met the Aryans on the battlefield with their army and lost. After the battle, the Aryans would kill the entire army and all the remaining elites without mercy. They would then depopulate the entire city-state by removing all the lower classes back to the central area of settlement, while turning many of them into slaves. Although the city-state would normally be abandoned, it was not uncommon for the Aryans or those loyal to the Aryans to then occupy the city-state once the local population was removed.

If the city-state continued to resist them after being defeated on the battlefield with the Aryan tribes having to lay siege to the city-state. Then no mercy of any kind was shown once the walls of the city had been breached. The Aryans would kill every man, woman, and child, in the city, leaving the bodies where they fell, sparing only the young female virgins to be taken as wives. After they had slaughtered the entire population, they would then loot the city of any items of value. Then they would destroy it, typically by fire, and then abandon the site forever. The famous ancient city of Mohenjo-Daro may be the best example of what happened to a city-state of the Indus valley whose population had resisted these Aryan tribes. Within its ruins, we find the gruesome evidence that the entire population was slaughtered with the bodies left lying in the streets where they fell. There is also ample evidence that the city was looted with much of it being destroyed by fire, with the entire site then being abandoned forever. [9]

Although the Harappan civilization collapsed under the weight of the Aryans, we have ample amounts of archaeological evidence that the assimilation and fusion of Harappan culture with the Aryans had a massive influence on the religion that becomes known as Hinduism. It is clear from the archaeological evidence that the Aryans did not bring a culture as advanced as the Harappans. Nevertheless, the religious beliefs of the Aryans combined with the beliefs of the Harappans laid the foundations of one of the world's great religions, Hinduism, including its rigid social system we call caste. [10]

By understanding who these Aryan speaking tribes were, allows us to understand that the religious and social structures they imposed on the local population give us our closest look at the original religious beliefs of these children of Israel. Although Hinduism is one of the world's great religions, it is a vastly different belief system than the traditional monotheistic religions of the western world or the people we normally think of as the Jews, in particular.

Our best source of information about this ancient time of Aryan India comes from the Rig-Veda and numerous Vedic hymns that have survived. Within these ancient texts, we find a world of Bronze Age barbarians with advanced bronze and iron weapons, mounted on horseback moving into the Indus Valley. Some archaeologists believe they can identify in the Vedic hymns references to the destruction of the Harappan city-states. The general setting of the Vedic hymns is a land that stretched from the western banks of the Indus River to the mighty Ganges River far to the east. It was a rich land inhabited by a light-skinned Aryan speaking people who made up the elite classes of rulers and religious leaders while living alongside the far more numerous darker-skinned natives. [11]

Before the coming of the tribes of Aryans, the ancient societies of the various people who lived in northern India and the Indus valley were formed by deeply rooted traditions centered around the family, clan, and tribal ties. Once the Aryan tribes had arrived and established control, this ancient pattern of life began to slowly give way to the Aryan social organization of society that we know as the "caste system." We must first look at this ancient Aryan system of caste to understand the later development of Hinduism. This process will also allow us to investigate the Israelites' original religious beliefs that composed this second phase of the great Exodus. [12]

The vast caste system that still governs much of India society to this very day appears to have been born out of the first-class divisions of early Aryan tribal society. This division of society consisted of a warrior-aristocracy ruling class, known as the "*Kshatriyas.*" This warrior-aristocracy shared power with a potently powerful priestly class, known as the "*Brahmans,*" both of which ruled over the ordinary peasant-farmers known as the "*Vaishyas,*" that made up the majority of the people. Movement between these first three classes of society appears to have been possible in the very beginning. The only unleapable barrier in these early times seems to have been between the native non-Aryans and the Aryans; one of the words used to denote the aboriginal inhabitants of India by the Aryans was "*dasa,*" which eventually came to mean "slave." One of the first categories added to this early class system was for non-Aryans, known as the "*Shudras,*" or the "unclean." These were the dark-skinned native people that could not study nor hear the Vedic hymns of the Aryans. This division of the Shudras from the Aryans clearly rested on the Aryans' wish to preserve their racial integrity from the native peoples. [13]

Over the centuries, this basic system of division of society based on three primary classes was slowly elaborated upon. As society slowly became more complex, further divisions and subdivisions appeared that were usually based upon occupation. Nevertheless, no matter how complex society became, the priestly class of the Brahmans was always the highest class of society that played a crucial role in all parts of society. The Brahmans quickly became so powerful that even the Kings of the Kshatriyas could not stand against them or question their actions. Soon, with the Brahmans' blessing, marriage and eating taboos were codified within each class, restricting them to marrying within them, eating only food cooked by fellow caste members, and, most importantly, obeying their regulations that governed their caste. These regulations typically limited who could belong to each caste and limited the members of each caste to one craft or profession. This lengthy process gradually led to the appearance of the caste system as we know it. Not only did the Aryans lay the foundations for the caste system that still governs Indian society, but with the help of this social system, they also laid the foundations of the religion that is still at the heart of Indian civilization, Hinduism. A religion that provides the moral framework and the religious reasons for the existence of the caste system. [14]

According to the archaeological evidence, before the arrival of the Aryans, it appears that the religious worship of the people of the Indus Valley Civilization was primarily focused on an Earth Mother or Mother Goddess figure, a male Shiva-like Sky-father god figure, with a Bull, along with numerous other gods and goddesses that were under these three. This simple arrangement of the worship of a Mother Goddess, a Male Sky-god, along with a Bull appears to be the common factor in the religions of every known Bronze Age civilization and culture. Once again, as they had done in Egypt, one of the first things the Aryans did was elevate the existing minor male fertility god to being the Supreme god of the entire pantheon. In this case, it was the god Shiva. Several seals have been found in the Harappan cities that appear to show a figure who looks like an early version of Shiva. These seals are also found with stones that appear much like the Lingam found in modern Hindu temples, the phallic cult-object that is the symbolic emblem of the god Shiva. [15]

This phallic cult-object is the next important way to trace the moment of these people and their Supreme god. Because once they have secured their political position over the local population, they always elevated the existing local minor male fertility god to the position of being the Supreme god of the pantheon along with his phallic cult symbolism. In ancient artwork, this symbolism of this Supreme god is commonly displayed as a male god with an unusually large erect penis. This phallic symbolism also leads to confusion on this new Supreme god's identity at later points in time in different cultures. Although it can lead to confusion, this unique phallic symbolism that is associated with this minor

56

fertility god makes him particularly easy to follow through the different cultures. As we go deeper into this second phase of the Exodus, this symbolism and how to follow it will become more understandable. In addition to elevating the minor male fertility god to being the Supreme god, he also becomes the mighty storm god, whose legendary weapon is the terrible thunderbolt. [16,17,18,19,20]

This brings us to our first example of how Aryans slowly fused and assimilated their religious beliefs with the local population's existing beliefs. Based on the evidence we have; the original Supreme god of the Aryans appears to have been the god known as *"Indra."* Before arriving in the Indus Valley, Indra was the Aryan god of the storm, thunder, and the life-giving rain. He was the great Lord of the heavens, the greatest of all warriors, and was above all the other gods in power and standing. His greatest weapon was a bolt of special lightning called *"Vajrayudh."* He was also known as a god who disguised himself to win over women and who went to any lengths of scheming to keep his position as the chief leader of the gods. These traits are the same traits of the Supreme god of many other cultures, with Zeus or Jupiter of Greek and Roman mythology being two of the best-known examples in the western world. These common elements of Indra appear to be the same as the earliest known versions of the Shiva-like god of the Indus Valley civilization. [21,22,23]

Our next step is to understand how the Aryans put this assimilating and fusing of the local religious beliefs with their own into practice. Once the Aryans had established themselves in the Indus Valley, they replaced their version of the Supreme god with the local one. In this case, the Aryan Supreme god Indra was replaced with the existing Shiva-like god of the native people. It appears that the Aryans kept their own mythology of Indra while superimposing it onto the Shiva-like god of the natives. Slowly over time, possibly centuries, these two gods fused into one god, creating the god Shiva as he is known today. Remarkably, although the two gods were fused into one, the Aryan god Indra was also fused with the local version of the god of the waters, a god remembered in the Vedic hymns as *"Varuna."* [24]

This existing native god of the waters, known as Varuna, was an almost exact copy of the Hyksos god Hadad and the Babylonian god Adad. In the Vedic hymns, Varuna was known as the ruler of the world and enforcer and upholder of law and order. He is said to have a thousand eyes and oversees the entire world of man. Hence, he is commonly known as the god of moral law that punishes those who transgress against the law but forgives them out of compassion and who loves it when they repent their transgressions, pray, and make a sacrifice to him. He is also the mighty Lord of the oceans, the waters, and all aquatic animals, in the same way as Poseidon or Neptune. He was also believed to be the Lord of the wind, which helps sustain life by bringing the rains to the crops. In the earliest Vedic writings, he was the Supreme King of the gods in the very beginning of time, but he yielded his position as Supreme King when he was fused with Indra with his kingship transferring to the new Supreme god Shiva. [25]

Although we are missing numerous details, this small bit of information allows us to understand that the Indo-European people were willing to reshuffle and modify their pantheon of gods as needed to accommodate the local population. When they began to assimilate and fuse with the beliefs, customs, and culture of the native population, they would not change the basic principles of the local belief to win over the hearts-and-minds of the lower classes that made up the bulk of the population. A modern example of this process can be seen in how the early Catholic Church assimilated, fused, and then ultimately Christianized pagan belief throughout Europe while keeping the basic ideas of Christianity and the teachings of the Catholic Church intact.

This willingness of the Aryans and the Indo-European people in general to modify their pantheon to fit with the local religious belief and customs adds numerous layers of confusion as these people slowly moved from place to place. Adding to this confusion, it appears that it was common for the other tribes to adopt some of these changes before they moved on to the next lot of land under the leadership of the twin brothers. Nevertheless, these things do make it difficult to follow which god is which in the many different religions of the ancient world. However, as we go farther into the second phase of the Exodus, we will be able to untangle much of this confusion.

The next primary god of the earliest Vedic pantheon of the Aryans is the god "*Agni*," he is the great master of fire, sacrifices, and wealth. The entire Vedic religion of the Aryans and with later Hindu belief is centered around sacrificial concepts. It was through sacrifice that the creation process, which the gods achieved at the beginning of time, had to be endlessly repeated to keep all of creation intact and functioning. It is believed that it was through Agni's holy sacrificial flames that men could reach the gods. He was thought to be the messenger of the gods as well as being the high-priest of the gods. These are the same traits of the later messenger gods of Greek and Roman cultures, Hermes, and Mercury. Agni is also one of the first places we see a reference to the twin brothers leading the second phase of the Exodus outside of the Dream Vision. In the Vedic hymns, it is said that Agni was the twin brother of Indra. As we go deeper into the second phase of the Exodus, we will see that this type of twin reference will show up in every culture they touched. [26,27,28,29]

What may not be evident is that within this ancient Vedic thought and even within modern-day Hinduism. We can see the earliest beginnings of the modern

Christian idea of the Holy Trinity, with the Father, the Son, and the Holy Ghost within these three primary gods of the Vedic Hymns of Shiva, Indra, and Agni. As with Egypt and the Theban triad this small realization provides us with a unique view into the minds of these ancient Israelites and our first chance to begin identifying each of these gods.

If we rely on our esoteric knowledge, we know that to our distant Cro-Magnon man ancestors at this ancient point in time, the mighty *"Heaven"* that was floating up above the clouds, looking down on humanity like it was the great eye of the Almighty Himself. At this early time, it was not the *"adobe of the Host of Heaven"* or a place where mortal men could go to and return. It is clearly stated within the earliest mythology that at this ancient time the "Heaven" was still viewed as a "thing" that passed overhead daily and not a "place." To our ancient ancestors, it was thought of as a "god" in and by itself. However, it was unlike any normal "god," for it was the Supreme god who was high above all the other gods as it looked down upon humanity as if it was the creator himself. Our next step is to realize that to our ancient ancestors, the mighty "Heaven" was viewed as the Supreme god, and that any of the ships that came from this Supreme god were thought to be some type of earthly incarnation of this Supreme god so it could interact with the mere mortals that walked upon the Earth. Although this idea will eventually undergo a major transformation, this idea of the Heaven being the Supreme god is always there somewhere in the back ground and never really ever goes away.

By understanding this, we can then realize that when our ancient ancestors interacted with one of these gods, they believed it to be an earthly incarnation of the great unknowable Supreme god they could see up above the clouds. For an example of this type of thinking, the Aryans believed that the messenger god Agni was an earthly incarnation of the unknowable Shiva high above so a mere mortal human could understand and interact with it, but at the same time, it was not the Supreme god. To our Cro-Magnon man ancestors, Agni was viewed as just a different, but often independent part of the larger whole that was the Supreme god that took the sacrifices of humanity back to the Supreme god. This might be a little bit confusing to our modern minds, but it does allow us to begin realizing that slowly, over time, the mighty "Heaven" becomes viewed as the "Father" of all the gods. Because all the other gods could be seen entering or leaving this Supreme god.

With our esoteric knowledge and knowing that the 'gods' were really advanced ships that interacted with humanity. We can understand that the ship that interacted with our ancestors far more than any others becomes known as the "King of the gods." This King of the gods was already known to our ancestors as the "Lord of the waters." Due to the constant interaction between this god and our ancient ancestors, he comes to be viewed as the "son" of the Supreme god, who then becomes viewed at the "Father" high above. The messenger god, that also interacts with humanity on a regular basis, slowly becomes thought of as the 'spirit' or 'Holy Ghost' as it is remembered in Christianity, that connects the earthly incarnation of the Supreme god with the unknowable Supreme god that looked down upon the mortal world of humans. Although this idea might seem a bit confusing at present, it will make more sense as we go farther into our journey.

In addition to these three primary gods, the Aryans had one more important god, "*Surya.*" He is the Lord of light and power. His brilliant radiating light keeps the terror of the darkness at bay. He is the maker of the light that illuminates the world of mortals, as well as the gods. He is also the destroyer of diseases and ill health; hence he is thought to bring good health. He is commonly depicted as golden in color with light radiating from his hair; he is customarily seen as riding swiftly across the sky in his great golden chariot drawn by seven divine horses. This description of Surya is remarkably similar to the Greek god Helios, who also has many of the same elements as the god Apollo. As with Apollo, Surya is believed to have great magical-like powers, with the ability to become invisible and is the holder of the most sacred text of the Vedas, the Gayatri. He was always addressed at his rising by every devout Brahman and held a high place among the priestly class. In contrast, for much of the native population, Surya was only a minor god and treated as such by them. Although this god of light is ubiquitous throughout numerous cultures, he is more of a mystery than most. He is commonly confused with the leader of the Fallen Watchers, the Lord-of-Light, also commonly known as Lucifer, the morning star. Even though he is commonly confused with leader of the Fallen Watchers, the mythology implies that he is an older version of the "Sky-Father" or Supreme god that the local people would not give up. So, he was incorporated into the pantheon as representing the Sun with its daily journey across the sky. [30,31,32]

Not only did the Aryans modify and fuse their pantheon of gods with the existing local gods. They also demoted the Earth Mother that figured heavily in all Bronze Age civilizations and cultures. It appears that this was always done by making her the wife of the Supreme god. To the Aryans, she becomes "*Devi,*" the heavenly wife of Shiva. The Aryans also took over the existing temples of the Mother Goddess and replaced her with one of the other primary male gods, normally Surya. These actions appear to be an attempt to connect the new religious beliefs of the Aryans with the older order to help to legitimize their claims with the native population. [33,34,35]

Another unique aspect of the Aryans and the Indo-Europeans in general, is that they would normally leave the existing female priesthood of the Temples dedicated to the Mother Goddess in place, if the priesthood accepted the change. If the female priesthood did not accept this change, which normally occurred because the local population would not accept this introduction of a new male god as the husband of the Mother Goddess. Then the Aryans would introduce a new female goddess with force upon both the priestesses and the local people. This new goddess would normally be the daughter of one of the three primary male gods. Once this new daughter goddess was established, they would then introduce a new male god, who would typically take the form of being the lover or husband of this new daughter goddess, which normally took the form of the original male god they tried to introduce.

This is but another example of how willingly and creatively the Aryans would modify their pantheon to suit local traditions, customs, and beliefs to cement their control over the native population. It is also an example of how the pantheon of gods grew as the Aryans became more creative when different tribes of the local population would not accept the Aryan gods in their original form. If neither option was acceptable to the native people, then the Aryans would destroy the temple, wipeout the entire female priesthood, and then move the people back to the central area of settlement. If the common people continued to resist, the Aryans would either kill them all or sell them into slavery, with both methods being used as an example of what would happen to people who resisted the Aryans. So, it was normally in the best interest of the female priesthood and the local population to just accept the changes without complaint. [36,37,38]

The Aryans also introduced one more important god named "*Yama*," who was the powerful god of the Underworld, also commonly known as the god of death. As with the other lords of the Underworld, Yama is not only the Lord of the Underworld, although he normally thought of as the embodiment of death itself, who wields a noose that he uses to seize the souls of those who are about to die, but he is neither good nor evil. In many ways, he was viewed in the same manner as our modern idea of the Grim Reaper. In so many ways, he is just the embodiment of the hard reality of a mortal existence and who performs a vital duty that helps maintain the balance of life. According to the Vedas, Yama is said to have been the first mortal who died. Which by virtue of precedence, he became the ruler of the departed dead. As with the gods Indra and Agni, Yama is also believed to be a twin of "*Sraddhadevea Manu*," who, according to tradition, was a mortal man that was warned of the coming of a great Deluge by the god Vishnu and instructed to build an Ark to save himself and his family in the same manner as Noah of the Bible. [39,40,41,42]

With our new esoteric knowledge and our understanding of the Dream Vision of Enoch, we now have the necessary information to begin understanding that many of the "twin gods" of mythology are a vague but direct reference to the legendary twin brothers leading this second phase of the Exodus. Although the twin brothers themselves may have been forgotten or wholly written out the mythology, their memory lives on embedded within the mythology, legends, and folklore as twin gods or semi-divine beings. It was also not uncommon for a great leader or king to be elevated to semi-godhood while still alive. Then upon his death, he would then be elevated to being a full "god." The Pharaohs of Egypt may be the best example of this ancient practice.

The next step is to begin realizing that the many "twin gods" of mythology are related to different aspects of these twin brothers and their exploits during the second phase of the Exodus. In the case of the Aryans and as we will see in other cultures, it appears that one brother was a great warrior, a bringer of death, while the other was a more thoughtful and peaceful man. The mythology paints a picture of where one brother was a warrior-king, while the other was the warrior-priest. This type of leadership structure would allow the twin brothers to control the military arm of the tribes and the religious priesthood, giving them total control of all the tribes. It is a leadership structure that appears to have been first established by Moses and Aaron at the beginning of the Exodus.

Before we move onto the next part of this story, we need to quickly explore what makes the six gods we have so far explored so essential and why they stand out from all the other gods the Aryans worshiped. One of the biggest factors that make these gods so unique is that they are found in every culture that the Indo-European people assimilated and fused with, in largely unchanged forms. Usually, only their names change, with some of the earliest symbolism related to each of these gods' also changing hands. One of the more interesting symbolic changes appears to occur just as the original Vedic religion of the Aryans begins transforming into Hinduism.

During this long transformation of the Vedic religion of the Aryans into Hinduism, many of the most familiar symbols associated with each of the gods, such as the trident being associated with the Lord of the waters or the crescent moon representing the Mother Goddess, were all associated initially with Shiva, the Supreme god. Unfortunately, the Vedas nor the many writings of later Hinduism give us any clue to why these symbolic changes occurred. Although the Vedas and Hinduism are silent on the subject, we know though our esoteric knowledge, that much of this symbolism represents various advanced weapon systems that were used by the gods. This allows us to speculate that these weapons were initially associated with Shiva, but, over time, they were transferred to various other gods to use as the political situations of the gods changed. Adding to the confusion is that this change in symbolism appears to also be a symbolic representation of the Aryans reshuffling and modifying their pantheon to suit the local population's existing traditions and customs.

By understanding that the Indo-European people and the ancient tribes of Israel who continued onward to other lands under the leadership of the divine twin brothers are the same people. We can begin to follow these people as they moved around the world. This also allows us to understand that the original religion of the children of Israel was not a monotheistic one but was instead a purely polytheistic religion. However, before we can explore how this originally polytheistic religion turned into a monotheistic one, we need to first finish exploring the rest of the journey of these people. But, before we can continue upon our journey, we must explore one last but equally important event that occurred due to the invasion-like settlement of these people that greatly aids in following their movements.

This event is that they always destroyed the existing Bronze Age economies of every culture they encountered. This economic destruction occurred because these ancient Bronze Age economies were command economies that were directly dependent upon long-distant trade for raw materials and products. The Bronze Age city-states' entire economic system was utterly dependent upon a highly organized central system of control. A system of control that was directly dependent upon writing and record keeping. When these tribes of the children of Israel killed the elites, they replaced them with their own illiterate people, this caused the existing economy's entire organizational structure to collapse. Not only did the local economy collapse, but the long-distance trade that it was dependent upon collapsed along with it. As the economies collapsed, so did all the institutions that were supported by the taxes these economies generated. [43]

One of the most visible signs of this general collapse of the Bronze Age economies and international trade was that the large-scale construction projects of the Bronze Age ended abruptly. The only new construction that occurs is not seen until long after the Indo-Europeans had assimilated and fused with the local population, transforming them into new cultures and societies. In the Indus Valley civilization, it is not until Hinduism is fully formed and firmly cemented at all levels of society that we see the formation of new kingdoms, which begin new large-scale construction projects. Even though we see construction begin again once these new societies had formed, it is generally at a vastly smaller scale, with much of it being confined to building temples, temple complexes, and the mighty towers that the gods once stood upon. [44]

Without long distant trade, one of the most important institutions that collapsed along with it, was writing. As the Bronze Age economies collapsed, there was simply no need for record-keeping or long-distance communication. Additionally, most scribes were in the service to the ruling class, with many of them were killed along with the elites they served. Additionally, these elites were replaced by a largely illiterate tribal people that had very little use for scribes. Without scribes and the general collapse of the economy, along with a new illiterate ruling class, writing quickly disappeared for the ordinary person. Only a small handful of scribes that happened to be in service of a temple that was taken over by the new priesthood retained the art of writing. In many areas of the world, writing wholly disappeared, including within the temples and the new priesthoods. This collapse of writing, except for a few small pockets of scribes who wrote exclusively for the priesthood, is one of the primary reasons this period after the collapse of the Bronze Age civilizations is usually known as one of the greatest Dark Ages of humanity. [45]

Although all the mighty Bronze Age civilizations collapsed, except for two, and a great Dark Age of ignorance fell upon humanity, this time became an age of religion that was much like the Medieval Dark Age of Europe of a thousand year ago. Although it became a time of religion with a complete devotion to the gods, we can see new religious structures and beliefs come into existence during this Dark Age. As the new religions began to take hold, a new economic model began to form that was based on a straightforward centralized agricultural system that is much like the feudal system of the Medieval Age of Europe. It was a simple system that conscripted most of the common people of the lower classes into a life of being simple peasant farmers that gave all they produced to the priesthood of the central temple in devotion to the gods. As we go farther along, we will see this is also an additional way to help track these people as they moved around the world during this second phase of the Exodus. [46]

Chapter 5

The Journey Continues

Once, the Aryan speaking tribes of the children of Israel had invaded and settled the Indus and Ganges river valleys in northern India, the rest of the tribes continued their journey to the east. Where they came upon the Mekong river system and its large delta, the world's seventh-longest river system. Unlike ancient India and the Indus Valley civilization, we know next to nothing about the people that occupied the territories of the Mekong river system before the arrival of the Indo-European speaking tribes.

It is believed that there were several small kingdoms located on the western side of the Tonle Sap river, which runs from the great Tonle Sap Lake in the west to the sea, joining the Mekong in the delta region. The scant archaeological evidence suggests that these kingdoms existed in a state of almost constant warfare with each other. Their art and overall culture appear to have been heavily influenced by India due to the long-established sea and land routes with the subcontinent. These people's actual origin is unknown because their original language, which is normally how historians trace the origins of early people, is unknown and was entirely replaced with an Indo-European language from India. After their arrival and just as they had done in northern India, once the Indo-Europeans had settled the area, they began assimilating and fusing with the local population. [1]

According to legend, ancient Cambodia came into existence through the union of a local Cambodian princess and an Indian Brahman named "*Kaundinya*." The princess was said to be the daughter of a mighty dragon king who ruled over a watery land far away. One day, as Kaundinya was sailing by, the princess paddled out a boat to greet him. Kaundinya then shot an arrow from his magical bow into her approaching boat, causing the fearful princess to agree to marry him. For the traditional dowry, her dragon father is said to have drunk up the waters of his land and presented them to Kaundinya to rule. Thereby creating the ancient kingdom of "*Kambuja*." Although this, like so many other legends, is historically opaque, it does give us a small look into the cultural forces that helped bring ancient Cambodia into existence. In particular, its close relationship with its great subcontinental neighbor, India. With almost all its early religious, royal, and written traditions stemming directly from ancient India and Hinduism. [2]

Unlike the Indus and Ganges river valleys, the people of Southeastern Asia revered the "*Naga*." The Naga are a unique class of semi-divine beings that are thought to be half-human and half-cobra. They are believed to be a robust and beautiful race of creatures who can assume either wholly human or fully serpentine form at will. They are believed to be potentially very dangerous to humans but are more often beneficial to humanity. They are also believed to have lived in a vast underground kingdom known as "*Naga-Loka*" or "*Patale-Loka*," which was filled with beautifully ornamented palaces covered in precious gems. [3]

The Naga is said to have been created by the native creator deity, known as "*Braham*." Braham appears to have been the original Father-god worshiped alongside the Mother Goddess and the Bull before the arrival of the Indo-Europeans and Hinduism. He, along with the other local gods, was gradually eclipsed by Shiva, Vishnu, with their version of the Mother Goddess, Devi. Braham is also closely associated with the Vedic creator god, "*Prajapati*," whose identity he later assumed. This provides us with another small insight into the fusing of the different gods of these children of Israel with the local gods of the native people they assimilated. [4,5]

As with the gods Indra and Varuna, where Varuna was the original King of the gods for the Indus Valley people, who was then replaced and fused with the similar Aryan god Indra. In case of Cambodia, it appears that the creator god or Supreme god of the tribe of Indo-Europeans who entered and eventually settled the Mekong river system was initially known as "*Prajapati*" who was then replaced with the local creator god Braham. These changes in the gods' names and identities give us another small look at the politics of this settlement and invasion of the Indo-European tribes and how flexible this early religious belief was. It appears that the actual names or manner of worship of the gods was unimportant, as long as the local people adopted the new belief system's basic ideas. The reason for this appears to be very similar to the replacement of the Mother Goddess. However, in this case, the native people would not accept the Indo-European Supreme god they called Prajapati, so the Indo-Europeans adopted the local creator god of Braham in place of Prajapati. Once they had adopted the local name and possibly even the local belief, they would slowly transform the local god into a version of their original Indo-European god, in time, the only real difference between the two gods ends up only being their names.

Although this only helps to add to the general confusion of the original identity of these gods. It also gives us another example of how the original pantheon of gods of these children of Israel changed and grew as they took over new cultures and people. By realizing that these children of Israel were made up of many different Indo-European speaking tribes, it makes sense that one of the reasons the names changed was because each tribe had their own language. For example, the tribe that spoke Aryan and settled the Indus and Ganges called the Supreme god Indra, but the tribe that settled the Mekong river system called this god Prajapati in their native language. This allows us to understand why the same gods go by so many different names. We will return to this subject after we have covered more of this journey.

By realizing that it was a different Indo-European speaking tribe than the Aryans that settled in Cambodia, we can quickly understand that as the many centuries went along, this had the effect of creating a slightly different form of Hinduism in Cambodia than existed in northern India. This slightly different Hinduism eventually led to the formation of the Khmer Empire and the building of the great temple site of Angkor-Wat. Although Angkor-Wat was built centuries after the initial settlement and invasion of the Mekong river and delta by these Indo-European speaking children of Israel. It provides us with another unique view into the original polytheistic religious belief of these people and the governmental structure they typically imposed upon the people they took over.
[6,7]

Initially, the people known as the Khmers were Hindus and are the people believed to have originally built the Angkor-Wat Temple complex and surrounding city. At the center of Angkor-Wat was a royal phallic cult dedicated to the supreme Hindu god Shiva that was centered around the phallic symbolism of the Lingam. Within Angkor-Wat, this Lingam was placed in the temple's central sanctuary. As with Shiva in India, this Cambodian version of Shiva is usually represented as a male fertility god with an unusually large erect penis. However, at a much later time and for unknown reasons, the god Vishnu became the most important Hindu god in Southwest Asia. His image was placed in the central sanctuary at Angkor-Wat, where it remained until the coming of Buddhism. Although it is unknown why this change took place, it is believed that it reflects some form of great political change that occurred within the Khmer Empire. [8]

Additionally, the Khmer Empire introduced the concept of *"Deyaraja,"* meaning *"God-King"* or literally *"The Lord of the Universe Who is King."* It refers to the cult associated directly with the rulers of Angkor-Wat, who, in time, came to be regarded as the earthly representation of the Supreme god, more commonly known in the Western world as the *"Divine Right"* of kings. Through a special consecration rite and a massive ritual, the kings were believed to be endowed with divine power and responsible for protecting the state and the people. This was accomplished by performing the same kind of role on Earth that the gods performed in the heavens. It was also directly linked with the Hindu idea that the earthly king was directly linked in a spiritually manner with one of the gods, typically Shiva or Vishnu. This *"Devaraja cult"* was very similar to Pharaoh worship in ancient Egypt, and as with Egypt, it was used to justify the state and why the population had to work to maintain the state and the King. [9]

This information provides us with a slightly better picture of these Indo-European speaking children of Israel and how they eventually assimilated the native peoples in Cambodia. By fusing, their culture, language, and religious belief, with the native one, they would eventually install a direct monarchy based on the idea of the Divine Right of Kings to rule the state and the people. Over time, the foreign Indo-European culture and the local culture fused into one. Thus, creating an entirely new civilization that incorporated local beliefs into a religious system that was exclusively based on complete severance to the gods. The primary focus was once again centered around the three primary gods, the Supreme god, that we know as the mighty Heaven, the direct earthly representative of this Supreme god who interacted with humans who was known as the Lord of the waters and in time became the King of the gods. With the third being the Messenger god that took the sacrifices, offerings, and gifts from humanity and transported them up to the Supreme god.

Although this fundamental process is seen every time these Indo-European speaking children of Israel settle a land, it does change slightly because each tribe speaks its own tribal language and has its own particular tribal god. Which for the Aryans was the god Indra that was replaced with local god Shiva, for the tribe that settled Cambodia it was Prajapati, who was changed to the local god known as Braham. Although they are all the same god, these small tribal and local differences help add to the confusion of the identity of the Supreme god.

This problem is only compounded with the next stop of these children of Israel, China. We also run into a bit of confusion on what route these Indo-European speaking people may have taken. Although it is easy to trace where they went, it is difficult to see what route they took once they began leaving the lands of Cambodia and the Mekong river system. This is primarily because we have evidence that at this point it appears their path went both to the north and to the south.

Given the scant evidence, it is reasonable to think that the tribes may have broken into two separate groups, with each group under the leadership of one of the twin brothers. With one group going north into China while the other went south into Australia and eventually to the many islands of the South Pacific that make up Polynesia. Additionally, we know that one bother was a warrior-king in this leadership structure with the other being a priest-king. This allows us to postulate that the group under the leadership of the warrior-king went north with the other group under the command of the priest-king went to the south.

Unfortunately, it is almost impossible to trace their moments south; the only evidence of their passing appears to be a few stories about twins in the mythology of the 900 distinct groups of Aboriginal Australians. It is highly probable that this is because they only encountered similar tribal societies as their own. But unlike their tribe, the Aboriginal tribes of Australia were spread out over a vast area with no central government or leadership with many tribes being isolated from one another. This would have made it next too impossible for the children of Israel to take over as they had before in the Land of Canaan, India, and Cambodia. It is also equally possible that by breaking into two separate groups, the numbers of each group were small enough that their chances of being able to conquer or unite the local tribes that were spread over the vast area of Australia were small. As we will learn shortly, the group that journeyed south was likely the smaller of the two groups. Because of their smaller numbers, they slowly intermarried with the local people, thereby losing their original identity to the point that only a few vague stories of twins are all that remain.

The only 'universal' myth within the Aboriginal tribes that seems to mark the passing of these children of Israel is the "Rainbow Serpent" myths. Unlike the Serpent Slaying myths will explore later in our journey, the main character of these myths, the Rainbow Serpent, is clearly a version of the Lord of the waters. In all the myths, the Rainbow Serpent is an unusually powerful, creative, magical, and often dangerous serpent that is closely associated with rainbows, rain, deep waterholes, and rivers. It is said that it descended from the dark serpent-like streak in the Milky Way and revealed itself to the people as a rainbow that moves through the waters. As it moved through the world, this enormous serpent shaped landscapes with water, sometimes drowning people or swallowing them whole. As with the more common Lord of the waters, there was a two-fold aspect to this Rainbow Serpent, sometimes he was healer, and the bringer of life through his rains, but he could just as easily blight others with sores, illness, and death. [10]

As for their path north, there is no doubt that the Indo-Europeans entered China and had a massive impact on ancient Chinese society and culture. However, in China, they encountered a radically different type of society than they had encountered before. Although the ancient narrative of China's earliest times is tough to recover, it can be outlined with some confidence. We know that before the arrival of these Indo-European speaking children of Israel, Chinese civilization was composed of two main tribes, known as the "*Shang*" and the "*Chou,*" with the Chou being more commonly known today as the "*Zhou.*" At the time of the arrival of the tribes of this second phase of the Exodus, the Shang tribe ruled much of China, with the Zhou occupying the lands to the west of central China. Both tribes were very similar in their thought, culture, and traditions. Nevertheless, the Shang tribe is the first name with independent evidence to support it in the traditional list of dynasties that was the basis of Chinese chronology and are the people we will examine first. [11]

Unlike the other lands that these children of Israel conquered, Shang China was not ruled by a small group of elites as a central power as with many traditional kingdoms. There were instead organized around a feudal-like system for the elites that was based upon a slave society for the countless peasants. Shang China consisted of hundreds, if not thousands of large estates that held vast reserves of human resources that were ruled over by powerful families, whose leaders operated as a warlord with them being the absolute ruler over their vast land holdings. The Shang domains' primary political arrangements seem to have depended on the uniting of the largest and most powerful landholding estates that were organized around obligations to a powerful king or Emperor-like figure. [12]

Although this arrangement is very similar to European Medieval vassals, it differs in the respect that the Emperor was not viewed as the supreme holder or owner of all the lands within Chinese society. In ancient Chinese society, the land was owned by the ruling families of the estates, with the Emperor only having ownership of his lands. The Emperor was normally just the most powerful of the current warrior landlords of the largest estates. Even if he took other estate lands by force, he would not be viewed as the rightful owner of the land by the other large estates' ruling families. These warrior landlords were the key figures of Chinese society, they were also the leading members of the many aristocratic lineages that claimed semi-mythical origins. Nevertheless, Shang China was not a simple Feudal state ruled over by warlord landholders, it had a highly advanced government that used scribes, standardized currency, weights, measures, and had a highly effective system of bureaucracy that could mobilize massive amounts of labor for the building of fortifications and entire cities if needed. [13]

The other significant difference was that both tribes of the Shang and Zhou, religion was incredibly crucial to early Chinese society, with it extending into the political, economic, and family spheres. The basis of the entire system was the family, which emerged as the legal refinement and subdivision of the clan. There were about a hundred clans, within each of which marriage was forbidden with members of the same clan. Each clan claimed to have been founded by a great hero or a god. The patriarchal heads of the clan's families and houses exercised special divine authority over its members. They were the only ones believed qualified to carry out its rituals and act as intermediaries with the powers controlling the universe on the clan's behalf. Over time, these persons came to be identified as the only people entitled to possess land or hold office due to the essential virtue of a descent whose origins were god-like. [14]

The common people of the lower classes and especially the millions of peasants were forbidden to take part in the clans' religious rituals. In turn, they founded their own religious outlets by maintaining the ancient worship of nature gods, which the elite, too, always paid some attention and respect for. The worship of mountains, rivers, and the spirits that were said to live among them became an essential imperial duty in the earliest of times. Although this worship was deemed necessary, it had less of an influence on Chinese religious thought than other religious traditions. [15]

This religious thought had considerable repercussions on the political forms of early Chinese society. The heart of the ruling house's claim for complete obedience was its religious superiority. It was through the maintenance of ritual, which gave it access to the goodwill of the unseen powers of the world, whose intention might be known from the oracles. Since the earliest days of Chinese society, all the great decisions of the state and many lesser ones were taken by consulting oracles that spoke to the ancestors. This was done by engraving turtle shells or the shoulder-blades of certain animals with written characters and symbols and then applying a heated bronze pin or rod to them that would produce cracks on the reverse side. The direction and length of the cracks in relationship to the written characters and symbols would then be read accordingly. This practice was so enormously crucial that these *"oracle-bones"* as they became known, were kept, presumably as records. [16]

These oracle-bones also provide us with the earliest evidence for the foundation of the Chinese language. Characters found on the oracle bones and some early bronzes are basically the same as those of classical Chinese. We know the Shang had over 5,000 such characters, though not all of them can be read. Furthermore, by the end of the Shang dynasty, the king had become the only one believed to be able to correctly interpret the oracle bones, thereby making him the primary shaman. Additionally, the Shang kings, who considered themselves divine rulers, also consulted with the great god *"Shangdi,"* the supreme being who ruled over all of humanity and nature, for advice and wisdom. [17]

One additional unique characterization of early Chinese religious thought was the practice of ancestor worship, not only were the gods honored by ritual, but also essential and powerful ancestors were also honored and sometimes worshipped. In many cases, the hero or god that founded the clan became just as important, if not more important, than the gods in befitting the clan. At the heart of this idea was the belief that only a nobleman could share in the cults that were behind the Chinese notions of kinship and the clans. Only a nobleman belonged to a family, which meant only he had ancestors. The reverence for ancestors and the propitiation of their spirits had existed long before the Shang. However, it does not seem that in the earliest times that many ancestors were believed to have survived into the spirit world. It appears that the only ones believed to exist in the spirit world were the spirits of particularly important or heroic individuals. With the most likely being the rulers themselves, whose ultimate origin, it was claimed, was itself godly. [18]

Early Chinese culture's unique character made Shang China a vastly different type of beast and next to impossible for these Indo-European speaking children of Israel to conquer and settle as they had before. However, located to the west of Shang China, there was the tribe known as the Zhou in what is now Shaanxi province. The Zhou tribe was very similar to the Shang in many respects, but they held very little political power at this early time. Historians have long debated the beginning of the Zhou, but it is known that they coexisted with the Shang. At various times they were a friendly tributary state to the Shang, but at other times they alternatively went to war with them. [19]

This tribe of Zhou living in western China are the people that these children of Israel fused with. However, unlike before, they were not the mighty conqueror that sooner or later killed the ruling elites, thereby replacing them with themselves. For the Zhou were organized much like the Shang, which put these children of Israel at a significant disadvantage. They had little choice but to move into the area peacefully, or risk being destroyed by the vastly more numerous Zhou, or be completely wiped out by the even more powerful Shang. Additionally, the vast difference in religious thought would also place these children of Israel at a great disadvantage since most Chinese, both the elites and peasants, would not accept a foreign religion that was not related to or included ancestor worship with the central ideas of the clan and family that made up the foundations of both Shang and Zhou society, culture, religion, and the political structure that supported it all.

Given the little information we have, it appears that these Indo-European speaking children of Israel were assimilated by the Zhou, primarily through intermarriage and by severing the most powerful clans of the Zhou. They may have fulfilled the position of being an honored foreign military or religious advisers to the ruling families. In the process of doing this, they completely lost their identity as a people. With their stories, religious thought, customs, and rituals being taken and transformed into uniquely Chinese interpretations, with Chinese characters, gods, and ancestors completely replacing the original beliefs. Their language was also uniquely transformed into Chinese, with the adopted words having similar meanings but different pronunciation and use. Although the tribe of these children of Israel that settled in China lost their identity as a people, including their religion, language, and culture, they never the less had a profound impact on the political, religious, and military thought of the Zhou. [20]

This fusing of the Zhou with the tribe of children of Israel that settled in China eventually led one of the Zhou ruling houses to devise a plan to conquer the Shang. After many years of bloody fighting, the Zhou were successful in conquering the Shang. However, a rebellion broke out before the Zhou could consolidate all the territory ruled by the Shang. Brutal fighting went on for three years before the rebellion was put down, allowing the Zhou to solidify their control over all of China. This was accomplished by taking over the Shang estates and creating an array of feudal states that maintained order with the new Emperor holding a claim on all the land. This was one of the first changes under the Zhou; they changed the idea of the king into that of a Divine Emperor whose power and claims to rule all lands of the world came directly from the gods, primarily the great god Shangdi and the ancestors. [21]

Remarkably, unlike most of the areas these children of Israel settled, Bronze Age China did not enter a long Dark Age, but it instead had a great flowering of cultural achievements that reflect the diversity of the feudal states that composed the Zhou Dynasty. The arts, in general, were essentially a continuation of those of the Shang Dynasty. Strangely enough, there was a deterioration of the variety and quality of the casting of bronze during the Zhou. Archeological evidence indicates that this decline in the quality of Zhou bronze was because the Zhou tried to maintain a monopoly on the metal with a new focus on military weapons and was not due to any general cultural decline. [22]

Not only was there a cultural flowering of the arts during the Zhou dynasty, Chinese society in general underwent dramatic changes. With the development and introduction of iron, ox-drawn plows, crossbows, horseback riding, and all of it on a large scale. There were also numerous large-scale irrigation projects undertaken, which significantly increased crop yields, with new roads and canals being constructed that connected the various feudal states together into a larger state. These changes led to more trade and the founding of new towns and cities along the trade routes. This development of trade led to the development of coinage, accounting, and greatly expanded the primitive writing system of the Shang period into the Chinese writing system still known today. There was also a tremendous philosophical flowering with the founding of many different schools of thought along with the unique Chinese system of Legalism. [23]

From the lands of China, the remaining tribes of the children of Israel under the leadership of the warrior-king brother then continued northward into Japan. Although, like China, much of early Japanese history is hard to uncover, it is clear these Indo-European speaking children of Israel entered Japan and had a tremendous impact on early Japanese culture and society. The current archaeological evidence suggests that Japan had initially been a country divided up among several powerful clans, which were presided over by an Emperor with an ill-defined royal supremacy based on an ancestry traced back to the Sun Goddess. As with the people of Cambodia and their form of Hinduism, the main thrust into Japan appears to come later after a similar system was fully developed in China. [24]

There was a significant influence from China with the introduction of iron technology and Chinese writing and characters, which provided a written form of the native language. There were attempts to bring about administrative changes that were directly based upon Chinese lines. Although there was cultural attraction and even dependence between China and Japan, it did not mean political submission by the Japanese nor an acceptance of Chinese culture. [25]

The Japanese central administration was already highly developed in scope and scale when these children of Israel arrived upon the shores of the islands of Japan. As they had done before in China, they were forced to assimilate and fuse with the largest tribe or clan on the island. In this case, they fused with the great Fujiwara clan. As with the Zhou in China, these children of Israel completely lost their identity with only their stories and some words being adopted and transformed into uniquely Japanese versions. [26]

After they fused with the Fujiwara clan, they begin to tie themselves very closely to the imperial household by marriage over a hundred-year period. Since it was common in Japanese society for the children to be brought up in the household of the mother's family, the clan could exercise a crucial influence upon the future emperors while they were children. Within just a few hundred years, the Fujiwara clan was effectively in control of the entire central government of Japan through marriage and alliances with other powerful clans that allowed them to hold key offices of the imperial court acting in the name of the Emperor. [27]

Japan allows us a small peek into how these children of Israel were able to slowly take over the central government systems through marriage, alliances, and holding court offices even though they had lost their identity as a people. As with China, these children of Israel could not impose their religious beliefs upon the elites nor the common people of Japan. This was because since the earliest beginnings of the historical era, even down to the present day, the keys to the continuity and the general toughness of Japanese society have been the family and the traditional religion known as Shinto. Whose essence was the worship at the proper times of specific local, personal, and clan deities who provide protection and favor to the clans. The clan was an enlarged family, and the nation the most enlarged family of all. In patriarchal style, the Emperor presided over the national family, just as a clan leader would over his clan or even the small farmer over his family. This provided a tremendous social unity to the Japanese people, with the Emperor being the focus. [28]

As with China, Japan did not enter a long Dark Age, but underwent a great flowering of culture during this time. Nevertheless, it was rather hermetically sealed from the world of the ordinary Japanese and the world at large by its materials, subject matter, and standards. It was essentially restricted to court art, which was shaped by court settings and events that were to be enjoyed by a relatively narrow circle of elites. The great majority of Japanese people would never even see the products of what is now believed to the first great peak of Japanese culture that laid much of the foundation of Japanese society. With its ideals of simplicity, discipline, good taste, and a love of nature that sometimes seem somewhat frivolous in our modern eyes, but always uniquely Japanese. [29]

Before we move on to the next leg of this great Exodus, not only did Chinese and Japanese culture flower after the arrival of these children of Israel, their societies were also transformed into a more militarist and warrior-based societies. This societal change adds significant weight to the idea that the original group of tribes had broken into two separate groups, with each one under the leadership of one of the twin brothers. With the group under the command of the warrior-king going north into the lands of China and Japan where they established the warrior-based societies we know so well. While the other group went south into Australia and then across the many islands of the Pacific Ocean, leaving only a few stories, rituals, words, and customs with the people they encountered.

Chapter 6

The New World and Beyond

After establishing themselves in China and Japan, the remaining tribes of the children of Israel continued their journey. There is ample archaeological evidence that they moved through the Bering Strait land-bridge into Alaska and down through western Canada into the Americas. There is also more recent archaeological evidence that some ancient people may have arrived by boat on the Pacific coast. This adds weight to the idea the tribes may have broken into two separate groups, with one going north and the other going southward through Australia and then across the many islands of the Southern Pacific. Where the second group eventually made landfall somewhere on the northwestern coast of the Americans. After arriving in the Americans, the two groups subsequently rejoined back into one large group. All available archaeological evidence indicates that these people then settled on the eastern coast of central Mexico. [1,2]

Unlike any place they had traveled before, we have no archaeological or historical evidence that there was any pre-existing Bronze Age civilization located anywhere in the new world. These Indo-European speaking children of Israel appear to have been the founders of the mother culture and civilization of almost all native American tribes, the mysterious Olmec. Many may find it surprising that one of the greatest mysteries surrounding the Olmec people are the mysterious artifacts that clearly show all the different races of humanity from all around the world. The most famous of these artifacts are the colossal stone heads that clearly show male individuals with heavy African facial features. These massive stone heads have been found in the Olmec heartland that lays on the eastern coast of Mexico within the modern-day states of Veracruz and Tabasco. [3,4]

These giant stone head sculptures are amongst the most mysterious and highly debated artifacts from the ancient world. Currently, there have been seventeen heads discovered, ten of which are from San Lorenzo and four are from La Venta, two of the most important Olmec centers. The other three with additional monuments were discovered at Tres Zapotes and La Cobata. All seventeen of the confirmed Olmec heads were sculpted from the same grey basalt known as "*Cerro Cintepec basalt*," named after a volcano in the Sierra-de-los-Tuxtlas mountains of Veracruz in eastern Mexico. Adding to the mystery is that these heads are up to nearly 3 meters (9.8 ft.) tall and 4.5 meters (14.7 ft.) in circumference, with an average weight of eight tons. Each of the heads was carved from a single boulder and then transported up to 150 kilometers (93 miles) through high mountains and valleys. It is unknown how the Olmecs moved the stones over such unforgiving hilly terrain since the Olmecs seem to have lacked beasts of burden and functional wheels. It is also highly unlikely they used any water transportation for the monuments, given the coastal currents and transportation limits within the few river estuaries in the area. [5,6]

Although there is great mystery surrounding these Olmec heads, there have been two badly damaged Olmec sculptures found that depict large rectangular stone blocks bound with ropes, with a largely destroyed human figure riding upon each block with their legs hanging over the side. Archaeologists have suggested that these figures may be Olmec rulers overseeing the stone's transport that would be fashioned into their monuments. This idea is highly unlikely, given the simple fact that rulers of all societies, both ancient and modern, do not take part in the actual physical labor of construction projects, much less sit upon the raw material as the laborers move it. Based on everything we know about human societies; it is much more likely the individuals seen sitting upon the stones are taskmasters or overseers in charge of the laborers that simply pulled the stones across the land with large numbers of people. [7]

Adding to the mystery is that we know the Olmecs possessed the necessary knowledge and organizational skills to commit a large number of people and resources to build large-scale earthworks. Based on the extensive earthworks that the Olmec's built, it has been proposed that they could have easily constructed temporary causeways using the very suitable and plentiful soils of the floodplains to move the massive heads. This would have allowed for a direct route across the floodplains to the San Lorenzo plateau where most of the Olmec heads have been found. However, this theory runs into problems, with the most important factor being that this idea does not appear to account for other Olmec sites, primarily due to the high mountains and steep valleys that litter the landscape. Unfortunately, the exact method the Olmecs used to move these great stone heads and other massive monuments remains a mystery. Although the great stone heads are well-known, they are just one example of the many mysteries surrounding the Olmecs. Another mystery that is found within the same archaeological strata with the African-looking Olmec heads are artifacts and stone carvings that depict bearded Caucasian figures and individuals that are clearly of Asia descent. Remarkably, within this stratum we find Olmec artifacts that depict every single racial group of people on the planet. [8,9,10]

Modern archaeologists and scholars are unable to elaborate upon the fact that all the races of humanity from around the world are so clearly depicted upon the ancient Olmec artifacts. Nevertheless, with our new esoteric knowledge relating to the second phase of the great Exodus of the Indo-European speaking children of Israel under the leadership of the divine twin brothers, this mystery can easily be illuminated upon. Because for the first time in modern history, we can understand that this these Indo-European speaking children of Israel was a uniquely diverse group of people; composed of people from entirely different races, cultures, traditions, languages, and technologies from all over the world. This knowledge allows us to understand that the Olmec artifacts reflect this diverse group under the leadership of the twin brothers. Additionally, these artifacts also appear to represent a critical change in society and how the "gods" viewed their human slaves. If we recall from the Dream Vision of Enoch, the First-Men were broken into three separate racial groups made up of white, red, and black colors. This original system appears to have given way to an entirely different system whereby this skin coloring is no longer critical or used by the gods. It is unknown why such a change occurred, but as we will learn later, it is reasonable to speculate that this change reflects some type of political change among the gods. It also just as equally possible that it was purely for adapting our ancient ancestors for the different environments they were to live as it is normally suggested by modern researchers. [11]

Although many will find the idea of the Olmecs being composed of all the different racial groups of humanity radical, it is supported by and explains the strange genetic mystery of the Native American people and their mysterious origins. One of the greatest problems of modern genetic science is that the Native American populations do not fit into the current genetic model or the theories of human origins. It appears that the Native American population has genetic markers from all over the world. There have been genetic markers found from Asia, Europe, the Middle East, and even Africa throughout the various tribes that make up the Native American population. The current genetic evidence seems to imply that they are the descendants of a large group of people that included all the different races of humanity from all around the world that settled in one central area and then spread out to the rest of the Americas. According to modern theories on genetics and human origins, this is an impossibility. Nevertheless, we can now realize that this "genetic mystery" can be easily explained by and is also direct evidence that Native Americans are the descendants of these ancient Indo-European speaking children of Israel from the second phase of the Exodus under the leadership of the divine twin brothers. [12,13,14,15,16,17,18]

Unlike all the other lands these Indo-European-speaking children of Israel settled. Their settlement in the Americas appears to have happened over a much shorter amount of time, possibly as short as a few decades instead of centuries. The reason for this is simply because there were no existing Bronze Age civilizations or any other type of civilization in the Americans that needed to be conquered and assimilated, by all accounts it was primarily virgin territory.

As with China and Japan, once the tribe that had inherited the Americas had established themselves and the other tribes had left, continuing their journey. We see an enormous explosion of building monumental architecture and the founding of towns and the building of cities. This monumental architecture also developed into a highly sophisticated style of stone sculpture that is unmatched in the ancient world at this early time. For many years it has been believed that the Olmecs did not possess writing. However, in the first decades of the 21st century, there has emerged evidence of Olmec hieroglyphs. Several examples of this hieroglyphic script have been found on roller-like stamps, very similar to the ancient Cylinder Seals of the old world. They have also been partially deciphered based on their similarity to later Meso-American scripts and symbolism. [19]

Even with the discovery of Olmec writing, very little is known about how Olmec society was composed or how much control was exercised by the rulers over what appears to be a widespread rural population. There is archaeological evidence that the Olmec rulers seem to have served in important religious functions as well as their functions as absolute leaders of the state. What exactly these religious functions were or how they were performed is unknown, but they appear to be centered around endless sacrifice to the gods. We do know that the Olmec foundation proved very important for all the Meso-American cultures that came after them. The calendars, hieroglyphics, and the practice of building large ceremonial sites that mark so much of the region in later times are all ultimately derived directly from the Olmecs. The Olmecs also knew the many gods that mark the different pantheons of Meso-American cultures. We also know that the Olmecs' successors built the first great American city, Teotihuacan, in what is now Mexico. It became a major trading center and was of outstanding religious importance with its huge complex of pyramids and great public buildings. We also know that the rather mysterious successors to the Olmecs greatly influenced the later Mayan, Aztec, and Inca societies and their complex religious beliefs. Additionally, the new world's religious beliefs, gods, and rituals are remarkably similar and have many parallels to Hinduism, with only the animal symbolism being different. [20,21]

This knowledge brings us to a point where we can answer one of the greatest mysteries of the ancient world and why we see the same monumental architecture, mythology, religious belief, symbolism, and the same gods from all around the world no matter the culture or civilization. It is simply because of this second phase of the great Exodus under the leadership of the legendary divine twin brothers as they journeyed around the globe. It also allows us to realize that as these Indo-European speaking children of Israel came into the new world of the Americas, they began to incorporate the local animals in place of the old-world animals in their script, artwork, and mythology. What is surprising is that Native American mythology drops the bull symbolism for the First-Men. They also speak of the First-Men as actual human beings and not in the traditional symbolic terms as cattle. This could be for the simple reason that there was no pre-existing civilization in the Americas. Since there was no pre-existing Bronze Age civilization, it is easy to understand why these children of Israel would have viewed themselves as the "First-Men" of this land, with no need for the old stories to explain their origin or hide it from the common people, as was so often case with the civilizations of the old world.

This brings us to the final leg of their journey. Even after traveling such a long distance over such a long period of time, there were still at least two tribes that had not reached the lands they had been promised. These last fragments of the original tribes then built boats and sailed across the Atlantic Ocean. Where they slammed into Europe, the Mediterranean, and western Africa with such great destructive force that they wiped out all the existing Bronze Age civilizations, except Egypt.

The Egyptians recorded the coming of these people and spoke of them as the mysterious *"Sea Peoples"* that came from far beyond the *"Pillars of Hercules."* According to the Egyptians, these mysterious Sea People came from the west across the great ocean and destroyed the existing Bronze Age civilizations of the Mediterranean, thereby plunging the survivors into a new great Dark Age. Until now, the origin of these people has been a complete and total mystery to scholars and lay alike. However, with our newfound esoteric knowledge of the second phase of the Exodus, this great mystery of the "*Sea People*" just melts away. To truly understand what happened once these people arrived, we must first go back and look at one of the most important of the Bronze Age civilizations when the original Exodus out of Egypt began, the Minoans. [22]

Minoan is a highly curious name and is a modern one taken from the name of King Minos, who is celebrated in mythology and legend, but he may not have existed in real life. The later Greeks believed or at least said that he was a great and powerful King of Crete who lived in the grand palace at Knossos. He is most famously known for his connection to the legendary Minotaur. It is unknown what the Minoans called themselves, but we know the Egyptians called them "*Keftiu*" or "*Kftjw*." Although the Minoans' trading relationship with Egypt is an indisputable fact, it is unknown what this Egyptian word meant. Scholars have proposed that the word is Greek in origin and is usually translated as meaning "*the nail of the earth*," with "*nail*," meaning "*the peak of a mountain*." Thus, the name "*Keftiu*" would primarily mean "*at the nail*," which is a term believed to have been used by sailors of the Bronze Age Mediterranean to indicated the dominant landmark of the island of Crete, which is the sharp peak located above the site of the highest open-air sanctuary on the island. During the Bronze Age, this was a well-known point of departure or destination among the ancient Aegean Sea seafarers and the Mediterranean in general. [23]

One of the things that makes the Minoans important is the evidence that the island of Thera experienced a tremendous volcanic eruption that almost destroyed the entire island and the city that once sat upon it. Although this massive eruption damaged the Minoan civilization of Crete, which lay a mere seventy miles away to the south, it was not the reason this grand civilization fell. Until recently, archaeologists and historians did not know precisely why the Minoan civilization collapsed in just a few generations after the destruction of Thera. According to the Linear B tablets, we now know that the Minoan civilization did not collapse in the traditional sense. The collapse of Minoan civilization was not because of the destruction of Thera, but it was primarily due to the Minoan elites assimilating and fusing with a new people that moved into mainland Greece, a people that came to been known as the "*Mycenean*." For us, the collapse of the Minoan civilization is not the critical point here but it is really Thera's destruction that we need to explore first. After this, we will take a closer look at the collapse of the Minoans. [24]

It has been proposed by many different people over the last few decades, both professional and amateur, that the eruption of Thera may be the reason behind the Ten Plagues of Egypt as recorded in the Bible since both events appear to date to about the same time. There have been numerous theories put forward that make compelling arguments that the after-effects of the eruption, as they spread out across the Mediterranean, would have provided the conditions necessary for the legendary Ten Plagues to happen.

Although there is debate that the eruption of Thera may, or may not, have been the real reason of the Ten Plagues, we do know that this eruption set in motion a series of events that eventually led to the collapse of the Minoan civilization. One of the direct results of the eruption was a great abandonment of many of the Aegean Sea islands and large numbers of people leaving the mainland of Greece. This was because the eruption destroyed much of the fishing and the settlements that depended on it. It also covered the fields with a thick layer of ash, which wiped out the crops and livestock. This alone forced most people to abandon their homes, settlements, and lands to search for food and new places to live. [25]

These events, like so many others we know little about, opened the door for new people to move into the mainland of Greece and then later, onto the many islands of the Aegean Sea. The arrival of these people brings us to a unique situation that does not appear to occur elsewhere on the planet during this time. This is because these new people who moved into the mainland of Greece and the surrounding islands as the Minoan civilization collapsed, appear to be an Indo-European speaking tribe of Israel. Which, as we will shortly learn, makes Greece the only land to suffer two separate invasions and settlements by the Indo-European-speaking children of Israel. [26]

For many, that idea may sound a bit strange, but there have been a few scholars and many laypeople that have proposed that these early invaders of Greece were from the Israelite tribe known as "Dan" from the biblical story. This idea appears to be based more on the idea that the surname of 'Dan' appears in so many places, names, and languages throughout southern and central Europe. It is also loosely based upon the Book of Judges and the Book of Isaiah that both mention that the tribe of Dan was the second largest of all the tribes and that the tribe broke into two groups, with one part of the tribe occupying a city known as Laish, located in the northwestern part of modern-day Israel, which they renamed Dan, while the other group is believed to had journeyed to other lands somewhere to the west.

Although the argument for the tribe of Dan being the original people who come to be known as the Mycenaeans is relatively weak, however, we do know that a Indo-European-speaking people moved into the Greek mainland and the islands of the Aegean Sea at about this time in history. These Indo-European speaking invaders brought with them advanced bronze and iron weapons, the horse, and the war-chariot, which, as we have already seen, are hallmarks of these children of Israel. We also have archaeological evidence that these invaders brought a new male-dominated religion centered around a male fertility god that helps lay the foundation for the later Greece pantheon of gods. Which again, is another important hallmark of the children of Israel and their travels. [27]

At the time of the collapse of the Minoan civilization, we know that the Minoan's primary religion focused on the worship of a great Mother Goddess on the mainland. On Crete and many of the Aegean Sea islands, Poseidon was the primary god of worship, with an Apollo-like god filling the role of the Sky-Father, which we know is a representation of the mighty Heaven up above, with the ever-present symbolism of Bulls. Many may find it surprising that at this early point in time, the mighty Zeus of Greek mythology was only a minor male fertility god that was worshipped on the mainland of Greece and Crete with no known temples or primary places of worship dedicated to him. As we will shortly learn, the worship of Zeus as the head of the Greek pantheon does not come until after the invasion of the Sea People. [28]

There is clear archaeological evidence that much violence came with these people and their new male god. The evidence shows us that this first group of Indo-European-speaking people were thought of as barbarians by the local population who mightily resisted the introduction of a new male god in place of the Mother Goddess. There is also clear archaeological evidence that these new people took over the existing temples and sites dedicated to the Mother Goddess by placing an idol of their supreme male god in place of the Mother Goddess. Although we do not know the original name of this god, the Linear B tablets refer to him as "*Diuja.*" Which appears to have been a very early version of Zeus. [29]

Remarkably, the few idols of this new male god that have survived show a striking similarity to the Greek god Apollo and not Zeus. Most of these idols have been found in the ruins of temples destroyed by the local population, led by the displaced female priesthood of the Mother Goddess's temples. The evidence suggests that this violent local resistance was led by the female priesthood and it went on for almost a century. The evidence also suggests that the destruction layer found in Knossos was not the result of ash raining down from the eruption of Thera, but is debris from the Minoan resistance to the Mycenaean incursions and their religion. It has been suggested that there were possibly local rebellions during this time that helped the Mycenaeans take over Knossos. The conflict seems to end once the new invaders had fully fused with the Minoan elites that then adopted the Minoan gods, becoming the civilization we know as Mycenean. Even after the Mycenean elites had secured their political power, they had to leave the female priesthood intact in most respects. This was primarily because the female priesthood held great sway over the local population. Although this female priesthood held great social influence, the new ruling class would only allow the female priesthood to remain in power if they adopted the Mycenean version of the Supreme god, which was an Apollo-like god. [30,31]

The female priestess who agreed to this change tended to gain even more political power than they held before. The world-famous Oracle of Delphi is by far the best example of this. During the time of the Minoans, the Oracle of Delphi was dedicated to the Mother Goddess and had always been controlled by an all-female priesthood. Nevertheless, after the invasion of the Indo-European-speaking barbarians and the fusing with the Minoan elites, the Oracle became dedicated to the god Apollo, but it still retained its all-female priesthood. In time, the Oracle of Delphi became one of the most important, powerful, and influential individuals in the ancient world. So powerful that no important decision was made by any leader of the Greek world or, for that matter, by any person, without first consulting the Oracle for guidance. [32,33]

After the Mycenaeans had taken over and fused with the local Minoan elites and while they established their political and religious control. They created an extraordinary, almost mythical civilization that would always hang in the shadows of the later Greek mind as a time of legends, great battles, and timeless heroes. The Mycenaean empire, if that term is permissible, became a prominent political and military power in the Mediterranean for a short time as Hittite power crumbled in the east and Egyptian power weakened in the south. For a short time, the Mycenaeans were a small group of people that were greatly enriched by trade that gave them a disproportionate importance while the great powers of the Mediterranean waned. [34]

As the great powers of the Mediterranean waned, the Mycenaeans established colonies on the shores of Asia Minor that greatly prospered through trade with other towns and city-states, most notably Troy. However, even as these colonies were being established and growing, there were signs that Mycenaean power was already beginning to weaken. Although the exact reasons are unknown, we do know a people known as the "*Achaeans.*" Which is one of the collective names for the Greeks in Homer's Iliad that come from the northwestern part of the Peloponnese peninsula and who occupied the coastal strip north of Arcadia. These people took part in a series of important attacks and raids on Egypt and many of the city-states on the shores of Asia Minor. With one of the most significant raids by them, with the help of other Greek-speaking tribes took place upon the shores of Asia Minor and was later immortalized as the legendary Siege of Troy. [35]

Against this troubled background of events, there was a series of dynastic upheavals in the Mycenaean city-states themselves. These upheavals appear to have been caused by a series of earthquakes that destroyed several Mycenaean centers of power on the mainland of Greece. This caused the remaining Mycenaean centers of power in the Aegean and Asia Minor to break up into disconnected city-states. As the city-states became independent entities, Mycenaean civilization collapsed, with many city-states being wholly abandoned. Not all the Mycenaean city-states were abandoned, but for those that survived, their life continued at a much lower level of achievement. The kingly treasures disappear, the palaces are not rebuilt. In some places, they hung on for centuries, while elsewhere, they were ruled as serfs or driven out by new conquerors. [36]

As the Mycenaean civilization was collapsing, we encounter the second settlement and invasion of the tribes of the children of Israel. Remarkably, these new conquerors were also speakers of an Indo-European language, who came from the north. Strangely, these new conquerors do not seem to have always settled the lands they ravaged but they did sweep away the existing political structures of the lands they entered. The future would be built upon their kingship and not on the Mycenaean political institutions or traditions. With their coming, we see the first glimpses of the ground plan that will later become classical Greece. What little we know of these people comes more from legend than archaeology or history. There are legendary accounts of one particular group among these newcomers, the *"Dorians."* They were said to be vigorous, bold, brave, and remembered as the descendants of the mighty Heracles. The language they spoke was *"Doric,"* and even in Greece's classical age, the people who spoke this dialect were what set them apart from other Greeks. In Sparta and Argos, it was Dorian communities that would become the future city-states that helped Greek culture to crystallize into a new civilization. [37]

The most successful of these new invaders were a people who were later identified as speakers of *"Ionic"* Greek. They settled Athens, which had either survived or had assimilated the invaders who came after the Mycenaean. From Athens, they set out and took root in the Cyclades and Ionia, the present-day Turkish coast of the Aegean Sea, where they laid the foundation of future city-states based upon a seafaring economy. They often chose sites that were once occupied by the Mycenaean, but they also displaced earlier Greek settlers. This coming of new peoples with the displacement of others creates a confusing

86

picture of a very confusing time, with only fragmentary evidence available for much of it. In order for us to make sense of this mass of confusion, we need to return to the coming of the Sea People and the incredible destruction they unleashed as they slammed into the Mediterranean civilizations like a hammer. [38]

Although the accounts we have are fragmentary, the Egyptians describe these Sea People as being composed of many different races and cultural groups. They describe them as being made up of tribes of different races of people that came from different cultures and who spoke different languages with each having a different dress, different customs, and even different weapons from one another. One of the unique things recorded within the Egyptian accounts is that these people also brought their women, their children, and even their livestock upon their countless boats coming from the west. They were not just an invasion force because they fully intended to settle the lands they conquered. [39]

The Egyptians were the only Mediterranean civilization that was able to resist their attempts to invade and settle their lands and, in the end, repel them from their shores. Nevertheless, it was at a high cost to the Egyptian state, with it significantly weakening Egypt. Repelling the 'Sea Peoples' is the event that started the long slow descent of Egypt from a great power to a minor player in world affairs, often occupied by foreign powers. However, the answers we seek do not lie with Egypt and its battles with the Sea People, but instead, we must look across the Mediterranean at what may seem at first an unlikely place, the founding of Rome in Italy.

It is within the ancient story of the founding of Rome that we find the critical piece of information that helps bring clarity to this great mass of confusion with the coming of the Sea People and its connection to the final phases of the second phase of the Exodus led by the divine twin brothers. Within the stories of the founding of Rome, we discover the first detailed story of the twin brothers that led this great immigration of the tribes of the Indo-European speaking children of Israel around the globe. In the Roman stories, the twin brothers are remembered as Romulus and Remus, the founders of the ancient city of Rome.

In the best-known Romulus and Remus story, we are told that the brothers were born in Alba Longa, one of the many ancient Latin villages and settlements that surrounded the future site of Rome. Their mother, Rhea Silvia, was a vestal virgin and the daughter of the former King Numitor. In Roman mythology, Numitor is said to have been the son of Procas, a descendant of Aeneas, the Trojan, who was believed to be the son of the prince Anchises and the goddess Aphrodite. [40]

When King Procas died, he was meant to be succeeded by his son Numitor. Instead, Numitor was overthrown and removed from the kingdom by his brother, Amulius, who had no respect or honor for his father's wishes or his brother's seniority and his right to the throne. Amulius also had murdered Numitor's sons to remove all power from his brother for himself. Once in power, Amulius forced Rhea Silvia to become a Vestal Virgin to render her unable to have children under pain of death. However, she is said to have been forcibly impregnated by the god Mars in a sacred grove dedicated to him. It is through their mother that the twins were said to be descended from Latin and Greek nobility. Upon Romulus and Remus's birth, their mother could not protect them from Amulius, who had ordered them killed. Their mother placed them in a small basket and sent them down the Tiber river so they would escape persecution by King Amulius. [41,42]

The small basket containing the twins was said to have been guided and looked after by the god Tiberinus, the Father of the River. Until it was brought to the shore of the den of the great mother wolf, who took the twins and raised them as her own at the site of what would eventually become Rome. In the best-known version of the story, the twins are believed to have been suckled by the great mother wolf in a cave known as the Lupercal. Eventually, the young twins were adopted by a local shepherd named Faustulus. They grew up tending their adopted father's flocks, totally unaware of their true identities. As they grew older and because of their semi-divine nature, they became natural leaders who attracted a large company of supporters from the local communities. [43]

When they became young adults, the brothers became involved in a dispute between the supporters of Numitor and King Amulius. As a result of their involvement, Remus was taken prisoner and brought to the city of Alba Longa. Both his grandfather and King Amulius suspected his true identity. Meanwhile, Romulus had a plan to free his brother with the help of the city. He organized an uprising among the people of the city to free his brother. During this time, the brothers eventually learned of their true identity and joined forces with their grandfather to restore him as the rightful ruler. Soon after joining their forces with their grandfather's, the brothers killed King Amulius. After Amulius' death, the brothers rejected the citizens' offer of the crown of Alba Longa and reinstated Numitor as the rightful king of Alba Longa. After these events, the twin brother then set out to build a city of their own. [44]

After searching many lands around Alba Longa, the brothers arrived back in the area of the seven hills by the Tiber river. The brothers soon began to quarrel over the location of the foundation of their new city. Legend says Romulus wished to build it upon the Palatine Hill, above the Lupercal, the centermost of

Rome's seven hills; Remus is said to have preferred the Aventine Hill, which is the southernmost of the seven hills. When they could not resolve their dispute, they agreed to seek the gods' approval through augury. Augury is a type of prophecy in which the entrails of birds are examined in order to determine what signs from the birds should be observed in order to know which actions the gods favored. [45]

In this case, the brothers were instructed to prepare a sacred space upon their respective hills and watch for birds to learn whom the gods would favor. Remus claimed he saw first saw six auspicious birds, but soon afterward, Romulus claimed he saw twelve and then claimed he had won with divine approval. Remus hotly disputed his brother's claim, with the quarrel escalating to the point that Remus is said to have been killed either by his brother or one of his supporters. After Remus' death, Romulus then founded the city of Rome, its institutions, government, religious traditions, and a great military tradition that would become the backbone of Rome's power. [46,47]

In another popular version of the story, Remus and Romulus remained at a standstill in their quarrel until Romulus began to dig trenches and build walls around his hill, the Palatine Hill. In response to Romulus' construction, Remus is said to have made a continuous mockery of the wall and his brother's city. After his brother had finished his work each day, Remus would boldly jump over Romulus' wall while endlessly belittling it and the city. This endless mockery angered Romulus to the point that he killed his brother. There are several versions of the story that speak of how Remus was said to have died on the fateful day of Rome's founding. In many of them, Remus is not killed by his brother but simply dies one day while jumping over the walls. In all cases, Remus' death is thought to be a sign from the gods of Rome's power and fate. Afterward, Romulus mournfully buries his brother, bestowing upon him full funeral honors. However, it should be noted; most sources convey the idea that Romulus killed his brother Remus. [48]

Although these stories about Remus and Romulus tell us more about the early Roman people's political thought and religious traditions, they tell us very little about the twin brothers themselves. Nevertheless, we can glean a few vitally important pieces of information that will help guide us through the last few steps of these legendary leaders.

One of the most critical pieces of information from the founding of Rome's stories is that the twin brothers were still alive and still leading this group of Indo-European-speaking children of Israel. Additionally, the traditional story of Remus and Romulus's birth is a vital connection to the original Exodus out of Egypt and Moses's birth. It is also a clue that a considerable amount of time had passed since the beginning of the Exodus's second phase. So much time had passed that the people do not seem to remember Moses or Aaron, but instead only knew the twin brothers' leadership. Over time, the tribes slowly incorporated them and then slowly replaced Moses and Aaron in the stories with the twin brothers. This provides us with another example of how the original story is remembered by each culture they fused with, but with each having slightly changed or different details as these children of Israel moved around the world.

The next critical piece of information is the death of Remus. It was common at this ancient time to view anybody that had left the community for any reason, with the expectation that they were never to return, as being dead. In the case of Remus's death, it is highly probable that once the city of Rome had been founded, he left and was not actually killed by his brother. The story of his death was just a simple way to explain away his absence. It is also a clue that the ones who stayed had no idea where Remus and the last tribes of the children of Israel had gone. It also highlights the common theme that runs through all the twin brothers' stories with their never-ending quarreling with one another, as only brothers can.

By realizing that one brother had left, we can now understand that the mysterious invaders that came from the north into mainland Greece must have been this last group of these Indo-European speaking children of Israel. It is evident that this last tribe moved north across Italy, going around the Adriatic Sea and then moving south into mainland Greece. We can also understand that the brother remembered by the Romans called Romulus and founded Rome must have been the warrior-king of the two with his brother Remus being the priest-king. What is now unsurprising is that ancient Greece has more stories related to twin brothers, divine twins, and twin gods within their mythology than any other ancient culture or civilization.

This small bit of information allows us to begin understanding that a large number of the Sea People were not the people who made up these last tribes of the children of Israel. But they were instead the people that made up the colossal baggage train that was composed of numerous non-related tribes, slaves, converts, merchants, and others that had become attached to the core tribes as they moved around the world. As the last remaining tribes of these children of Israel settled into Italy and Greece, this large baggage train of people scattered across the Mediterranean. These appear to be the Sea People that are remembered by the Egyptians. These are also the people that brought upon the Bronze Age collapse across the Mediterranean, primarily because every city-state and civilization of the time who resisted them, they destroyed. They followed the same pattern as the tribes had before. They would destroy any city-state or settlement that resisted them. In the case of the Bronze Age civilizations of the Mediterranean, it appears that almost every single city-state, settlement, and civilization resisted them and were ultimately destroyed by them in the end, except for Egypt.

Remarkably, the historical evidence tells us that neither the Egyptians nor the Myceneans had any idea who these mysterious Sea People were or where they had come from. This is an important clue that a large amount of time had passed, possibly centuries, if not thousands of years, since the original Exodus out of Egypt. So much time had elapsed that the first settlements of the children of Israel, the Myceneans, and the later Greeks did not recognize each other. Additionally, the Myceneans suffered greatly at the hands of their fellow tribesmen, with almost all their primary cites being destroyed with their coming.

Understandably, many people from this great baggage train scattered deep into Europe once the last tribes of the children of Israel had settled, where they assimilated and fused with the countless local tribes. As they fused with the local tribes, they followed the same pattern as the children of Israel they had been following. Once they had established political control over the local population, they would elevate the minor male fertility god to being the Supreme god. To the many tribes of northern Europe, this was the Horned god, commonly known by his Celtic name "*Cernunnos.*" He is also commonly known in southern Europe as the god Pan. Pan was the most common version of the minor male fertility god throughout southern Europe before the coming of the Sea People. It is believed that the god Pan was a god of an earlier people or tribe that lived somewhere in the northern areas of mainland Greece. He was a god of great power and influence over these people, but they disappeared, becoming lost to history. Although these mysterious people who originally worshiped Pan may have lost their identity and are completely forgotten by history, their god managed to live on within the Greek pantheon. [49,50]

With our new esoteric knowledge, we can understand why the Roman and Greek pantheons are so very similar. It is because they are based on the same pantheon of gods from the same group of people, with only the names being different, primarily due to local customs and small differences between the tribes. This is the same pattern we have repeatedly seen as these Indo-European-speaking children of Israel moved around the world during this second phase of the Exodus. This also allows us to see a small but essential change in how the gods slowly change from the beginning of their journey with their first settlement-invasion in the Indus Valley to the last settlements in Italy and Greece. This change is that the gods become much more human in their actions, their appearance, and representation among humanity.

It is difficult to know why this change occurred, but we know that it profoundly impacted the later thinking of both the Greeks and the Romans which had an enormous influence on western thought and civilization. Using mythology and our esoteric knowledge as our guide, we can speculate that this change came about because of more interaction between the tribes and the gods. A large body of mythology is directly related to the twin brothers that depict the brothers in constant conflict with numerous and nameless vengeful gods. In many myths, the gods work through powerful kings that are always trying to kill or imprison the brothers in some gruesome manner. In Meso-American folklore, there is a common theme of the brothers conflicting with the gods of the Underworld and its powerful Lords of death.

In these Meso-American myths about the twin brothers and the Underworld, we can gain a sense of this change in how the gods became more human and less otherworldly. Remarkably, the general concepts of the Underworld are very similar to the stories of the creation of man, the star that fell from heaven, the great deluge, and even the mighty Heaven floating up above the clouds. As with those stories, the stories of the Underworld are found in every single ancient civilization, culture, and society across the world. The idea of the Underworld is so universal that it has been put forward that it *"may be as old as humanity itself."* This could be correct, but as we learned from our journey through the Dream Vision, there are numerous symbolic aspects of the ancient mythologies of the Underworld that have been overlooked. [51]

As with the other mythologies we have explored, to properly understand the ancient mythology of the Underworld, we must always be aware of and look at the common esoteric symbolism within the stories. However, unlike the other stories we have examined, when exploring the Underworld's mythology, we need to always keep in mind that our ancient ancestors' ideas of "death" and our modern-day concept are two vastly different things. We must always keep the idea in the back of our minds that our ancient ancestors viewed death differently than we do today. In our modern world, "death" usually refers to the actual physical death of the body. However, in the ancient world, death was not quite as specific in its meaning. An individual who had been exiled, banished, sold into slavery, or taken into bondage, with the idea that this individual was never to return to the community, would be thought of as dead to those left behind. This general idea applied to anybody that had no expectation they would return. It also included individuals who may have set-off for long journeys or voyages to unknown lands and who did not return until long after they were expected. The legendary story of Odysseus is a perfect example of this.

Within the myth, Odysseus is not able to return home for twenty years. Although this wife, Penelope, believed that he may still be alive. The community of Ithaca believed him to be dead, with numerous requests that Penelope remarry. In the end, Odysseus returns and claims his household and reasserts his place as the rightful King of Ithaca. Nevertheless, his wife cannot believe that her husband has really returned with her fearing that he is perhaps some god in disguise. She eventually tests him by ordering her servant Euryclea to move the bed from their wedding-chamber. Odysseus protests that it cannot be moved, for he made this bed himself, and one of its legs is a living olive tree. After this test, Penelope finally accepts that her husband had indeed returned to her. Once Penelope accepts that her husband had returned, the people of Ithaca also accept that Odysseus had returned. [52]

Unfortunately, in the ancient world, most individuals that had been thought of as being dead were not as lucky as Odysseus. For most, if by some chance, one of these "dead" individuals happened to return for some reason, their families, friends, and the community would still treat them as they were physically dead. Their property, their household, and their claims would have been given away or taken over by others. It would also not be uncommon for the family or the community to physically kill them if they returned. Ancient folklore is filled with countless tales of the dead returning and being dealt with harshly, generally in a violent manner.

Understanding that being "dead" in the ancient world did not necessarily mean a "physical death," we can understand that this state of being dead is more of symbolic death. It was reserved for people that were believed by others that they would never be seen again, although they were most likely still very much alive. By understanding this, we can then realize that the Underworld's traditional interpretation of being populated by the "*spirits or souls of the physically dead*" is incorrect. It is more likely that the Underworld was populated by individuals who were very much physically alive but symbolically dead to their family, communities, and society in general. They became the "*damned souls*" with no place or future within accepted human society and were treated as if they were physically dead. In time, these damned souls came to be viewed as the walking dead. Once they became viewed as the walking dead, it is not difficult to imagine how our ancient ancestors symbolically came to also view them as spirits or ghosts that were damned to walk the Earth if they happened to return.

This esoteric knowledge allows us to understand that because of the real threat of actual physical death if they did return to their community, most individuals in the is state would stay away from their old communities. If, for some reason, one of these symbolically dead happened to return, it would have been likely they would only come at night under the cover of darkness to try and contact family, loved ones, or close friends. It is highly probable that these individuals would have been in bad shape with torn and dirty clothes, possibly starving or ill. It does not take much imagination to see how an individual that had been exiled and believed to be symbolically dead by their family, friends, and community, that happened to come sneaking around in the inky darkness of moonless night, in unkempt, dirty clothes, possibly carrying a small light source, like a small lantern that threw off an eerily glow as they moved through the darkness. This would, of course, scare anybody who happened upon this poor soul. This would in turn, be spoken of as seeing a dead person walking around. Again, it does not take much imagination to see how these symbolically dead people were turned into the idea of lost souls or lost spirits that come to be viewed as ghosts of the dead. Our modern-day lore related to ghosts and spirits of the dead still contain these same elements.

By keeping this general idea in mind, we can begin interpreting the mythology of the Underworld in an entirely new way. In addition, and due to our esoteric understanding of the Dream Vision of Enoch, we have something that those who came before us did not, which is being able to place the ancient myths in their proper order both within the esoteric and more traditional historical timelines.

Our first step is to understand that there are two basic concepts of the Underworld. The first comes directly from the oldest surviving written story in its original form that we know of, the Epic of Gilgamesh. Within its text, we are told of an Underworld that is a dark, gloomy, and dreary place where all the dead go, no matter their social standing. In this most ancient of stories, we are told that the Underworld "*is a house of darkness, where the dead drink dirt and eat stone.*" The second idea, which comes from a much later date than the Epic of Gilgamesh, is the more traditional idea of the Underworld being a multi-level Hell-like environment. Where wrongdoers, criminals, sinners, and those who blasphemed against the gods were sent as punishment for their transgressions. This change in the general concept of Underworld can first be seen in ancient Mesopotamia, in the Sumerian and Akkadian poems which were written long after the time of the Epic of Gilgamesh. In these poems we are told of "*Ereshkigal,*" the queen of the dead and sister of "*Inanna,*" who is better known by her Akkadian name as "*Ishtar.*" Ereshkigal was said to have ruled over a vast seven-level Underworld with each level being separated from each other by a great gate. [53]

Our first clue to understanding these two different ideas of the Underworld and how they are related to the twin brothers comes from a few different sources, but primarily from the mythology of Meso-American cultures. In almost all the known Meso-American myths, legends, and folklore of the Underworld they usually refer to the legendary twin brothers of mythology in some manner. In many of these myths, it is due to the actions of the brothers, but the more common theme found within the mythology is that they were born into this world because of the direct actions of the gods or lords of the Underworld. Remarkably, in these myths, we can see the ideas about the Underworld undergo their change from a dark and gloomy place we find in the Epic of Gilgamesh to the terrible Hell-like Underworld where the wrongdoers of this life are punished in some horrible fashion fitting their transgressions and sins.

Within the myths of the Maya, we learn of "*Xibalba*," (Shee-bal-ba), which is the name the "*K'iche*," or more commonly known as the Quiche Maya gave to their Underworld, a name that meant the "*place of fear and fright*." Within these myths, we also learn of an important creation story about the birth of the Maya Hero Twins, "*Hunahpu*" and "*Xbalanque*." Within this myth, we are told that when the great Maize god, "*Hun-Hunahpu*," and his brother, "*Vucub-Hunahpu*," were playing a game of "*Pokatok*," the gods of the Underworld had become greatly annoyed by the noise and were also very envious of the brothers' talents. Pokatok was the violent ball game that both mortals and the gods were equally obsessed with and that was played with a solid rubber ball, which typically weighed up to 4 kg (9 lbs.). It is said that the original stone ball court was situated just above the entrance to Xibalba. Upon this ball court, the gods of the Underworld summoned the two brother gods to put them through a series of games or tests to see if they were as good as they claimed to be. [54,55,56]

We are told that the brother gods outwitted all the gods of the Underworld in all their tests. They also made it through the nine-levels of the Underworld. Their final test, and reason for all the other tests, was to play the first game of Pokatok among the gods of the Underworld upon the great stone ball court over Xibalba. Although the brothers played with great skill and swiftness, in the end, they lost to the gods of the Underworld. The gods of the Underworld then sacrificed the brother gods by cutting off their heads and then buried their bodies beneath the ball court. The myth then tells us that the head of the Maize god Hun-Hunahpu, was placed in a calabash tree, where it was later found by a goddess of the Underworld known as "*Blood-Moon*." It is said she became miraculously pregnant after the head spat into her hands, and she subsequently gave birth to the legendary Maya Hero Twins, named Hunahpu and Xbalanque. [57]

The myth says that as these twin brothers grew, they became excellent hunters and very accomplished Pokatok players. It is also believed that they had magical powers that were given to them by the creator gods that lived up above in the sky. The myth speaks of how one day the brothers caught a rat while they were out hunting. However, this was no ordinary rat, but it was a magical rat of the gods. The magical rodent then tells the twin brothers what truly happened to their father and uncle at the hands of the Lords of the Underworld. It is unknown if learning the truth about their father and uncle or their irresistible love of the game of Pokatok and the chance to challenge the gods of the Underworld with a game is what lured the twin brothers to Xibalba. [58]

Upon arriving at the entrance, the brothers allowed themselves to be drawn down into Xibalba, just as their father and uncle had done. As their father and uncle had done before, the twin brothers easily survived all the brutal tests of the Underworld. They are said to have spent their last night in the "*House of Bats*," where a monstrously vicious bat bit off the head of the brother Hunahpu. The gods of the Underworld then forced Xbalanque to play a game of Pokatok with his brother's head as the ball. Somehow, Xbalanque cleverly switched his brother's head with that of a large rabbit. After easily winning the game, he reattached his brother's head to his body and then magically brought him back to life. [59]

Although Xbalanque had won the game of Pokatok, the mighty Lords of the Underworld still wanted the twin brothers dead. The twin brothers eventually outwitted the Lords of the Underworld by using their magical abilities to make it appear that they had allowed themselves to be sacrificed upon a great fire. After returning to life, the twin brothers then slew all the gods and lords of the Underworld but one, "*Hun-Came*," or "*One Death*." After killing the gods of the Underworld, the brothers then returned to the surface and resurrected their father, Hun-Hunahpu, the Mazie god. After the twin brothers had left Xibalba, the last surviving Lord of the Underworld, Hun-Came, brought back "*Vucub-Came*," the "*Seven Death*." With whose help brought back the other ten Lords of the Underworld. [60]

As with the Remus and Romulus stories, these stories from the Quiche Maya tell us more about the political and social interactions between humans and the gods than it does about the twin brothers themselves. But, unlike the Remus and Romulus stories, the Meso-American myths show us that there was a highly "political" situation that was occurring between these children of Israel and the gods on Earth. With it being rather straight forward that the second phase of the Exodus was causing a massive political upheaval among the gods and a shift in power. Not only is this political situation reflected in the mythology, but we also

96

get a clue to why the Messenger god was eventually replaced with the Lord of the Underworld in the original Trinity of gods. These myths also provide us with the information that allows us to reconstruct a small piece of what may have happened once these Indo-European-speaking children of Israel entered the Americans.

According to the myths, as the tribes moved across the Americas and began their settlement, they encountered the Underworld and its rulers. As reflected in the Meso-American myths, this contact resulted in massive political and social upheaval for both the tribes and the rulers of the Underworld. The myths tell us that eventually, the Underworld's Lords are defeated by the twin brothers in some manner. Although many details are missing, we can see the same pattern of substitution of gods within the pantheon and reflected in the mythology. But instead of reflecting a change to make peace with the local population, this change is representing a political change with the gods themselves. This allows us to understand that this change of the Messenger god being replaced by the Lord of the Underworld reflects some type of peace settlement between the Lords of the Underworld and the Sky-gods that the tribes followed. Remarkably, this change is carried across the Atlantic Ocean and is seen in Greek and Roman mythology. We will return to the Underworld a bit later, but, before we can go any farther in our journey, we need to pause and take a more in-depth look at this polytheistic religion of the children of Israel and their many gods.

Although many believe that the religion of the ancient Israelites was always monotheistic. Scholars and historians have known for decades that the earliest Israelites followed some type of polytheistic religion. The question has always been what was this mysterious polytheistic religion? As we have learned through our journey, this mysterious polytheistic religion of the early Israelites was the foundation of all the polytheistic religions we are aware of worldwide. This naturally leads us to the critical question of how this original polytheistic religion developed into the monotheistic belief we know of today? For us to start answering this question and many others, we need to first return to the early Proto-European people who settled in the ancient Land of Canaan and the gods they worshipped.

One of the more remarkable things about this ancient polytheistic belief system of the earliest Proto-Indo-Europeans and the later Indo-Europeans is that there are always twelve primary gods, with the three most important ones always forming a trinity. Amazingly, scholars and laypeople never seem to notice the symbolic connection between these twelve gods and the Bible's twelve tribes of Israel.

As with the seventy Shepherds we encountered within the Dream Vision, the number twelve provides us with important esoteric knowledge. In this case, the connection between the gods and the tribes of Israel by the number twelve. This provides us with the reason why there were twelve tribes remembered in the Bible and that it was simply because there were twelve gods. With each god having one tribe that it controlled or oversaw. Then each individual tribe would view this god as their tribal god who they held above all others, while they would also worship the other eleven gods of the other tribes. This allows us to understand that to keep the peace between the tribes; each god was included in the pantheon, thereby creating the twelve primary gods that all the tribes worshipped or honored. Although this is a simplistic understanding of a highly complex subject, it provides us with enough information on how the original pantheon came together for the tribes to allow us to take the next step in reconstructing some of the original polytheistic religion of these people.

Due to the Indo-European people's willingness to modify and substitute gods in their pantheon, it makes it very difficult, if not impossible, for us to reconstruct the original pantheon of the earliest Proto-Indo-European people entirely. Although we will not be able to fully reconstruct the original pantheon, we now have enough information to at least reconstruct the original trinity of gods and identify a few common threads that run throughout all the mythologies.

Our starting point is returning to the biblical story of Moses, with him first encountering his God, the God of Abraham, Jacob, and Isaac during his exile from Egypt. As we have already discovered, this was the god Hadad of the Hyksos, commonly known as the Lord of the waters. In time, this Lord of the waters becomes known as the King of the gods. The next point is to understand that the leadership of the twin brothers was based directly on the leadership of Moses and Aaron, with one being a warrior-king and other being the priest-king. This understanding will allow us to see an important connection between this Lord of the waters, Moses, and the warrior-king of the twin brothers very shortly.

The next step is our understanding that these early tribes of Israel each spoke different languages, but they had a common tongue that allowed the tribes to speak with one another. This common language is the language we call Proto-Indo-European. Within this ancient language, it is believed that this Lord of the waters and King of the gods was known as "*Neptonos*," a name that literally means "*Grandson of the Waters*." This god Neptonos is the original 'Lord of the waters' that all the later gods of the waters like Varuna, Poseidon, and Neptune can trace their origins. [61,62]

This brings us to a connection that has been missed by all. By understanding that it was the divine twin brothers who had finally settled in Rome and Greece, we can see the direct connection between the Lord of the waters, Neptonos of the Proto-Indo-European people, and the god Neptune of Rome. When compared to all the other Lords of the waters, Rome is the only culture that kept the name of this god that was very close to its original Proto-Indo-European name of Neptonos. This connection allows us to realize that the warrior-king of the twin brothers was following a belief that must have been very close to the original belief and the god of Moses. It is also reasonable to assume that he like Moses, was unyielding in those beliefs. Simultaneously, the brother who was priest-king that had finally settled in Greece appears to have been much more open to modifying and substituting the pantheon of gods to make peace with the native population. As we have already explored, this Lord of the waters is the God of the Bible that leads the Hebrews out of Egypt. He also the god that leads the twin brothers around the world. It is this long period of interaction between this god and humanity that is one of the primary reasons why he becomes known as the "*King of the gods.*"

While at the same time as the Lord of the waters was turning into the "*King of the gods*," the ever-present Heaven orbiting high above becomes the "*Supreme god*" that is always looking down upon humanity like a great eye observing of all creation. To the Proto-Indo-Europeans, this Supreme god was known as "*Dyeus-Pater*," the Sky-Father. As we have learned, this Supreme god goes by many names, with Shiva, Zeus, Jupiter, or Ahura Mazda being the best known. This Supreme god is always associated with the mighty storm with him being commonly remembered as the "*Storm god*" with his powerful thunderbolts. [63,64]

The next important god was the Messenger god. This god is normally associated with fire in some manner. According to mythology, this god was the primary means of delivering messages, offerings, and sacrifices, to either the King of the gods or directly to the Supreme god high above humanity. Since we understand that these 'gods' were technologically advanced craft, we can easily recognize that the fire symbolism associated with this god must be due to it using a rocket-like propulsion system that generated a large cloud of fire and smoke upon launching or landing. As with all the gods, this Messenger god went by many different names like Agni, Hermes, Mercury, among others. It is believed that the Proto-Indo-Europeans may have called this god by some version of the word Hermes who was normally "*seen from afar and untiring*." In later cultures, this Messenger god becomes associated with the symbolism of the "*Ram*." With our knowledge of the esoteric symbolism, we know that the symbolism of the Ram is normally related to a leader that has been raised above his fellow man in some divine manner with the help of a god. This symbolic connection allows us to realize that it is likely that this Messenger god may have been the god responsible for elevating individual humans to kingship. [65,66,67]

These three gods become the basis of the Trinity of gods that still survives today in Christianity. The idea of the Trinity is easier to understand once we think of the second phase of the Exodus and the twin brothers being guided by the "King of the gods," just as they had been since leaving Egypt. With the "Supreme god" always high above, looking down upon all of creation as if it was the great eye of the creator himself looking down upon all of humanity. With the "Messenger god" moving between the two regularly. So regular it became imbedded within the mythology, which over thousands of years, survives today as the Christian Trinity of the Father, the Son, and the Holy Ghost or Spirit.

This then brings us to one of the most significant misunderstandings related to the mighty Heaven. Because if Dyeus-Pater, Shiva, Jupiter, Zeus, Shiva, and Ahura Mazda, among others, is the mighty Heaven floating above, then where do all the other Solar deities come from? This great mystery disappears when we remember the '*Fall of the Watchers*' and the fact that many of the people taken over by these "*children of the men who saw God*" already had names, customs, and beliefs related to the mighty Heaven up above. Many of these solar gods are leftovers from the time when the gods walked among humanity, during the time between the Fall of the Watchers up to the Great Deluge and the reconquest of Earth. While others are local versions of Sky-Father god during the time between the Great Deluge and the coming of the children of Israel, with 'solar-deities,' like Helios, Cronus, Aten, or Apollo being some of the more common ones.

The gods of Light, like Apollo, Surya, or Yu-Yi from Chinese mythology are always associated with being a Solar deity or the Solar disk itself. They are commonly believed to be the god that pulled the sun across the sky in a magical chariot. Which as we know is not the 'Sun' or 'Solar disk' but is really the mighty Heaven, the abode of the Host of Heaven from an earlier time and older traditions. We can also understand that the magical chariot's symbolism was used to represent the god that was in control of the mighty Heaven as it moved across the sky as if he was driving a chariot across the sky.

Additionally, we must also remember the Fall of the Watchers, of when a "*star fell from Heaven*" on that one early morning and who brought freedom and knowledge to an enslaved humanity. This was the "*Lord-of-Light,*" known as Lucifer, the morning star in the biblical tradition and the Book of Enoch. Over thousands of years, this original "*Lord-of-Light,*" who was also the first '*Savior*' of humanity, became directly associated with the Heaven. This great 'Lord-of-Light' had such an incredible impact upon humanity that he was deeply embedded into the existing cultures and societies that these Indo-European-speaking children of Israel took over. These beliefs were so embedded that they had little choice but to assimilate and fuse any existing versions of the Lord-of-Light being the mighty Heaven above into the new Supreme god so the local population would accept the new pantheon of gods they introduced. Overtime, he was slowly demonized and transformed into an evil character that is often mistakenly remembered within the biblical tradition as Satan or the Devil.

As we learned with the fusing of the Aryan god Indra with Shiva and then later with the god Varuna, these earlier versions of the Lord of Light or the Sky-Father were already associated with the mighty Heaven. They typically become an almost mirror image of the new Supreme god. However, they tend to lose much of their power and standing in so many ways while also gaining new ones in the process. As we saw earlier with the god Apollo being used as a substitute for Zeus at the Oracle of Delphi. Since the female priesthood and the local population would not accept Zeus, the children of Israel substituted him with a god they would accept, in this case the ancient god of light known as Apollo. This was primarily because the local population knew who he was and his connection to the Minoans and the Mother Goddess of that civilization. Over time, Apollo slowly lost his standing, eventually being replaced with Zeus.

This pattern of substituting the gods as needed into and out of the pantheon to bring peace among the cultures and societies they took over is seen repeatedly. It also helps explain why there are so many similar but different gods of Light, Sky-Fathers and Solar deities that are all related to the mighty Heaven. They are essentially leftovers from a much earlier time that were changed as needed. With many of them being a version of the existing Sky-Father that was worshiped alongside the Mother Goddess and the Bull long before the arrival of the Indo-European speaking children of Israel. While others tended to be combination of the older Lord-of-Light and the god that overthrew him during the Great Flood. This modifying and substitution of gods in the pantheons is what has led to much of the confusion when identifying some of these ancient gods. Another factor that adds to the confusion is our esoteric knowledge that to our ancient ancestors when one of these ships landed and the occupants exited the ship, they viewed this event as the "god" transforming into something else, typically a Bull, the symbolic representation of the First-Men. This duality adds another layer of confusion that can only be understood through the esoteric knowledge of the symbolism of Dream Vision of Enoch and the secret history of creation it holds.

One final factor that we have not addressed in much detail is the type of thinking that our ancient ancestors applied to the mighty Heaven floating high above the clouds and the various ships that were seen entering or leaving this mighty abode of the Host of Heaven. To our ancient Neanderthal and then later

Cro-Magnon man ancestors, they would view any ship leaving the Heaven and coming down to Earth was the great unknowable Supreme god of the heavens was breaking off a small piece of itself to come down and interact with humans. It was thought of as small earthly incarnation of the Supreme god that was created so mere mortals could understand it and interact with it. So, the "god" that came down was believed to be a part of the unknowable Supreme god's essence, but in just a smaller, more understandable version. This type of thinking is still seen today within Christianity and their idea that Jesus Christ, the man, is of the same essence of the Father above, or more simply, he was God made into flesh so humans could understand the unknowable God up above. As we can now easily understand, this has only added to this great mass of confusion about the gods and how there are related to one another, sometimes, across cultures.

Although we are missing numerous details, this once again allows us to put together a more realistic chain of events that helps explain one of the greatest mysteries of the ancient world and why all the cultures of the ancient world appear to such similar beliefs, customs, traditions, and architecture. It is directly related to the second phase of the Exodus under the leadership of the legendary divine twin brothers moving around the world to occupy the lands, which according to the biblical tradition, each tribe had inherited by lot. As each tribe settled in their new lands, they removed the elites of every group of people they encountered and replaced them with members of their tribe.

Once this political change had been accomplished, they would then begin imposing a new religious belief upon the local people. A belief that was built around the twelve primary gods that the tribes worshiped. However, they also uniquely modified, fused, or substituted these twelve gods with the local gods as needed to achieve peace between the new rulers and the native population. They would also incorporate local customs, rituals, and traditions into their new pantheon of gods as necessary to assimilate the local culture and society. This, in turn, built the numerous different polytheistic pantheons we see worldwide, with each being centered around the trinity of three primary gods, the Supreme god, the King of the gods, and the Messenger god.

Chapter 7

The Land of Canaan

T he next step in our esoteric journey is to return the ancient Land of Canaan that is spoken of in the Bible with the realization that it was in the area of what is today the modern nation-state of Iran. With its primary areas of settlement being located within the many valleys of Zagros Mountains and across the great plain of the Iranian highlands, commonly known as the Iranian Plateau. As stated before, from a historical point of view, we know very little about the original Proto-Indo-European people that settled this ancient land. We will take a much more in-depth look at the known historical information shortly. However, we must first start with the biblical account of the Israelites settling the Land of Canaan and the events that came later as they established the Kingdom of Israel to properly understand how the biblical account is based upon historical events.

According to the Bible, after the twin brothers and the other tribes had left on their journey to the distant lands they were to inherit, the remaining tribes that had stayed in the Land of Canaan had settled into a simple pastoral way of life broken along tribal and clan lines. The common factors holding these tribes together were their collective experience of the Exodus out of Egypt and their devotion to the Tabernacle that housed the holy Ark of the Covenant, also known as the Ark of the Testimony. Within the Book of Judges, it is said that during this early time the Israelites were a tribal people without a King or any central government for "*In those days there was no king in Israel: every man did that which was right in his own eyes.*" [1]

According to the Book of Judges these early Israelites were viewed as a "*stiff-necked people*" that routinely fell away from the teachings of their fathers and corrupted themselves by "a *whoring after and bowing down to strange gods.*" When this happened, their Lord-God would raise a "*Judge*" that would then lead them back from their sinful ways to the Tabernacle and the Ark of the Covenant. This general cycle of the people falling away and their Lord-God raising a Judge that leads them back, goes on for untold generations. Until one day, the people of Israel began to demand a King so they could be like the other peoples of the world.

The Book of Samuel tells us that the Lord of the Israelites, speaking through Samuel, tried to warn the people of Israel against wanting a king and that their Lord would turn His back on them if they lost their way once again. Nevertheless, as we all know, the people of Israel would not listen to their Lord and demanded a king to rule over them, to judge them, and to fight their battles. Soon after these events, the Book of Samuel speaks of how their Lord raised a man named Saul to be the new leader for Israel's tribes, to be the first King. Saul is presented as a man that was a competent and highly successful military leader that defeated several of the enemies of this new Kingdom of Israel. Although he appears to be an excellent general, he proves to be a poor king in time. As his reign went on, we are told that he became increasingly paranoid and began abusing his power. As the years went by, King Saul slowly begins to turn against the people of Israel. During the later years of his reign, the Lord of Israel then raises a new "*Ram*" to become a king for His people.

This new 'Ram' was, of course, the ever-famous King David. The biblical account goes into great detail about the life of King David with his many human faults. Out of his many accomplishments as King of Israel, his most significant was the uniting of Israel's tribes into one people and establishing the new Kingdom of Israel. The biblical account speaks of how King David had a great desire to construct a great "*House*" for his Lord and God to house the holy Ark of the Covenant, but he was unable to begin its construction during his reign. That task would fall to his son, Solomon.

After ruling for forty years, King David's remarkable life came to an end. Upon his death, his son Solomon assumed the throne. King Solomon's reign was and still is, believed by both Jews and Christians to have been a *Great Golden Age* for the people of the Kingdom of Israel. Although King Solomon is remembered as a good, just, and wise ruler, his most important act as King, was the construction and incredible dedication ceremony of the Temple and Citadel he had built to house the Ark of the Covenant, more commonly known as King Solomon's Temple, it is also commonly referred to as the First Temple. As with his father, the Bible also goes into detail about King Solomon's long, wealthy, and legendary reign that lasted for forty years, but like all good things, King of Solomon's wise rule was not meant to last forever.

Upon King Solomon's death, his son, Rehoboam, assumes the throne. Unlike his father, the Bible presents Rehoboam as more of a spoiled child than a man who would be a wise king. Although the biblical account is vague, we are told that the new King Rehoboam refuses to listen to the older advisers that served his father, but instead listened to his younger advisers and friends. These younger men advised King Rehoboam to place a *"heavy yoke"* upon the people of Israel. The Bible never states what this *"heavy-yoke"* was; it only says that it was much greater than the one his father had placed upon them. This heavy-yoke is traditionally believed to be related to some form of service to the throne. This act of placing a heavy yoke upon the people was rejected by all the tribes of Israel, except for the tribes of Judah, Benjamin, and Levi in the Land of Canaan. This mysterious event was serious enough that it had the effect of breaking the Kingdom of Israel into two separate kingdoms, with one being the Kingdom of Judea composed of the tribes of Judah, Benjamin, and the Levi priesthood in the Land of Canaan. With the other being the Kingdom of Israel, which consisted of the other tribes of Israel spread around the world.

From this time onward, until the destruction of King Solomon's Temple, the Bible speaks of a slow general decline of both kingdoms. This slow general downfall of the two kingdoms eventually leads to both kingdoms being invaded. The first to be invaded and conquered was the Kingdom of Israel, with its capital city of Samaria being taken by the Assyrian Empire. With understanding that the Kingdom of Israel was actually numerous kingdoms spread around the world. We can surmise that biblical account is referring to a city-state that was viewed as the 'capital' for the numerous kingdoms that made up the Kingdom of Israel. Once this capital had been taken by the Assyrians, the Kingdom of Israel ceased to exist as a unified state and broke into numerous kingdoms spread around the world. Over time, this original connection was forgotten and eventually lost, thereby creating the myth of the lost tribes of Israel.

The Kingdom of Judah centered around Jerusalem and King Solomon's Temple is believed to have existed for a couple more centuries as an independent state until the Neo-Babylonian Empire conquered it under the reign of King Nebuchadnezzar. After King Nebuchadnezzar conquered the Kingdom of Judah, he famously takes all the elites captive. He then loots the great Temple and Citadel of King Solomon, taking its treasures along with the elites back to the city of Babylon. Soon after these events, King Nebuchadnezzar once again invades the Land of Canaan which results in the destruction of King Solomon's Temple and Citadel, with it being burned down along with all the palaces with any remaining *"goodly vessels"* being destroyed with the rest of the elites being taken captive and returned to city of Babylon, thereby starting the Babylonian Captivity.

This is the point where we need to pause the biblical account and return to history and explore the Proto-Indo-European people who occupied the ancient lands of the Iranian Plateau and the Zagros Mountains. This will significantly aid us in understanding how these mysterious ancient people known as the Proto-Indo-Europeans and the ancient Israelites of the Bible are categorically the same people.

Once again, historically, we know very little about these ancient Proto-Indo-European speaking people who settled in the lands of the Iranian Plateau and the Zagros Mountains. We do not know what language they spoke. However, we know that this unknown language was the mother tongue that later became the Indo-European language that went on to provide the foundation for dozens of the languages that we speak today. Although it should be noted, this later Indo-European language is just as mysterious as the original Proto-European language that it originated from. We also have learned that the Aryan language group that later became what we call *"Vedic Sanskrit,"* that is still preserved in the ancient texts of the Vedas and is the foundational canon and language for Hinduism, is just one language of the vast Indo-European language group. [2,3]

Although we do not know what this original Proto-Indo-European language was, we do know it became the basis of what is known as the Proto-Indo-Iranian group of languages. This Proto-Indo-Iranian language is the ancestor of the later Iranian languages such as Persian, Pashto, Kurdish, and Sogdian, in the same manner as the Aryan language was the basis of Vedic Sanskrit. We also know that these people were a tribal-based society that was organized around clan and kinship. The rest of the information we have about these people comes from the stories that have been reconstructed by scholars and historians based on the similarities of the comparative mythologies of the various later cultures that were the descendants of these original Proto-Indo-European people. [4,5]

It is generally agreed that these early settlers' common political arrangement was hierarchical in structure, with some form of social ranking based on social status. It is thought that it was unlikely that they had a rigidly stratified social structure broken into castes, as we see later in India. At this early time there appears to a general distinction made between free persons of the tribe and slaves, who were typically prisoners of war, but debtors who were unable to repay their debts also filled their ranks. The 'free' people of the tribe were composed of an exclusive elite class of kings, priests, warriors, and commoners who were members of various clans that composed the tribe. Each tribe followed a Chief who oversaw the religious ceremonies and day-to-day activities of the tribe. It was common for several smaller tribes to band together, forming a much larger tribe, whereby the Chiefs of each of these smaller tribes would then choose a 'King' to rule over them with the elders of the various tribes then acting as advisers to this King. [6,7,8]

Although this individual would be called "King" by the various clans and tribes that made him king, he tended to be little more than a local warlord that only had power over the tribes that had appointed him as king. It was common for this individual to be the oldest male leader of the most powerful family of the largest clan from the largest tribe. However, unlike the typical ancient warlord, these tribal kings were expected to sponsor the great feasts and be the religious leader who oversaw the High-priest and the priesthood as they performed the sacred religious ceremonies and sacrificial rites that established favorable relations with the divine realm of the gods. In these early Proto-Indo-European tribal societies, it appears that religion and government were always directly connected through this King and the Head-priest. A relationship that appears similar to the one we encountered with Moses and Aaron of the Bible. [9,10,11,12]

Within this early society, the religion was centered around the ritual sacrifice of cattle and horses. The animals were slaughtered during the religious ceremonies and dedicated to the gods in the hope of winning their favor. Scholars believe this ritual sacrifice of cattle, in particular, the heifer, was at the center of their beliefs. It was a symbolic representation of the primordial condition of the world order. Scholars base this idea on the great number of ancient creation myths from the area that have the common story of a great warrior or king, normally the son of a god or goddess, that involves the liberation of cattle and wealth that had been stolen by a monster, commonly a three-headed creature named "*Ngwhi.*" Once the cattle had been saved, they are turned over to the High-priest of the temple to be properly sacrificed as the gods had intended. [13,14,15,16]

With our esoteric knowledge that "cattle" normally symbolize the First-Men who had fallen from grace. We can realize that the scholarly interpretation could be incorrect. Because these 'cattle' that were being sacrificed by these Proto-Indo-European people could have been the First-Men or Neanderthal. This appears to add weight to the idea we touched upon in our journey through the Dream Vision of Enoch that there may have been an active program under the command of the gods for Cro-Magnon man to remove Neanderthal from the population by this point in time.

The next important aspect of this ancient religion was the ritual sacrifice of horses. These rituals did involve the actual mass sacrifice of horses. This tradition appears to have been for the renewal of kingship that involved the ritual mating of a queen or king with a heavenly horse, which was then sacrificed and cut-up for distribution to the ritual participants. Within the earliest mythologies, this mating of a queen or king with this heavenly horse produced the divine twin brothers of legend. [17,18]

This close association of the twin brothers and horses is found throughout the mythology of the Proto-Indo-Europeans and their later Indo-European descendants. This ancient connection between the twin brothers and horses is an incredibly important clue to one of the greatest mysteries of ancient mythology and why horses are always connected to the mighty Lord of the waters. In every single ancient culture that contains horses within their mythology, they are always associated with the Lord of the waters in some manner, with the Greek god Poseidon and the Roman's Neptune being two of the best known. The question has always been, why are horses always associated with or directly connected to the Lord of the waters throughout so many cultures and mythologies? Now, with our knowledge of the esoteric symbolism of the Dream Vision and this final clue, we can provide an answer to this age-old mystery. [19,20]

As we have learned from our journey, the Lord of the waters also commonly known as the King of the gods, and the Lord-God of the Bible are the same god. This remote connection then allows us to realize that once these Proto-Indo-European speaking children of Israel had reached the Land of Canaan and first began settling it. The twin brothers must have been presented with domesticated horses by the Lord of the waters. With our knowledge of the second phase of the Exodus, we can understand that this must have been done for no other reason than to aid them in their long journey guiding each tribe to their inherited lands across the globe.

This knowledge then allows us to understand and explain how and why horses became associated with the Lord of the waters and the divine twin brothers. It is also highly probable that this is the point in time when the large-scale domestication of horses by humans began. It would also explain how horses became so widespread across the ancient world and why they were originally only available to royalty or wealthy elites. This was simply because they were given only to the ruling class by the gods through the twin brothers and not the commoners. This also explains why throughout history owning a

108

horse has tended to be viewed as a status symbol of wealth and power. It is easy to imagine the fear and awe people must have felt when these children of Israel under the leadership of the twin brothers arrived in their lands with all the elites of the tribes sitting atop horses. As these children of Israel begin settling the area and removing the local ruling class, it would have only reinforced the idea of the power and status of anyone who was in command of such an animal.

Another interesting aspect of the twin brothers was their close association with the goddess of the dawn or *"Dawn Goddess,"* known as *"Hausos"* to the Proto-Indo-Europeans. In almost all the ancient traditions we know of, the twin brothers are the younger brothers of this Dawn Goddess, with the great Sky-Father, Dyeus-Phater, as their father. Surprisingly, the Earth Mother is not their mother, as many may have suspected. Instead, their mother tends to be some divine horse that normally takes the form of a great white horse with incredible magical power and wisdom that comes directly from the waters or out of the foam of the sea. In these stories, the twin brothers are normally represented as young men sitting upon their mighty steeds, pulling the sun across the sky. Because of our unique understanding of the esoteric symbolism, we can easily understand that this is another connection that symbolizes the twin brothers' divine connection to horses. It also shows their direct connection to the Sky-gods and the Sky-Father or Heaven itself, which ultimately gave them their claim to leadership. [21,22]

In addition to being the sister of the twin brothers, the Dawn Goddess was also known as the *"daughter of heaven,"* or *"Sky-Daughter."* With her being depicted as opening the gates of Heaven when she appears at the beginning of the day. She was believed to be never-aging with her being reborn anew each morning. She goes on to be remembered as Eos in Greek mythology and as Aurora in Roman. Within the mythology, she appears to be an early version of the Messenger god. In later mythology she is seen as a reluctant goddess of the dawn. In many stories, she is beaten for tarrying or lingering in her divine duties. This seems to present the idea that she was replaced with a male Messenger god after somehow failing in her duties. Although she was a popular goddess throughout the ancient world, she quickly becomes a minor goddess. [23,24,25,26,27]

The single most important god of these earliest settlers was *"Dyeus-Pater,"* whose name literally means *"Sky-Father."* He is the best known and well-attested of all the ancient Proto-Indo-European and later Indo-European deities. His dwelling place was the skies, high above the clouds. He was also the Supreme god and the gateway to the other gods. As we know, this Sky-Father, who was above all other gods, was the mighty Heaven in low Earth orbit, appearing as a great all-seeing-eye looking down upon humanity. [28,29,30]

The next important god for these ancient people was the Lord of the waters, "*Neptonos.*" As we already know, this god becomes the King of the gods and is also known as the God of the Bible. Additionally, now that we understand his connection to the twin brothers and the horse, it is slightly easier to understand why he was viewed as the King of the gods. This King of the gods also becomes closely associated with the Messenger god, who was always associated with fire and sacrifice to the gods. As we have already seen, these two gods, along with the Sky-Father, become the basis of the Trinity of three gods.

This allows us to easily understand that within this basic arrangement with the Sky-father being the mighty Heaven that is far above the clouds and was always looking down upon all of creation became the unknowable Supreme god. The Lord of the waters was the 'Son' of the Supreme god that came to interact with humanity in a more understandable form. With the Messenger god being the one that moved between the 'Son' on Earth and the 'Father' in the sky. Hence, we can easily see that from the earliest times of the Proto-Indo-Europeans the beginnings of the Trinity as we still know it today and why the number three held such importance for our ancient ancestors.

The last important god or goddess we will explore at the moment is the Earth Mother, also commonly known as the Mother Earth or the Mother Goddess. To the Proto-Indo-Europeans, this goddess was known as *"dhéǵhōm,"* which is believed to be the root Indo-European word for "Earth." She was the Earth herself conceived as a divine entity, rather than a goddess of the Earth. At this early time, the Earth Mother was portrayed as the vast and often dark house of mortals on Earth, while in sharp contrast with the Sky-father Dyeus-Pater, which was the bright sky and seat of the immortal gods. She was likely the consort or wife of the Sky-father. She is commonly associated with fertility and growth, but she is also deeply connected with death, with her dark soil being the final dwelling place of the deceased. Thus, the Earth Mother is portrayed as the giver of all good things and viewed as a prophetess that shall offer good harvests to the community. In the earliest mythologies, not only was the soil of the Earth Mother the final resting place for the dead, but she was also usually the supreme ruler of the Underworld. At some unknown point, she loses her position as ruler of the Underworld to a male Lord of the dead. [31,32]

Unfortunately, the mythologies do not explain the reason for this change, nor have scholars offered any real explanation for this change. However, we are now aware of a great 'political' change in the Underworld that occurred during the second phase of the Exodus with the twin brothers. Although there are few details, we can speculate that this political upheaval of the Underworld may have resulted in this Earth Mother being removed from power as the supreme ruler of the Underworld and of Earth with her taking a place beside the Supreme god as his wife or consort. We will examine this political change in greater depth at a slightly later point.

The next important historical information that we have about these people comes centuries later from the Assyrian Empire, which were the only other Bronze Age people outside of the Egyptians who were able to resist these Indo-European speaking children of Israel as they moved around the world in their great Exodus. It appears that the primary reason the Assyrians were able to resist the tribes was simply because the Assyrians were more brutal than the Israelites. We have ample evidence and numerous stone reliefs that commemorate the Assyrian Kings' great deeds that repeat, monotonously, the gruesome tale of sacking, enslavement, impalement, torture, and the final solution of mass deportation and enslavement of conquered peoples. The entire Assyrian Empire was built on a brutal foundation of conquest and sheer intimidation of other people. They also created the best army the world had seen until that time. This army was fed by conscription of all males and armed with iron weapons and siege artillery that could breach city walls that were impregnable until this time. This army also included some mailed and armored cavalry with an effective command that coordinated this force of arms across the battlefield. It is believed that the Assyrians had a religious fervor behind their conquests, with their god Assur commonly being shown hovering over their armies as they went to battle against the unbelievers. [33]

We also have additional information from Herodotus' "*Histories*" about the tribes that lived in the valleys of the Zagros Mountains and across the Iranian plateau at this time. However, it should be noted that both the Assyrian and Herodotus sources are viewed as highly biased, with much of the information being little more than propaganda designed to demonize these people. Although these sources are very biased against these people and the later Persians. Scholars and historians, with the help of surrounding cultures, have reconstructed some of the history of these somewhat mysterious people with some confidence.

According to the Assyrians, the people who lived in these lands were known as the Medes, who spoke the Median language. As with the Proto-Indo-Europeans, we do not know what this Median language was, for no writing has survived, except for a few names. The Assyrians' earliest records present these Medes as little more than a small vassal state to the Assyrian Empire that was made up of various small tribes scattered across the Iranian Plataea and the valleys of the Zagros Mountains. However, although they were thought of as a vassal state, the Assyrians never directly ruled these people, but they did pay tribute to the Assyrians. The Assyrian records also commonly report that they had to send troops to the border areas with these Median tribes to primarily protect the important East-West trade route that ran through northern Iran. A trade route that would one day become known as the "*Silk Road.*" In time, the Assyrian Kings imposed "*Vassal Treaties*" upon the tribes of the Medes in return to protect them from the many predatory raids of the marauding Scythians and Cimmerians. [34,35,36,37]

For some unknown reason, but possibly due to political actions of the more powerful societies of Elam, Mannaea, Urartu, and the Assyrians, the six largest tribes of Medes came together under one banner and king. Herodotus called this first king, "*Deioces,*" known to the Median people as "*a just and incorruptible man.*" According to Herodotus in chapters 95 to 130 in book 1 of his Histories, this King Deioces acted much like a "*Judge*" as recorded in the Bible. Herodotus recounts that as a young man, he was asked by the leaders and elders of the six largest Median tribes to solve their disputes, which he agreed too, but only upon the condition that they make him "King" of the Median tribes, which they quickly agreed to. [38]

Although King Deioces united the six primary tribes of the Medes into one independent kingdom and fought many battles against the Assyrians, the Medes were still in many ways little more than vassal state to the Assyrian Empire, with King Deioces still sending yearly tribute to the capital city of Nineveh. However, unlike before, the tribute that King Deioces sent to Assyria was not for protection from the marauding Scythians and Cimmerians but it was now to keep the Assyrians out of Median lands. Even under the watchful and often brutal eye of the Assyrians, King Deioces was able to expand the newly formed Median kingdom's borders at the expense of the Assyrians. Much of this expansion was primarily in the lands to the south and east far from Assyria's direct influence. Soon after he formed the tribes into a unified Median state, King Deioces began constructing his capital city at Ecbatana, which means "*the place of gathering.*" It is situated at the foot of Mount Alvand in north-western Iran. Scholars believe that the ruins found in and around the modern-day Iranian city of Hamadan are the remains of this ancient capital of Ecbatana. [39,40,41]

According to Herodotus, King Deioces ruled for fifty-three years, and upon his death, his eldest son, Phraortes, assumed the throne. Next to nothing is known about Phraortes the man or his rule. We do know that he, like his father, started wars against the Assyrians and expanded the borders of the Median kingdom by subjugating the Persian tribes to the south along with the tribes of the Parthians. We also know that he had to deal with several internal quarrels and was not well-liked by his subjects. After twenty-two years of rule, he was defeated and killed on the battlefield by King Ashurbanipal of the Assyrian Empire. Upon his death, the Median tribes were invaded by the Scythians, who controlled the area for twenty years. [42,43,44]

During this time when the Scythians controlled the area, a man Herodotus called "*Cyaxares*" or "*Good Ruler*" who longed for revenge against the Scythians came to power. He somehow managed to organize a force that killed the leaders of the Scythians, thereby forcing them from Median lands. After expelling the Scythians, Cyaxares proclaimed himself "*King of the Medes.*" After defeating the Scythians, he began preparing for war against the Assyrian Empire. In the process, King Cyaxares reorganized his army, becoming the first military commander in history to divide his troops into separate specialized sections of spearmen, archers, stone-throwers, bowmen, and heavy cavalry with armored horses, that were supported by highly trained infantry that were armed with advanced bronze and iron weapons. He was also the first military commander to break each of these specialized sections into individual units with their own command structure, thus greatly reducing the chances that the entire section would break apart if its commander died in battle. By anybody's standards, King Cyaxares was a great military mind that still influences how we organize our armies and fight wars to this very day. [45,46]

After reorganizing his army, he allied with King Nabopolassar of Babylon, a mutual enemy of Assyria. This alliance was formalized through the marriage of King Cyaxares' daughter, Amytis, to the son of King Nabopolassar, Nebuchadnezzar II. Nebuchadnezzar II is famous for building the Hanging Gardens of Babylon, so his beloved wife, Amytis, would not feel so homesick for her homeland's mountains and forests. [47,48]

Soon after forming this alliance, according to Herodotus, King Cyaxares united most of the remaining small Median tribes into a fully unified state. The few tribes that resisted, as with neighboring territories, he conquered, thereby transforming the Median Kingdom into the Median Empire, becoming a regional and world power. He even formed a new alliance with the Scythians even though they had battled each other just ten years earlier. At this point, King Cyaxares, with the aid of the forces of King Nabopolassar, and the Scythians, he was able to conquer the Assyrians at Assur, and soon after, he sacked and destroyed the capital city of the Assyrian Empire, Nineveh. Although there is no doubt about King Cyaxares' military might, much of this victory was because the Assyrian Empire was already in a state of collapse, with much of their mighty Empire crumbling with many parts of it in a general state of revolt when King Cyaxares' army fell upon them. [49,50,51]

After King Cyaxares had conquered the Assyrians, he, like so many other rulers, began undertaking large building projects and constructing roads to unite the various people of his newly formed Median Empire. All known accounts present King Cyaxares not only as a great military leader, but he was also thought of as a good King and an excellent Statesmen that was beloved by his people. Even the people he conquered appear to have the utmost respect for the man, with no known reports of them ever trying to revolt while under his rule. [52]

A large part of King Cyaxares' power came from the priesthood of the Median people, known as the *"Magi,"* that he strongly supported by giving them special rights and protections. He also provided them with a workforce to build *"Tepe Nush-e Jan,"* a site which was located approximately 50 km (31 miles) to the south of the Median capital of Ecbatana, located by the modern-day city of Hamadan in north-western Iran, upon a small hill that overlooks the surrounding area. This was the primary site of the Magi leadership, as with the biblical tribe of Levi, all the priests came from one Median tribe known as the tribe of Magi, that provided all the priests for the Medes and the later Persians. They made up the *"priestly caste,"* which passed their religious functions from father to son. These Magi played a significant role in the Median court, where they were *"advisers, dream interpreters, soothsayers, and prophets"* to the King and his court. [53]

According to Herodotus, after a very successful reign of fifty-three years, King Cyaxares was succeeded by son *"Astyages."* As with his grandfather, almost nothing is known about King Astyages' reign or the man himself. The ancient sources we have are obviously biased, with Herodotus painting the man as a cruel despotic ruler, while Ctesias' account presents him as a caring king beloved by his people. Other accounts fall somewhere between these two extremes, making it impossible to make any type of judgment about him or his reign. We do know that soon after assuming the throne, King Astyages began losing control of the lands his father, grandfather, and great-grandfather had conquered. By the end of his thirty-two-year reign, the mighty Median Empire was but a former shadow of itself, only ruling over the traditional lands of the original six Median tribes that were first united under King Deioces. Based on this information alone, it appears that King Astyages may have been closer to the cruel and despotic ruler Herodotus presents in his Histories. [54,55]

We also know that when King Astyages assumed the throne, he inherited a large and mighty empire that he ruled with an alliance with his two brothers-in-law, King Croesus of the Kingdom of Lydia, and King Nebuchadnezzar II of Babylon. As with his father, these alliances were based upon marriage, with King Astyages marrying Aryenis, the sister of King Croesus. The Babylonian alliance was due to Nebuchadnezzar's marriage to Astyages' sister, Amytis. Nevertheless, this alliance appears to have been very weak and was quickly broken soon after King Astyages took the throne. The breaking of this alliance seems to support the idea that Astyages may have been despotic in his rule. [56]

Classical historians typically accept the account given in the "*Cyropaedia*" of Xenophon. Although Xenophon's account of King Astyages is no more reliable than any other ancient sources we have. With that said, Xenophon does appear to give us some information about the end of King Astyages' rule, and strangely, as we will explore in the next chapter, Xenophon also presents Cyrus the Great as the grandson of King Astyages. Which according to Xenophon, results in the founding of the mighty Achaemenid Empire by Cyrus. Although we do not know the circumstances surrounding King Astyages' death, Xenophon claims that after thirty-two years of relative stability, King Astyages' lost his nobles' support during a war against his grandson Cyrus where he was captured by Cyrus. All the other accounts we have differ with Xenophon; in some, the captured King Astyages was treated with clemency; in others, he was imprisoned, while in others he was murdered. [57,58]

Although there much we do not know about King Astyages, there is one point that all the ancient accounts do agree upon and that King Astyages had embraced and was a devout follower of a religion that was very similar to the religion of Zoroastrianism, but with a slightly different doctrine. It has also been proposed that his father, King Cyaxares, may have followed a similar religion derived from Zoroaster's teachings. This is because it is highly probable that King Cyaxares is the man responsible for constructing the mysterious temple site known as "*Takht-e-Soleyman*," which means the "*Throne of Solomon.*" This mysterious site is located approximately 240 km (150 miles) northwest of the city Hamadan, near the present-day town of Takab, Iran. The site sits in a broad valley with a rectangular platform like-structure about 60 meters (197 ft) above the surrounding plain at its center. The site itself measures approximately 350 meters (1,150 ft) by 550 meters (1,800 ft). Remarkably, these dimensions are very similar to the ones given in the Bible for the outer-courtyard of King Solomon's Temple and Citadel, which are given as being approximately 244 meters (800 ft) by 488 meters (1,600 ft). [59,60,61,62]

At one time, a large building stood upon this site, but today, located were the original platform that this building stood upon, there is now a small lake fed by springs hidden beneath the surface. The water is saturated with minerals and heavy metals, making the water undrinkable and so toxic that it cannot support life. An ancient volcano, known as "*Zendan-e-Soleyman*," which means "*The Prison of Solomon*," located about 3 kilometers (1.8 miles) to the west, is believed to be feeding the site's springs. According to local folklore, King Solomon used the volcano to imprison monsters and demons inside its 100-meter (328 ft) deep crater, which is believed to have been filled with water at that ancient time. Given the stunning natural landscape, the entire area must have been perceived as a mystical site by the ancients. [63,64]

Map of the location of Takht-e-Soleyman.

What is truly remarkable about this mysterious site is that everything about this entire place is either named after or related to Bible's King Solomon and the First Temple he built in some fashion. There have been numerous temples and shrines discovered in the area, which are all claimed to be related to King Solomon or his Temple in some manner. Many of them date back thousands upon thousands of years. Modern archaeologists and scholars have no explanation for why this entire site is named after or related to King Solomon or his Temple. However, as we have been learning, the answer to this mystery was simply because this was part of the ancient Land of Canaan. This knowledge

116

allows us to begin understanding that this site could be the original location of King Solomon's Temple. For us to do this, we must first take a few moments and explore not only the strange site of Takht-e-Soleyman, but we must also take a closer look at the priesthood of the Magi and their Zoroastrian faith. [65]

Classical historians have *"unanimously"* regarded the Magi as the priests of only the Zoroastrian faith. They believe the site of Takht-e-Soleyman was originally built by and for the Zoroastrian priesthood during the reign of King Cyaxares, with the final construction of the site being completed under his son, King Astyages. Nevertheless, as we have already learned, the original Proto-Indo-Europeans that settled the area and the later Indo-European people practiced a polytheistic religion based around sacrifice to the gods. This understanding of the original religion of these people allows us to begin realizing that the faith of Zoroastrianism was not and could not have been the Magi's original belief system. This would also mean that the Magi must have adopted the religion of Zoroastrianism during the reign of King Cyaxares or King Astyages. However, before we can understand how and why this might have happened, we must first look at the man remembered as Zoroaster and the religion he founded. This will also allow us to learn how this non-traditional religion of Zoroastrianism might be why King Astyages lost his nobles' support and why the Median Empire began to crumble under his rule. [66,67]

Zoroaster, also known as Zarathustra, was an ancient spiritual leader who founded the religion known as Zoroastrianism. We know very little about the man Zoroaster nor we do know when he may have lived. Scholars have placed his life anywhere from seventeen-hundred BC to the sixth century BC. We also do not know where he was born, but it is believed that it was somewhere in the far eastern parts of the Iranian plateau. Nevertheless, Zoroaster is recorded as being the son of a man known as Pourusaspa of the Spitamaids or Spitamans clan, of the Dugdow tribe, with it being said that his great-grandfather was a chief called Haecataspa. However, it is unknown if any of this information is true. It is also said that he had had four brothers, two younger and two older, but all this information and their names come from a much later Pahlavi work of the Sasanian Empire, written centuries later. [68,69,70]

According to Zoroastrian tradition, Zoroaster began training for the priesthood around age seven. According to the *"Gathas,"* which are seventeen *"Avestan"* hymns believed to have been composed by Zoroaster himself, he became a full priest around the age of fifteen or sixteen. He claimed that he had gained secret knowledge from other mystical and religious teachers when he left the household of his parents at age twenty and began traveling around the Median lands visiting each of the tribes. This traditional belief that Zoroaster was trained as a priest of the Magi, while also becoming a priest at such a young age is quite mysterious. Because as we have already learned, the tribe of Magi provided all the priests for the Medians and the later Persians, and there is no known historical or archaeological evidence that supports the idea that Zoroaster was part of this tribe of Magi. This alone would have made Zoroaster a religious outsider who would have been viewed as a false priest or heretical teacher by the Magi priesthood. This is our first clue that allows us to begin understanding for the first time that the claim that Zoroaster was trained as a priest is most likely false, with it being used to provide a legitimate claim or connection to the Magi priesthood. [71,72]

Around age thirty, Zoroaster claimed he experienced a vision and a grand revelation during a spring festival. It was this grand vision that would become a template for all other claimed visions and revelations of later religious teachers and cult leaders, including those of today. Zoroaster claimed that while standing on the bank of a river, he saw a great shining Being, who revealed himself as "*Vohu-Manah*" or the "*Good Purpose*" and revealed the knowledge of "*Ahura-Mazda*," the "*Wise Lord*," and Supreme god of the world and all of creation, along with five other radiant figures of light. He also learned of the Destructive Spirit known as "*Angra-Mainyu*," the terrible enemy of Ahura-Mazda, and the great order of creation. [73,74]

From this vision and further revelations from Vohu-Manah, Zoroaster developed a new and highly complex theology, where he openly rejected the polytheistic belief of many gods. He then broke the great gods into two primary groups with one being known as the "*Asha*," which represented order and righteous behavior, with the other being the "*Drui*," which represented deception of the evil ones. Over many centuries, these two categories of divine beings became known and remembered as Angels and Demons in the biblical tradition. [75]

He also began teaching about an individual judgment of the individual person based upon their actions in this life. He developed the basic ideas that would later become the concepts of Heaven and Hell, the resurrection of the physical body, the Last Judgment, and of everlasting life for the reunited soul and body, all of which depended on the behavior of the individual in this life. He essentially created the first human-centered religious belief that was not focused on the whims of the gods, but on man's own free will and choices. All his teachings are believed to be contained within the Garths and Avesta writings. Zoroaster also openly rejected and publicly condemned the mass sacrifice of animals to the gods as a cruel and brutal practice. He also openly opposed the use of mind-altering drugs that the Magi priesthood used during rituals. His complex theology and religious teachings borrowed heavily upon the early Abrahamic religion. It was often claimed that Zoroaster was trying to return the people to the original religion and worship of the one true god he called Ahura-Mazda. [76,77,78,79]

As one can imagine, these new and radical teachings of Zoroaster were not well received by either the Magi or the majority of the Median people. Eventually, around the age of forty-two, Zoroaster made his most important conversion when Queen Hutaosa and her husband King Vishtaspa, of the far eastern Kingdom of Bactria, converted to Zoroastrianism. They provided him with patronage and protection that allowed Zoroaster to establish a highly faithful community of devout believers who would move across the Median lands proselytizing this new belief after his death. According to tradition, Zoroaster lived to the age of seventy-seven under the protection of Queen Hutaosa and King Vishtaspa. However, some sources claim he was murdered by a *"Karapan,"* or a *"priest of the old religion."* [80,81]

What is truly remarkable is that the religion of Zoroastrianism did not die with its founder. However, much like Christianity would later, it expanded and spread among many different people through his devout followers. There was a great appeal in its strict doctrine and code of behavior that focused on the individual and their choices, then blindly serving the gods or earthly rulers. This strict code of behavior governed how an individual dressed, ate, worked, and, most importantly of all, how to worship the one true and only god Ahura-Mazda. Although the Magi initially resisted Zoroaster's teachings and this new religion, they quickly adopted it in a remarkably short amount of time, possibly in less than one generation. By all accounts, once Zoroastrianism appeared, it quickly and completely took over the Magi priesthood of the Medes. Once it had taken over the priesthood, it quickly became the primary belief of all the Median people throughout the Empire. Soon after the reign of the last major Median King, Astyages, until the coming of Cyrus the Great, the religion of Zoroastrianism with its strict reforms and doctrine spread with remarkable speed across the western lands of the Medes and into the surrounding lands with it displacing the original religious beliefs of all the Median tribes. [82,83,84]

As you have no doubt already noticed, there are several parallels between the biblical story of the first four kings of the Kingdom of Israel and the first four kings of the Medes. Additionally, there are also parallels between the priesthood of the Magi and the priesthood of the Levi spoken of in the Bible, with our first hints that Zoroastrianism could be the corrupting factor of the original polytheistic belief system that was put into place by the events of the Exodus. In the next chapter, we will explore how the religion of Zoroastrianism ultimately ties into an entirely new understanding of the Exodus and the Kingdom of Israel in a way never imagined before. It will also answer many of the mysteries surrounding King Solomon's Temple and Citadel and a few of the lingering mysteries of the Dream Vision of Enoch.

Chapter 8

Understanding the Mystery

W e have finally reached the point where we have enough information to begin reassembling the events starting with the Exodus up to the destruction of King Solomon's Temple and Citadel. In this process, we will also begin to answer several of the greatest mysteries about the Exodus in general. Additionally, we will finally answer the few lingering mysteries related to the Dream Vision of Enoch we have not yet explored.

Our starting point are the tribes that had settled the Land of Canaan just after the divine twin brothers had embarked upon their incredible journey across the world. For countless generations, these Proto-Indo-European-speaking children of Israel lived a relatively simple tribal life with each tribe and individual living and worshiping as they saw fit. Both history and the Bible tell us that they had no central government at this early time, nor did the tribes always agree or get along with one another. If we return to the biblical account, we can see that the only thing holding these tribes together was their shared experience of the great Exodus out of Egypt and the Tabernacle that housed the holy Ark of the Covenant. This shared experience also applied to the tribes that had continued their journey under the twin brothers.

As the divine twin brothers and the tribes moved around the world, establishing new kingdoms. They and their descendants would naturally begin to send offerings and gifts back to the Tabernacle and the holy Ark of the

Covenant it housed. As can be imagined, these offerings and gifts would have been small and infrequent in the very beginning. Nevertheless, slowly over the centuries, as each of these new kingdoms became established, their offerings would have grown in value and size. Due to the limits of long-distance travel at this ancient time, these offerings must have consisted of gold, silver, gemstones, and other small objects that held great value but could easily be transported by a small group over a long distance.

As the centuries slowly went by and as these offerings slowly grew, so did the Tabernacle's wealth and, more importantly, the wealth of the priesthood of the Magi that controlled it. As the Magi's wealth grew, so did their political power. Historically and within the traditional biblical account, the priesthood was always the real power behind the political leadership of the tribes. Be it a simple tribal Chief or the Kings who commanded mighty armies, their claims to rule relied upon the priesthood's approval and backing. As we have already discovered at the beginning of our journey into the Exodus, the High-priest and the Chief usually worked very closely with one another to lead the tribes. This arrangement was based upon Moses and Aaron and how they depended upon one another to lead the earliest tribes and how each of the tribes in general were politically structured.

Over an unknown amount of time, this arrangement of the tribal Chief or King and the High-priest working closely together to lead the people broke into two separate distinct roles and classes. Why exactly this happened is unknown, but it was probably due to the needs of their society, government, and religious belief, simply growing far beyond the ability of one or two people to fulfill. There must have also been numerous quarrels, disagreements, and general economic and societal pressures that aided in the separation of powers of the King and the High-priest into different roles and classes. Additionally, the general pressure of raising and leading an army creates a situation where the King is far away from the general population and unable to fulfill his religious functions. During these situations, the High-priest would have to assume the King's religious responsibilities in his absence. These situations would have significantly helped break up the traditional roles of the warrior-king and head-priest into two separate societal classes that were heavily dependent upon one another for their power.

One of the most important functions the Magi priesthood performed was the great ritual sacrifices of animals to the gods to gain their favor. They also looked after and guarded the great "*Sacred Fire*" used to communicate with the gods during a mysterious "*fire ritual*" that was at the center of the great festivals and ceremonies. It is unknown what form this fire ritual took, but it is believed to have been performed in a manner similar too Hinduism's fire rituals and beliefs, which are focused around an altar located within a sacred *"fire temple."* It is believed that there were three Sacred Fires, commonly known as *"Great Fires,"* or *"Royal Fires,"* that figured heavily within this ancient society. Almost everything we know of these Great Fires and the ancient temples that housed them comes from the much later Zoroastrianism that took over the Magi priesthood and their temples and from even later Arab sources. According to Zoroastrianism's traditions, there were three sacred Royal Fires that came directly from Ahura-Mazda, the Supreme god of their religion. However, it is clear from both the historical record and the archaeology that the ideology, folklore, customs, and the traditions surrounding these three sacred and holy Royal Fires came from the much older religious tradition that Zoroastrianism took over. [1,2,3,4]

There are numerous stories about miracles occurring at the sites of these sacred fires. Many of the myths are of the sacred fires themselves and how they become associated with numerous legendary local folklore heroes and mythology that reaches deep into the Proto-Indo-European religious traditions and mythology. The ancient Proto-Indo-European mythology appears to agree with Zoroastrianism that there were originally three sacred Royal Fires that came directly from the gods. The earlier mythology also agrees that the priesthood maintained and protected each of these Royal Fires as they competed with one another for pilgrims and converts by promoting the miracles purported to have occurred at their respective sites. Within the ancient traditions, it is said that these three sacred fires mirrored the social and feudal-like divisions of the tribes and of society in general. With one fire being for the priesthood and their direct supporters, one was for the warrior-king class, while the last one was for the agriculturists or common people that made up the bulk of society. [5,6,7,8,9,10]

This basic outline of how ancient Proto-Indo-European society was organized is a classic example of how all the societies that were created by the coming of the divine twin brothers during the second phase of the Exodus were broken into a simple three-class system. A system that is seen in the earliest caste system of the Aryans in the Indus Valley with their fundamental class-divisions of a settled agricultural society. Within the earliest Aryan society, there was a warrior-aristocracy class known as the *"Kshatriyas,"* a priestly class known as *"Brahmans,"* and the ordinary peasant-farmers, known as *"Vaishyas."* Remarkably, unlike the Hinduism that came later, these earliest class divisions of society do not appear exclusive, and movement was possible between them. The only unleapable barrier in the earliest times seems to have been between the non-Aryan locals and their Aryan overlords. In time, a fourth class was created out of the Vaishyas that denoted India's aboriginal inhabitants as *"dasa,"* which eventually came to mean "slave." These non-Aryans also became the *"Shudras"* or 'unclean,' who were forbidden to study or hear the Vedic hymns. [11]

Although Hinduism gives us a small look at how this ancient Proto-Indo-European society was structured, it unfortunately, gives us no information about the original sacred Royal Fires that figured so heavily in the earliest mythology. Thankfully, we know the location of one of these sacred fires, a place we have already touched upon in the last chapter, the site known as Takht-e-Soeyman or the Throne of Solomon. This site was the location of the Royal Fire for the warrior-king class and the aristocracy that supported it. From the earliest Proto-Indo-European tribes until the destruction of the Temple that once sat upon this site, any King who wished to rule the surrounding lands and tribes had to go and be blessed by the Magi priesthood as he humbled himself before the sacred flame housed within the Holy of Holies deep in the Temple before he could ascend the throne and take the title of King. [12,13]

As for the original locations for the other two Royal Fires, they are unknown, although many different sites have been proposed over the years. The Magi priesthood's sacred fire is believed by many to have been located at a site known as *"Rhaga,"* which is more-or-less the modern-day capital city of Iran, Tehran. It is known that this was the site where much of the leadership of the Magi resided. It has also been suggested that the priesthood's sacred fire was far to the southeast, possibly somewhere in the eastern parts of modern-day Afghanistan. The agriculturists' sacred fire is like the priestly fire and is believed by many to have been originally located somewhere in northern Iran. In contrast, others believe it was located somewhere far to the south of the city of Rhaga on the southern part of the Iranian Plateau. Later Arab sources only add to the confusion of where two other sacred fires' actual locations may have been. It appears that at this point time, both sites have truly been lost to history. [14,15,16,17]

What makes these Royal Fires so important, is that one for the warrior-king and the aristocracy is described in great detail within the Bible and remembered as the holy Ark of the Covenant. Now, that might sound rather strange at first, but the key to understanding this connection is found in Chapter 25, verses 17-22 of the Book of Exodus, where the Lord instructs Moses in constructing the Mercy Seat that sat upon the Ark of the Covenant.

"And thou shalt make a mercy seat of pure gold: two cubits and a half shall be the length thereof, and a cubit and a half the breadth thereof. And thou shalt make two cherubims of gold, of beaten work shalt thou make them, in the two ends of the mercy seat. And make one cherub on the one end, and the

other cherub on the other end: even of the mercy seat shall ye make the cherubims on the two ends thereof. And the cherubims shall stretch forth their wings on high, covering the mercy seat with their wings, and their faces shall look one to another; toward the mercy seat shall the faces of the cherubims be. And thou shalt put the mercy seat above upon the ark; and in the ark thou shalt put the testimony that I shall give thee. And there I will meet with thee, and I will commune with thee from above the mercy seat, from between the two cherubims which are upon the ark of the testimony, of all things which I will give thee in commandment unto the children of Israel."
(Exodus, 25: 17-22. KJV)

As we can see, the last sentence is our first clue, for it tells us that God *"...will commune with thee from above the mercy seat, from between the two cherubims which are upon the ark of the testimony."* Our next clue comes from the Bible's descriptions of the Holy of Holies in the Tabernacle and that it could only be accessed through the veil that separated it from the Holy Place. Within the Book of Exodus, we are told that *"The Golden Lampstand illuminated the Holy Place."* However, we are also told that there was no artificial lighting of any kind within the Holy of Holies in the Tabernacle, nor was it permitted. Additionally, the Holy of Holies was absent of any windows, openings, or other means to allow any natural or artificial light to enter that most holy and sacred space. We are also told that the light in the Holy of Holies was furnished by the *"Shekinah"* or "Glory of God."

The word *"Shekinah"* does not appear within the Bible; it comes from later Jewish texts outside of the Bible that describe it as the *"Light of God,"* or the *"Glory of God*, with instances of it appearing beyond the Holy of Holies. Within Jewish tradition, it is this *"Shekinah"* that illuminated Moses's face in Exodus 24:29-35. It was also seen again at the Tabernacle's dedication and later at King Solomon's Temple. It was the *"Shekinah"* that caused Moses to leave the Tabernacle in Exodus 40:34, and it was the *"Shekinah"* that filled the Temple and caused the priests to move away from the Temple when the Lord came down from heaven and stood upon the Temple during its dedication in 2 Chronicles 5:13-14. In the Book of Ezekiel, Judah's tragic state and the people of Israel are illustrated by the *"Shekinah"* or *"Light of God"* departing from the Temple. [18,19,20]

As we can now understand that the Bible and Jewish tradition do speak of these sacred Royal fires, but they are commonly interpreted as the *"Shekinah"* or *"Light of God."* This is the Sacred Fire which sits upon the *"mercy seat, from between the two cherubims,"* also commonly known as the *"Glory of God"* instead of a Royal Fire. Additionally, as with Zoroastrianism, both the Bible and Jewish tradition tell us this "*Shekinah*" was how their God communicated directly with the priesthood.

Remarkably, the Biblical story also symbolically speaks of the other two Royal Fires. They are represented symbolically by two of the three objects that were placed inside the Ark of the Covenant. Which, according to Hebrews 9:4, was "*the golden pot that had manna, and Aaron's rod that budded, and the tablets of the covenant.*" Aaron's rod that budded is a symbolic representation of the agriculturists.

To understand how Aaron's rod is connected to the agriculturist class we need to examine the curious story of "*The rebellion of Korah*" and the "*two hundred and fifty princes of the assembly, famous in the congregation, men of renown*" that rose-up before Moses and Aaron that is found in the Book of Numbers 16: 1-40. This story speaks of how a man known as Korah led two-hundred-and-fifty princes of the congregation to question why Moses and Aaron had put themselves above the congregation when "*seeing all the congregation are holy, every one of them, and the LORD is among them.*" Soon after, the conspirators were punished for their rebellion when the Lord sent fire from heaven to consume all of them. Three accomplices of Korah were also punished when the Lord caused the ground to split open beneath them, swallowing them, their families, and anyone who had been associated with Korah, along with all their possessions. Furthermore, there were many Israelites who did approve of what had happened to the families of the three accomplices and objected to Moses, saying, "*Ye have killed the people of the LORD.*" The Lord then commanded Moses to depart from the congregation as He then smote 14,700 of the people of Israel.

This rebellion of Korah has always been quite the mystery, with many arguments put forward over the years of why Korah and the two-hundred-and-fifty princes had rebelled against Moses and Aaron. The secret to understanding this rebellion is found in the next chapter of the Book of Numbers. Within this chapter, the LORD commands Moses to:

"Speak unto the children of Israel, and take of every one of the them a rod according to the house of their fathers, of all their princes according to the house of their fathers twelve rods: write thou every man's name upon his rod. And thou shalt write Aaron's name upon the rod of Levi: for one rod shall be for the head of the house of their fathers. And thou shalt lay them up in the Tabernacle of the congregation be the testimony, where I will meet with you. And it shall come to pass, that the man's rod, whom I shall choose shall

blossom: and I will make to cease from me the murmurings of the children of Israel, whereby they murmur against you. And Moses spake unto the children of Israel, and every one of their princes gave him a rod apiece, for each prince one, according to their fathers' houses, twelve rod: and the rod of Aaron was among their rods. And Moses laid up the rods before the LORD in the Tabernacle of witness. And it came to pass, that on the morrow Moses went into the Tabernacle of witness; and, behold, the rod of Aaron for the house of Levi was budded, and brought forth buds, and bloomed blossoms, and yielded almonds. And Moses brought out all the rods from before the LORD unto all the children of Israel: and they looked, and took every man his rod. And the LORD said unto Moses, Bring Aaron's rod again before the testimony, to be kept for a token against the rebels; and thou shalt quite take away their murmurings from me, that they die not. And Moses did so; as the LORD commanded him, so did he. And the children of Israel spake [spoke] unto Moses, saying Behold, we die, we perish, we all perish. Whosoever cometh any thing near unto the Tabernacle of the LORD shall die: shall we be consumed with dying"?"
(Numbers 17: 2-13.)

This is a highly symbolic story of placing the High-priest of the priesthood and the Chief of the tribes above the rest of the people, who will later become the agriculturists and farmers of the lower classes of this society. The Rod that Budded, symbolizes how the farmers are dependent upon the priesthood for their livelihood and are responsible for the abundant crops that are given by their Lord. With a reminder that they will be put to death by their Lord if they question or rebel against the Chief or the High-priest. Symbolically, the golden pot of manna represents the time when the Israelites could not grow or gather their food during the Exodus, which also symbolically connects it to the agriculturists and common people of the tribes being taken care of by their Lord when they could not feed themselves. The two Tablets of the Covenant, commonly known as the Ten Commandments, symbolized the warrior-king by directly connecting them to Moses and their Lord.

Although the other two Royal Fires are symbolically remembered in the biblical story, they do not hold the same place of respect as the Royal Fire of the warrior-king class that was housed in the temple that once stood upon the site of Takht-e-Soleyman. Will we return to Ark of the Covenant shortly and explore what may have happened to this most sacred of lost holy objects once we reach the destruction of King Solomon's Temple.

In addition to maintaining the Royal Fires that allowed them to communicate with the gods, the Magi priesthood also provided for all the Proto-Indo-European people's spiritual needs, along with the later Medes and Persians. Like all other societies at the time, the Magi priesthood was at the center of all economic activity, which also added to their political and social power. This allowed the priesthood of the Magi to directly control a large portion of society with the Royal Fires being a central focal point of this control and religious belief in general. By realizing the connection to the Ark of the Covenant, which, according to the Bible, was under the control of the Levi priesthood and was also the major focus of the Israelites. We can begin understanding that all the new kingdoms that were established by the divine twin brothers during the second phase of the Exodus would have had a reason to send offerings and gifts back to the Tabernacle and the Ark of the Covenant or Royal Fire as a direct offering to their gods.

Once again, we can quickly realize that these offerings would have been small and little more than symbolic offerings or gifts in the beginning. However, slowly, over the generations, as these new kingdoms and societies grew, their offerings and gifts to the Tabernacle would grow. In time, pilgrims from all over the world would journey back to the holy Tabernacle and the Ark of the Covenant to pay their respects, perform sacrifices, and give personal offerings and to place idols of their tribal god in the Tabernacle to help win favor with all the gods. This resulted in the Tabernacle and the priesthood that controlled it gaining massive wealth and power. This wealth, after many generations, eventually grew to such a point that it became necessary for the priesthood to raise a king and an army to protect it. This allows us to realize for the first time that this is the most likely source of all the money that supported not only a kingship but also provide the funds for a large professional army.

The next step is understanding that the first four kings of the ancient Medes are the historical individuals that the first four kings of the Kingdom of Israel that are recorded in the Bible were based upon. This then allows us to understand where the great wealth came from to pay for the weapons, horses, men, supplies, and all the other items needed to maintain and field a professional army of King Solomon. It also explains the great biblical mystery of where King Solomon's legendary treasure and great wealth came from.

The following step is to realize that the first two kings of the Kingdom of Israel in the Bible appear to be in a slightly different order when compared to the first two kings of the ancient Medes. In the biblical story, the first King of Israel, Saul, was not related to David, but the first two kings of the Medes were father and son. So, why the difference? This is simply because of ancient tribal traditions and customs. If a son was an embarrassment or had brought shame to his father, he would be disowned in order to "Save Face" for honor, pride, and social standing within the tribe. This ancient custom allows us to easily understand that the biblical story is slightly different because of these largely forgotten tribal customs. Based upon this, it allows us to understand that King David of the Bible was most likely the first King of Israel, and not Saul. This also provides us with a clue that the second Median King, Phraortes, the son of King Deioces, must have been a poor king and a distasteful man. Because it appears that he was so disliked, they changed the story to remove the father-son relationship by making him the first King of Israel in the biblical account. This slight change allows King David to be presented as a savior-like figure who came to save his people in the name of his Lord from a petty king that oppressed his people. Simply put, it makes for a much more enjoyable and memorable story.

These events then bring us to the legendary wise King Solomon. As we have already learned, the legendary King Solomon of the Bible is based upon the equally legendary King Cyaxares of the Medes. This is a point where history, mythology, and the Bible come together in one place. It will also allow us to understand for the first time in modern history what the genuine corrupting factor that ultimately led to the destruction of King Solomon's Temple and Citadel really was.

To understand the events that led up to the destruction of King Solomon's Temple we must first realize that the ancient temple complex in northern Iran known as Takht-e-Soleyman claimed to have been built by King Cyaxares of the Median Empire and King Solomon's Temple and Citadel of the Bible are the same building. Not only does the site of Takht-e-Soleyman closely match the description of King Solomon's Temple given in the Bible, but it was also the location of the most sacred of the three Royal Fires, which is remembered as the Ark of the Covenant in the Bible. However, unlike the traditional interpretation of the biblical story, we know that the original Israelites or Proto-Indo-European people followed a purely polytheistic religion based around animal sacrifice with complete service and devotion to the will of the gods. What follows next is the single most crucial event that sets in motion all the other events that eventually ends in the destruction of King Solomon's Temple and then later, everything.

According to the biblical account, the primary problem was that the people of Israel and the priesthood had become corrupted. The biblical story clearly states that this corrupting factor was because the priesthood had turned away from the religion of their fathers and began *whoring after strange gods their fathers did not know.*" It is unknown when this corruption of the priesthood begins, but it comes to its first climax soon after King Solomon's death when his son, Rehoboam, takes the throne. With understanding that the fourth king of the Medes, King Astyages, and the Bible's King Rehoboam are the same man. We can for the first time in modern history, understand that the real corrupting factor of the priesthood that controlled King Solomon's Temple was the religion of Zoroastrianism. In the last chapter, we learned that King Astyages was a follower of a religion that was based upon a strict interpretation of Zoroastrian doctrines before he became King of the Medes. He also directly supported the priesthood of this new religion of Zoroastrianism. It is this support of King Astyages that allows the priesthood of Zoroastrianism to enter and take over the First Temple.

This allows us to understand that the religion of Zoroastrianism with its strict and uncompromising monotheistic belief of only one God is the religious belief that corrupted the priesthood of King Solomon's Temple and then the people of Israel as recorded in the Bible. Zoroastrianism is the belief that leads the people away from the polytheistic religion of Moses. Although, it is unknown if Zoroaster came up with this monotheistic cult by himself or if he may have had help from one of the other 'godly' factions. Nevertheless, as we continue our journey, we will see that it is more probable that Zoroaster may have created the entire belief system from scratch. Additionally, we will also see that it ultimately does not matter if Zoroaster made up the religion or if he had help from one or more of the gods. Because in the end, it is not about who created the belief that is important, but that it was the religious belief that corrupted the original polytheistic religion of the First Temple.

In order to understand how and why Zoroastrianism had such great appeal, we need to remember that by this point in time, this was a simple tribal society that had undergone an almost unbelievable change in a remarkably short amount of time. According to the biblical account and Median history, in less than a hundred years, this society went from being a simple society based around tribe, clan, and kinship that was strictly governed by tribal tradition and custom—to becoming one of the largest empires to have existed up to that time and a major world power.

In our modern world, it is easy to understand the massive upheaval this tribal-based society underwent as it quickly transformed itself into the Median Empire. We can also easily understand that the incredible political, economic, and general societal changes that occurred would have had an enormous impact on ordinary people as their traditions and tribal customs were thrown to the wayside. We can also understand that many of these changes would not have been viewed positively by the average person especially as traditional tribal law and custom began being superseded by the king, the priesthood, and a newly formed professional army.

Not only was there significant social, economic, and political change for the average person, but more importantly, we can understand that their religion, which was the basis of their entire society and existence, also underwent a radical change. In less than a generation or two, it went from being a simple polytheistic belief with only a few thousand fellow tribal members taking part in the required worship of their tribal god at the Tabernacle that held the Ark of the Covenant or Royal Fire through ritual animal sacrifice. To it being transformed into a massive affair at a large new Temple complex that may have included tens of thousands of people who were not direct tribal members. Many of these new people were the elites of conquered people, converts, and elite members and pilgrims of the other tribes from far-away lands, who now seemed to have strange and quite different beliefs of worship than their own. Due to this influx of people, the sacrifice of animals also grew from being a small, highly religious affair with great personal meaning to the people into a massive slaughter of tens of thousands, if not hundreds of thousands of animals with vast amounts of blood, gut-piles, and burning piles of fat, blood, and meat that lasted for days.

The massive need for animals for sacrifice led to the next significant development, a business to supply the needed animals for the great sacrifices. As we are told in the Bible during the Second Temple Period, hundreds of vendors were selling all manner of animals to the thousands of pilgrims that came to the Temple, especially at the time of Passover. This was a big business that was highly profitable, with it all being controlled by the priesthood of the Temple. It is easy to imagine how this business of supplying the animals, selling the animals, blessing the animals, and then sacrificing them, quickly turned into a corrupt "Temple Cult" of sorts.

It is not difficult to understand that for the average person in this society who saw their religion, their customs, and their dearly held traditions that had lasted for countless generations quickly turn into something they did not recognize, relate too, or want to be a part of. What was once a private and highly meaningful ritual of sacrifice quickly turned into a business of mass slaughter that would only add to the average person's general disgust. This allows us to understand why Zoroastrianism would have had such a great appeal to so many people. There must have been many people that felt lost with a longing for a simpler more personal tribal life. Zoroastrianism with its simple but stringent tribal-like doctrine, with its focus on the individual and of being part of a larger community of like-minded people with the return to a simple worship of only one tribal god must have seemed like a chance to return to a more traditional time and way of life.

According to the Bible, almost as soon as the First Temple was built, a disagreement quickly arose among the people and from within the priesthood. When an unknown number of the younger priests began practicing a religion in the First Temple that was not the same religion as their fathers. It is highly probable that one of the primary reasons that the First Temple was built was to counteract this new heretical monotheistic religion of Zoroastrianism. It is easy to imagine that it was hoped that this grand Temple that would house the holy Ark of the Covenant would help unite all the different kingdoms that were created under the divine twin brothers into one worldwide super-kingdom that was focused on providing sacrifice and service to the gods. Unfortunately, it had the opposite effect that would, in time, be directly responsible for breaking apart this short-lived super-kingdom into two separate and very different kingdoms.

One of the main factors behind the rise of this new monotheistic religion of Zoroastrianism appears to be that the gods had vastly underestimated the complete revulsion and disgust that the average human has when seeing thousands upon thousands of animals being brutally slaughtered, drained of their blood, gutted, with much of it being burned over many days, sometimes weeks. It is not difficult to understand how this would have naturally drawn many people to Zoroastrianism with its outright rejection of large-scale animal sacrifice. As we will learn, this also lends weight to the idea that Zoroaster developed the belief by himself and why the doctrine contains elements from different belief systems.

Historically, the turning point appears to be when King Astyages, the son of King Cyaxares, who is known to have been a devout follower and supporter of a rather strict and often violent sect of Zoroastrianism and who is the historical person that the biblical King Rehoboam, son of King Solomon, is based upon, ascends the throne. Upon assuming the throne, he uses his power to replace the traditional priesthood of the tribes, the Magi, with the priests of the strict sect of Zoroastrianism that King Astyages followed. Soon after, these corrupted Magi then try to establish this new monotheistic religion upon all the people of the Kingdom of Israel. All the tribes, except for the original six Median tribes in the Land of Canaan that King Astyages and the Magi had direct control of, rejected this new teaching. This rejection of this new heretical religion by the majority of the tribes led to the breaking up of the Kingdom of Israel into two separate kingdoms, the Kingdom of Judea in the Land of Canaan, and the Kingdom of Israel, being the rest of the kingdoms spread around the world that were established by the twin brothers.

This allows us to understand that the "*heavy yolk*" that the Bible speaks of and that King Rehoboam tried to place upon the people is referring to this new monotheistic religion of Zoroastrianism. This allows us to understand that from this point in time until the destruction of King Solomon's Temple, the Bible's Books of Kings, of Chronicles, and many of the prophets of the Old Testament are speaking of the back and forth power struggle between the traditional polytheistic religion of Moses and this new heretical monotheistic religion of Zoroastrianism. Understanding this allows us to finally place the biblical story into the proper context with also understanding the real esoteric knowledge of King Solomon's Temple and Citadel. In the process, we will also begin answering numerous mysteries surrounding the ever-mysterious Shepherds of the Dream Vision of Enoch and the gods themselves.

According to the Bible, after the Kingdom of Israel had split into two kingdoms, King Solomon's Temple, and the Ark of the Covenant it housed, was not the central focal point of this new monotheistic religion, with the building quickly falling into disrepair. This was simply because Zoroastrianism's religious teachings fiercely rejected animal sacrifice, which, according to the Bible, King Solomon's Temple was the epicenter of this ritual. Additionally, once the other kingdoms of the Kingdom of Israel broke away from this newly formed Kingdom of Judea, the offerings, gifts, and the pilgrimage of the faithful to King Solomon's Temple and the Ark of the Covenant would have ended abruptly, which would have cut off all the wealth flowing into the First Temple and, more importantly, the priesthood. This simple lack of funds is one of the primary reasons why the priesthood loses much of its influence and power with the First Temple falling into disrepair.

Although the First Temple falls into disrepair, the Books of Kings and Chronicles tell us that during this back and forth power struggle, the First Temple was repaired at least twice when Kings who followed the religion of their fathers came back into power. Remarkably, not only does the biblical account give us a detailed description of the repairs undertaken on the First Temple, but it also gives a remarkably good description of the new sites of worship that the followers of Zoroastrianism used when they were not in control of the First Temple. Surprisingly, the description of these sites of worship given in the Bible matches the archaeological evidence of known Zoroastrianism shrines and temples.

These ancient Zoroastrian sites have several unique features that show an essential connection to the biblical story of Abraham and Isaac. These sites typically sit upon a small hill, or high platform, with a small temple built around an altar, surrounded by groves of trees and bushes. This matches the description of the small hill that Abraham was commanded to sacrifice his son Isaac upon in the Book of Genesis. What may be surprising to many is that not only does the Bible give an accurate description of these Zoroastrian sites of worship, but it also makes several direct references that some of these sites were used for the ritual of "*passing through the fire*." Which was the gruesome ritual where parents would sacrifice their children to an idol by burning them alive. Although there does not appear to be any supporting evidence for this ritual of child sacrifice in Zoroastrianism or its writings. There is no denying that the evidence that the Zoroastrian sites of worship match the description of the hill that Abraham was to sacrifice Isaac upon. This seems to give weight to the biblical descriptions and claims that the followers of this new monotheistic religion practiced this ritual of human sacrifice. It also makes sense when we consider that Zoroastrianism was trying to return to some form of the original religion they believed was practiced when their ancestors first settled in the Land of Canaan and long before the Exodus out of Egypt.

It appears that the followers of Zoroastrianism believed the polytheistic religion of Moses that was being practiced was corrupt because of the massive animal sacrifice that was occurring at the First Temple. It is easy to understand that these people would have viewed themselves as the righteous ones as they tried to return an earlier purer time of worship. While at the same time, viewing the traditional followers as cruel, brutal, sinners that were insanely killing animals in drug fueled rituals. Given the doctrines of Zoroastrianism, it is not hard to imagine that some might want replace the animal sacrifice with humans, as a form of justice to pay for the never-ending slaughter of Ahura Mazda's creatures.

At present, there is currently no supporting evidence that the followers of this sect of Zoroastrianism practiced human sacrifice. Although, it does make sense when we consider that there must have been some people that still practiced this earlier form of belief. With our esoteric knowledge, we know the story of Abraham and Isaac is vital because it is a story about ending the practice of ritual human sacrifice to the gods. We also discovered through our journey through the Dream Vision of Enoch that human sacrifice appears to be one of the primary differences between the two main god-factions at the time. With one side seemly requiring it to prove loyalty to them, while the other viewed it as an abomination. Remarkably, Zoroastrianism's followers make the same claims against the followers of the traditional polytheistic religion of Moses. Although both sides make the same claim of human sacrifice against the other and the entire idea appears to be little more than propaganda. It does give us a small glimpse into the vicious back and forth power struggle between these two religious camps. A cycle that eventually leads to the destruction of King Solomon's Temple.

The destruction of the First Temple brings us to one of the two most critical points of our esoteric understanding of why we have the traditional biblical story we do. However, first, we must look at the events that led up to the destruction of the First Temple and the famous Babylonian Captivity that came from it. With our starting point being the last King of Judea that restored Moses's traditional polytheistic belief and repaired the First Temple, King Josiah.

Within the Books of 2 Kings and 2 Chronicles, we are given details of how King Josiah repairs King Solomon's Temple and, in the process, finds the Book of the Law, which was then imposed upon the people. He also abolished idolatry and reinstituted the Passover or great sacrifice. We are also told that King Josiah:

"And like unto him was there no king before him, that turned to the LORD with all his heart, and with all his soul, and with all his might, according to all the law of Moses; neither after him arose there any like him."
(2 Kings 23:25)

According to the biblical account, King Josiah was a very devout and faithful follower of the original polytheistic religious belief of the Israelites, more commonly known as the religion of Moses. Upon his death, his son, Jehoahaz, assumed his throne and quickly went to work dismantling all that his father had done to establish the old religion. At some point, King Jehoahaz comes into conflict with Egypt and is captured by Pharaoh. Pharaoh then places Jehoahaz's brother, Eliakim, upon the throne. For some unknown reason, Eliakim's name is changed to Jehoiakim. He appears to be little more than a puppet ruler for Pharaoh to ensure that tribute is paid to Egypt. However, it also appears that he tried to somehow undermine Pharaoh. The biblical account says that he taxed the land and then gave that money to Pharaoh's army commander. We are also told that Jehoiakim either became or was already a follower of Zoroastrianism, for he "*did that which was evil in the sight of the LORD.*" During this time, Nebuchadnezzar, King of Babylon, forces the Egyptians back into Egypt proper and takes control of all the lands they ruled, including the Land of Canaan and their vassal King Jehoiakim.

Although the biblical account is rather vague and does not give any real details, after three years under King Nebuchadnezzar, King Jehoiakim openly rebelled against him, which leads to the first of two invasions by King Nebuchadnezzar. This first invasion resulted in King Nebuchadnezzar looting the First Temple of its treasures and taking the elites connected to King Jehoiakim back to Babylon. He also places King Jehoiakim's son, Jehoiachin, on the throne, who was quickly replaced with his brother Zedekiah. It is during this time from King Josiah to the invasion of King Nebuchadnezzar that a very strict, extremist, and violent sect of Zoroastrianism arises in the Land of Canaan.

According to the Dream Vision of Enoch and the Bible, it is at this point that the Lord-God calls forth and sends an unknown number of messengers and prophets to His people, one of which was Enoch. The Dream Vision also tells us that all these messengers and prophets, except for Enoch, were mocked and eventually murdered by the people.

> *"And again, I saw those sheep that they again erred and went many ways, and forsook that their house, and the Lord of the sheep called some from amongst the sheep and sent them to the sheep, but the sheep began to slay them. And of the was saved and was not slain, and it sped away and cried aloud over the sheep; and they sought to slay it, but the Lord of the sheep saved it, and brought it up to me, and caused it to dwell there."*
> (Book of Enoch, 89:51,52)

> *"Moreover all the chief of the priests, and the people, transgressed very much after all the abomination of the heathen; and polluted the house of the LORD which he had hallowed in Jerusalem. And the LORD God of their fathers sent to them by his messengers, rising up betimes, and sending; because he had compassion on his people, and on his dwelling place: But the mocked the messengers of God, and despised his words, and misused his prophets, until the wrath of the LORD arose against his people, till there was no remedy. Therefore he brought upon them the king of the Chaldees, who slew their young men with the sword in the house of the sanctuary, and had no compassion upon young man or maiden, old man, or him that stooped for age: he gave the all into his hand."*
> (2 Chronicles, 36:14-17)

Unlike before, we can now understand that it was the followers of this strict, extremist, and clearly violent sect of Zoroastrianism that murdered the messengers and prophets sent by the Lord. This also allows us to realize that these followers of this strict sect of Zoroastrianism were in power at the time and controlled the First Temple. This new understanding of "who" was in control of the First Temple allows us to understand something that will be very shocking and highly radical to many. That one of the Bible's most famous prophets, Jeremiah, was a devout follower of this violent extremist sect of Zoroastrianism.

The first piece of evidence for this radical claim is found in chapter three of the Book of Jeremiah. Where the prophet openly speaks of the "*backsliding of*

Judah" during the reign of King Josiah, the last restorer of King Solomon's Temple. A man that the Bible claims in the Book of 2 Kings, had *"...turned to the LORD with all his heart, and with all his soul, and with all his might, according to all the law of Moses."* The Bible also states that King Josiah was the last King of Judah that followed the traditional religion of Moses and who had found and reinstated the Book of the Law. This claim of the *"backsliding of Judah"* by Jeremiah seems rather strange. Because why would Jeremiah complain that restoring the First Temple by King Josiah, and the finding of the Book of the Law as causing the backsliding of the people, unless he was a follower of Zoroastrianism?

The next and by far more damning piece of evidence that the prophet Jeremiah was a devout follower of Zoroastrianism is found in chapter twenty-three of the Book of Jeremiah. In this chapter, Jeremiah spends thirty-one verses attacking the *"messengers sent by the Lord"* who he calls *"false prophets and priests that walk-in wickedness."* He also calls for the people of Israel not to listen to these false prophets and to openly mock them. He also heavily implies that they should be executed for their *"false teachings."* These are the messengers spoken of in the Dream Vision of Enoch and 2 Chronicles and who were eventually murdered by the people, except for the one known as Enoch. This alone proves that Jeremiah must have been a prophet or priest of this strict, extremist, and clearly violent sect of Zoroastrianism.

Understanding that Jeremiah was a devout follower of Zoroastrianism allows us to realize that the equally famous prophet Isaiah was also a devout follower of this extremist sect of Zoroastrianism. Within the Book of Isaiah, the prophet Isaiah also attacks the one King during his lifetime that was a restorer of the old traditional religion of Moses and repaired the First Temple, King Hezekiah. This again, makes no sense, unless Isaiah, like Jeremiah, was a devout follower of Zoroastrianism.

As we know from the Dream Vision of Enoch, the messengers and prophets are murdered by the people. This slaying of the messengers of the Lord by the people of Israel, along with the rebellion of King Zedekiah against King Nebuchadnezzar, results in the second invasion of the Land of Canaan and the destruction of the First Temple. Interestingly, according to 2 Chronicles 36:12, another reason that is given for this invasion by Nebuchadnezzar was because King Zedekiah would not humble himself to the prophet Jeremiah. This implies that King Zedekiah was not a follower of Zoroastrianism but was a follower of the traditional polytheistic religion of Moses. Unfortunately, neither the Bible nor the Dream Vision provides us with enough information, but is clear that this entire situation was vastly more complex than has been traditionally believed.

According to the Bible, it is during this second invasion by King Nebuchadnezzar that King Solomon's Temple and Citadel are once again looted with the building completely destroyed with it being burned to the ground. After the destruction of the First Temple, King Nebuchadnezzar then "*broke down all the walls*" surrounding the First Temple and then "*burnt the palaces*" of the priesthood and elites. His final act was to take all the remaining elites, the priesthood, and their servants captive, returning with them to the city of Babylon, thus, beginning the great Babylonian Captivity. The critical piece of knowledge for understanding the importance of this event is realizing that the people that King Nebuchadnezzar took back to Babylon were the priesthood and the elite classes that were devout followers of this strict, extremist, and often violent sect of Zoroastrianism that had taken over the First Temple.

Once these people were taken to the cosmopolitan city of Babylon, both history and religious tradition tell us that they began trying to protect and preserve their identity as a people and as a religious community. They did this by living apart from the rest of the population in a tight-knit community that only included themselves. They essentially created the first ghettos. The next step was by far the more important, with these exiles, as they became known, began codifying their beliefs and writing them down for the first time. This was the first step in composing the Torah or Old Testament in the form we know it. It is also the point in history of when this new religion began to be referred to as Judaism with its followers being called Jews.

With our new esoteric knowledge, we can now understand that these Jews were not the followers of the traditional polytheistic religion of Moses, but they were followers of an extremist sect of Zoroastrianism that had corrupted the First Temple. We can also understand that during the Babylonian Captivity, this radical and extremist sect of Zoroastrianism was slowly transformed into the monotheistic religion known as Judaism. As radical as this idea is, the next part of this saga will help provide the next critical piece of information to understand why we have the story we do.

The next critical event that occurred was the coming of "*Cyrus II*" of Persia, more commonly known as "*Cyrus the Great*," the founder of the mighty Achaemenid Empire, the first Persian Empire. We know a great deal about Cyrus the Great and his many accomplishments, with countless history books exploring his many exploits and rule. However, although we know a great deal about Cyrus the Great and his Achaemenid Empire, there have always been two questions about his rule that seem to stand above all others and have never been truthfully answered. The first is how was Cyrus the Great able to conquer all the lands of the Medes and all the surrounding lands they once controlled at their height, so quickly and generally with little to no bloodshed? The other and by far the more famous question is why Cyrus was so generous to the Jews once he had conquered Babylon and freed them from their captivity? Outside of us lacking one small piece of information, we now have more than enough information to easily answer both questions that have plagued historians for centuries. [21]

We can quickly and easily answer the first question with our new understanding that the ancient Land of Canaan was the area known today as modern-day Iran and that the Medes are the historical people that the biblical story is based upon. The critical piece of information that we are lacking was when Cyrus came to power. As Cyrus was securing his position, one of the first things he did was to start a campaign to suppress the political power of the Magi. He stripped them of the special privileges, rights, and took their vast landholdings. More importantly, he stripped them of all their political power, making them directly dependent upon Cyrus' kingship for their authority. This suppression of the Magi is why Cyrus was able to take over the Median lands so quickly and easily. He simply began restoring the original traditional polytheistic religion while striping the Magi priesthood of their economic, social, and political power over the people. For this alone, the common people of the Median tribes loved him and supported Cyrus without question once he had freed them for the strict extremist sect of Zoroastrianism that had taken hold across the land. This simple act of suppressing the Magi priesthood and restoring the old polytheistic religion allowed him to create the largest Empire the world had seen up until this time. [22]

Our new esoteric knowledge also allows us to realize that Cyrus the Great appears to have been attempting to rebuild the original worldwide Kingdom of Israel that briefly existed under King Cyaxares, who is remembered in the Bible as the legendary and almost mythical reign of King Solomon. We can also understand that this idea of restoring the Kingdom of Israel under King Solomon may have been a central focus point of Cyrus and his drive to power. This idea would have been used to motivate the people to his cause. It also helps explain why so many different people supported Cyrus and allowed him to create the largest Empire that had existed up to that time. This knowledge also explains why Cyrus the Great claimed he was directly related to the Median Kings.

This understanding then allows us to easily answer the question of why Cyrus was so generous to the Jews once he had conquered the city of Babylon. It was merely because he was related to, or at least claimed to be related to these people, thereby meaning they were fellow tribesmen, clansmen, and possibly even kin and had to be treated as such. Tribal law, custom, and tradition would have demanded that Cyrus be respectful and generous to his fellow tribesmen, especially after their long captivity in a foreign land.

Although Cyrus the Great may have been related to these people, he was by no means a stupid man. It is plainly evident that he could not risk allowing these radical religious zealots to return to what was now the heartland of his Achaemenid Empire. These Jews, as they were now referred to as, would have simply presented too much of a religious, economic, and political threat to his rule. So, being the prudent ruler that he was, Cyrus issued a decree that allowed these religious radicals to leave Babylon. However, he did not allow them to return to the original site of the First Temple.

Although Cyrus the Great had freed the Jews, both the biblical story and the historical account state that most of these people did not wish to leave the city of Babylon. This was simply because they had created new lives for themselves that had become intertwined with Babylonian society and economic life, typically by intermarrying with the local population and adopting local beliefs. It was only a small group of the most zealot and devout followers of this new religion of Judaism that wished to leave to rebuild the Temple. Even with our new esoteric understanding, it is unclear if Cyrus the Great sent the Jews to the far western edge of his Empire or if they chose it for themselves. Nevertheless, it seems that there was already a small community of people that held very similar religious beliefs to these followers of Judaism in the land of Judea, in the area of the modern-day nations of Israel, Jordon, and parts of Syria. According to the Books of Ezra and Nehemiah, around 50,000 Jews made the initial journey to the land of Judea, located in modern-day Israel. At a later point, an unknown number of these exiles came from Babylon with the prophet Ezra himself.

These events bring us to the second critical part of understanding of how we came to have the Bible as we know it today. Within the biblical Books of Ezra, Nehemiah, Haggai, and the Dream Vision of Enoch, we are told that once these exiled Jews had settled in these new lands, primarily in the area of the modern-day nation of Israel centered on the city of Jerusalem. They ran into significant opposition from the local and surrounding people when they tried to rebuild their Temple. It has always been quite the mystery of why the local and surrounding people so strongly resisted the building of the Second Temple as it was to become known. However, with our new esoteric understanding, this great mystery just melts away. This is because we can now easily understand the reason why the local people opposed the building of the Second Temple was simply because they knew their lands were not the Land of Canaan, nor was the city of Jerusalem the original site of King Solomon's Temple and Citadel. It was not until the Jews had gained complete political power over the area and had converted a large number of the local population to their religion of Judaism that they were able to complete the building of the Second Temple.

This allows us to understand why we have the Torah or Old Testament of the Bible in the form we know today. It is simply because the followers of this new religion known as Judaism, a religion that was directly based on a radically heretical, extremist, and often violent sect of monotheistic Zoroastrianism, are not only the people that built the Second Temple in the city of Jerusalem, but they are also the people that first wrote down the Torah or Old Testament of the Bible as we know it.

This knowledge allows us to understand why the biblical stories of the great Exodus out of Egypt up to the building of the Second Temple has so many contradictions contained within them. It is because the followers of Judaism altered the stories to make it seem like the lands of the current nation of Israel was the ancient Land of Canaan and that the city of Jerusalem as the site of King Solomon's Temple and Citadel. It was all done simply to legitimatize their claims to rule. This is also why the legendary divine twin brothers and the entire second phase of the Exodus were carefully removed from the biblical story. It was simply because it would have shown that these Jews were not following the original polytheistic religion of Moses but were instead following a heretical belief that was viewed as evil in the eyes of their tribal Lord.

As we know from history, after building the Second Temple, these people established an independent Jewish kingdom that lasted until the coming of Alexander the Great and then later, the Romans. By understanding who these Jews were, we can now understand why the Greeks and the later Romans had such a poor view of these followers of Judaism who only worshiped one God. Although it appears that both the Greeks and Romans had forgotten about the First Temple or its location, they knew there was more than one God, primarily because they saw and interacted with them on a regular basis. Therefore, many people of the time thought these Jews worshipping only one God was not based on reality with most thinking these Jews were a little crazy and even possibly a danger to society.

We can now easily understand that this common viewpoint of the Jews by the Greeks, the Romans, and just about every other culture that came into contact with them at this time was because they knew from firsthand knowledge there were many gods, just because they had seen them coming to take their ritual sacrifices away at the grand religious ceremonies. So, this Jewish idea of that there was only one God, with it being the Supreme God, with all the other 'gods' being a lesser part of that one Supreme God, with the other gods also being changed into the form of an Angel or Demon, was a bit too much for the average person of the time to accept. With also understanding that this group could be very violent in defense of their radical monotheistic religious beliefs, we can finally understand why the Greeks, the Romans, and the other cultures who came into contact with these Jews viewed them as a strange people who would use violence to defend themselves against anybody who tried to tell them differently. As history tells us, these Jews were considered so strange, touchy, and generally violent that most decent people of the ancient world, including powerful governments like Rome, tried to avoid them at all costs.

Now, before we move on to the next chapter, we need to take a moment to step back and explore one of the greatest mysteries of all time, and what happened to the holy Ark of the Covenant? In the process, we will also gain a slightly better understanding of how the followers of Zoroastrianism viewed this most holy of objects.

Traditionally, most modern scholars, historians, and a surprisingly large amount of the faithful believe that the Ark of the Covenant disappeared during the first invasion of King Nebuchadnezzar and his looting of King Solomon's Temple. However, upon a closer look at the Bible combined with our new esoteric understanding of the back-and-forth power struggle over the First Temple between the priesthood of the traditional polytheistic religion of Moses and the priesthood of the new radical monotheistic Zoroastrianism. We will quickly discover that it is highly probable that the Ark of the Covenant was removed from the Holy of Holies in the Temple long before the coming of King Nebuchadnezzar.

Our starting point to understanding this mystery starts during King Josiah's reign, the last good King of Judah before the events leading up to the first invasion of King Nebuchadnezzar. We are told in the Book of 2 Chronicles that during the repairs of the First Temple, King Josiah orders the priesthood of the Levites to return the holy Ark of the Covenant to the Temple.

"And said unto the Levites that taught all Israel, which were holy unto the LORD, Put the holy ark in the house which Solomon the son of David king of Israel did build;"
(2 Chronicles 35:3)

This often-overlooked line provides us with the clue we need to understand what was happening at the time. If we consider this one small line of text and combine it with our new knowledge of the constant power struggle over the First Temple between the two priesthoods. It allows us to easily understand that the priesthood of the traditional polytheistic religion of Moses would not have wanted or have allowed the Ark of the Covenant to stay in the hands of the priesthood of the unbelieving monotheistic religion of Zoroastrianism. Additionally, we can also understand that the Zoroastrian priesthood would not have wanted it and would have taken steps to remove it from the Temple.

This idea is supported by chapter three of the Book of Jeremiah, which also adds more evidence to the idea that Jeremiah was a zealot follower of this radical, strict, and often violent sect of Zoroastrianism. In this chapter, while Jeremiah is complaining of Judah's backsliding under the reign of King Josiah, he openly speaks of how the day will come that the people of Judah and Israel will no longer care about or even think about the Ark of the Covenant.

"And it shall come to pass, when ye be multiplied and increased in the land, in those days, saith the LORD, they shall say no more, The ark of the covenant of the LORD: neither shall it come to mind: neither shall they remember it; neither shall they visit it; neither shall that be done any more. At that time they shall call Jerusalem the throne of the LORD, to Jerusalem: neither shall they walk any more after the imagination of their evil heart."
(Jeremiah 3:16,17)

These verses from Jeremiah clearly support the idea that the priesthood and the devout followers of Zoroastrianism disapproved of the Ark of the Covenant and would have taken steps to remove it from the First Temple and from the very minds of the people. This allows us to realize that the Ark of the Covenant must have been removed from the First Temple shortly after King Josiah's death, which was years before the coming of King Nebuchadnezzar and the looting of the First Temple. Although it is now straightforward to understand why the Ark of the Covenant would have been removed, it still does not answer the question of what may have happened to it once it was removed from the First Temple. The answer to this question depends on whether the Art of the Covenant was removed in secret or not.

If the Ark was removed in secret, this would significantly limit how far it could have been moved from the First Temple site, which we now know to be Takht-e-Soleyman in the northwestern part of modern-day Iran. If we look at a map of the area surrounding Takht-e-Soleyman, we will find that it is surrounded by mountains, ranging from 3 to 10 km (1.8 to 6.2 miles) from the site. Common sense tells us that if it was quietly moved, possibly at night, it must have been hidden somewhere in the valley's surrounding mountains, either in a natural or man-made cave and possibly still sitting there today.

If it was removed with public knowledge, then the truth is, it could have been moved anywhere within borders of the ancient Land of Canaan or what is today, the modern nation-state of Iran. Nevertheless, since there are no records or evidence that it was ever located at a different site or that it ever left the Land of Canaan. It would seem to lend a tremendous amount of support to the idea that if it was removed secretly or not, it is hidden somewhere in the lands of northwestern Iran. If we consider the stories of how dangerous the Art of the Covenant was, if it was mishandled, this would also place significant limits on how far it would have been moved. Which would still keep its final location somewhere within the borders of the ancient Land of Canaan.

Although understanding this does not give us an actual location of the Ark of the Covenant, it does give us a general idea of the area of where it might be, if it still actually exists. This then allows us to understand why so many nations, especially those with a strong esoteric tradition, have such a great interest in the modern-day nation of Iran. It is because, to the followers of the esoteric and even the faithful of both Judaism and Christianity, the very idea that the Art of the Covenant, the holiest of all holy objects, could be in an Islamic country is by itself an unthinkable abomination. Combined with the possibility that these unbelievers could find it, sends shockwaves of terror through them all. Because as we all know, the Bible tells us that an army that walks with the Ark before it is invincible.

Chapter 9

The Mystery of the Gods

As we discovered in our journey through the Dream Vision of Enoch, the 'gods' of our ancestors were not divine, nor are they extraterrestrial aliens from some unknown planet orbiting some distant star, as they and their supporters would like everybody to believe. However, as we learned, it is highly probable that they are the last intelligent species to have evolved and develop on Earth long before ourselves. We also learned that both of our species have a common ancestor, which is why our two species are so similar. We also learned that they began moving out into the solar system and were settling on the Moon, Mars, and an unknown number of other bodies orbiting the sun, when they destroyed their civilization on Earth approximately twelve million years ago. The lucky ones on Mars managed to not only survive but in time, they became a highly technologically advanced people that created an entirely new and unique civilization after their civilization was wiped out back on Earth.

We also discovered that this unique civilization that had developed on Mars over millions of years were the ones that eventually returned to Earth hundreds of thousands of years ago, primarily to exploit it for resources as their traditional sources of raw material began to run low. This return to Earth and the resource extraction by these people gave rise to a significant number of creation stories. Additionally, and possibly more important, we also discovered that these 'gods' that our ancient ancestors worshiped were the technologically advanced craft that flew and interacted with humankind, and not the individuals inside, flying these craft. The primary gods were composed of the few advanced flying ships that came and talked or interacted with individual humans in some manner. Nevertheless, even with this knowledge, there are still a few missing pieces to the puzzle, and the story is far from complete. Now, with our new esoteric understanding of the events surrounding the great Exodus and the many kingdoms established by the divine twin brothers, we will finally be able to fill in many of the missing pieces of the overall story and place these events into their proper order and context.

To properly begin this part of our journey, we must first change how we refer to these 'gods.' In "Unlocking the Dream Vision: The secret history of creation" the 'gods' were broken into two primary factions or camps, the "Lord-of-Light faction," and the "Lord-God faction." Although this simple break-down worked well for explaining the overall events that unfolded as presented in the Dream Vision of Enoch, it falls short for this part of our journey. So, we will need to be more accurate in describing these so-called 'gods.' To accomplish this, we will now refer to the ancient gods in general as the "*Terrans*." For those who may be unaware, the word "*terra*" is an ancient Old English word for Earth. It seems like a fitting word when it is put into the context of our esoteric knowledge of the ancient world with "*Terrans*," roughly meaning "*Ancient Earthling*."

The second change is that we need to realize that the "Lord-of-Light faction" virtually disappears after the Great Deluge and reconquest of Earth, with it only applying to the time of the Fallen Watchers. Once, overthrown, the great "Lord-of-Light" was replaced with a new 'god.' Within Greek mythology, the Lord-of-Light faction is remembered as "Ouranos" or "Uranus," who was overthrown and replaced with the Titan Cronos. In time, Cronos is overthrown and replaced by Zeus. We also need to understand that these 'changes' are actually representing 'political changes' occurring with these Terrans over control of the mighty Heaven.

As we discovered, the mighty Heaven was a massive space-station that was the Terrans primary manufacturing and resource hub in low Earth orbit that appeared like a great 'all-seeing-eye' that looked down upon all of humanity. It is easy to understand that this massive space-station would have had countless lights on it for various reasons; that helped create the illusion of it looking like a great eye to our ancient ancestors looking up from the surface of the Earth. It is also easy to understand that the Terrans may have changed some aspect of these lights to represent the political change, much as we do to show a change in government or ownership. The simplest change would have been just been a change in the color of the lights to represent this political change. Which, to our ancient ancestors witnessing this change, it must have seemed like it had completely changed into a new and different god.

We also need to remember that one of the primary reasons for the first political upheaval that resulted in the Fall of the Watchers was due to some form of strict population control this civilization practiced. As we learned from our journey through the Dream Vision of Enoch, these population controls were necessary simply because they had great difficulty feeding their people due to the natural limits of the low gravity on a fully habitable Mars. This limiting factor of the Terrans not being able to provide enough food and resources for their people seems to be the primary reason for most of their actions and behavior. As we will now begin learning, this is also the critical piece of information that has been missing.

For us to begin to piece all of this together within the proper context, we must return to that ancient point in time that occurred just after the Great Deluge, when the reconquest of the Earth was completed by what appears to be the Terran government. In both the Book of Enoch and within the biblical tradition, the Lord-God faction or Terran government, took steps to ensure that the Fall of the Watchers would never happen again, especially the interbreeding with humanity. What little information we have, speaks of how the Terrans viewed the actions of the Fallen Watchers as an abomination and a terrible crime against creation itself. Because of this crime against man and nature, the Fallen Watchers were physically changed, with most, if not all of them being physically altered in some manner so they could never mate with humans again. Not only were the Fallen Watchers punished, we learned that there were other significant changes made to their society to help make sure such crimes would not reoccur.

Although we do not know the exact details, our esoteric knowledge allows us to speculate with some confidence that one of the major changes must have been how they controlled their population growth by allowing more marriages and children. With the reintroduction of the Heaven and the resources provided from Earth after the reconquest, and regardless of the economic system they used, it would have produced a massive economic boom and a time of plenty for their society. It may have been viewed as a clear indication that it was time for them to change their ways. As expected, these changes slowly led to an increase in their population. At first, it would have been easily and efficiently dealt with, especially with the resources provided by the Heaven. But as the centuries passed and their numbers slowly increased, the same age-old problem would begin to return.

The economic and political system installed on Earth right after the Great Deluge appears to have been a simple straightforward political arrangement

147

supported by an equally simple religious system to control our Neanderthal ancestors. Based on what little information we have, this system seems to have been made up of a simple three-part belief that consisted of the great Sky-father up high above the clouds, the great Earth Mother here on Earth, both of which were centered around the symbolism of the Bull. Our esoteric knowledge of the symbolism allows us to place this simple arrangement within its proper context, as we take our first steps to strip away much of the confusion.

We can easily understand that this basic arrangement consists of our ancient Neanderthal ancestors that are represented symbolically by the Bull, bringing offerings and sacrifices to the great Earth Mother. Afterward, Earth Mother would then send these sacrifices up to the great Sky-father up above the clouds with the help of the Dawn goddess. Although there is little evidence, it is highly probable that the Earth Mother would bestow gifts and needed items or services to our Neanderthal ancestors in return for their offerings. This seems to be supported by the significant number of Mother Goddess artifacts that date from this time. These artifacts are generally small figurines or statues of a faceless female with extremely large breasts and belly. These artifacts are believed to portray a pregnant Mother Goddess related to fertility, with the idea that she was the giver of life. Based on the scant evidence, it appears that this Earth Mother figure or Mother Goddess was by far more important to our ancient ancestors at this time than the distant Sky-father high up in the sky.

This then allows us to take the next step to begin stripping away the mythology to understand that after the Great Deluge, the Terran government had reestablished their control over the group of Terrans on Earth that controlled our ancestors. Remarkably, within the mythology, the Earth Mother figure is the only one of the 'gods' that seems to always be present, no matter the epoch, including before and during the Fall of the Watchers. This seems to support the idea that since the creation of the First-Men, the Terrans always had some presence on Earth to exploit our ancient ancestors with it always taking the form of, or being viewed as a Mother-like figure.

This appears to have been done so our Neanderthal ancestors would gather food and resources for them to be transported up to the Heaven or Sky-father and then to the rest of their civilization. Although the mythology clearly tells us that our Neanderthal ancestor were being exploited by the Terrans, they were not the primary source of resources. According the mythology, the Terrans employed massive machines for industrial extraction of metals and other mineral resources that they needed to support their civilization. Remarkably, the mythology also implies that these great machines were not under the control of the Terran government nor the Terrans on Earth, but were in fact controlled by an unknown third party. It also is very apparent that for much of the time, the Heaven itself was under the control of this unknown third party.

Although we are clearly missing countless details, this basic arrangement appears to have existed from the end of the Great Deluge and the reconquest of Earth at about 72,000 BC to the coming of Cro-Magnon Man at approximately 39,000 BC. This simple system appears to have been very stable with no evidence that it changed in any meaningful manner for about thirty-three thousand years. However, as we already know, starting around 39,000 BC, the political situation begins to change. Based upon this information, it appears that it took approximately thirty-three-thousand years for the Terrans' population to grow to a point where they began once again having problems supplying enough food and other resources from the Earth to feed their people and maintain their civilization.

By understanding that a large part of the Terrans motivation on Earth was centered around food production to feed their people and metal resources to sustain their civilization. We can now easily understand that the coming of Cro-Magnon Man must have been the direct result of their need for greater production to feed and supply their ever-growing population. It is rather apparent that Neanderthal simply could not keep up with the ever-increasing demand for more resources. This demand is why the Terran government decided to improve the stock by breaking Neanderthal into at least two separate sub-species. With one being our more intelligent immediate ancestor Cro-Magnon man, who could produce more and handle a more complex society, with the other being the ever mysterious Hairy-Man of legend.

This change resulted in some type of war among the Terrans. This is the war that is vaguely remembered in the Book of Genesis as the war of the kings that resulted in the destruction of the cities of the plains forever remembered as the sinful cities of Sodom and Gomorrah. It is this almost forgotten war that left the first radioactive spike found in the ice-cores that date to about 39,000 BC. This first radioactive spike and the biblical story of the destruction of the cities of plains shows us that the Terrans did not have much of a problem using nuclear devices or weapons against one another and our ancestors. This will also give us our first glimpse into a few of the other possible political motivations behind the Terrans on Earth.

This first radioactive spike proves that the Terrans used nuclear technology and weapons in this little war. According to the biblical account, it is rather clear they had no problems using such weapons against our helpless ancestors with the detailed description given of the destruction of cities of Sodom and Gomorrah. The use of these weapons appears to be the direct result of the Terran government changing our ancestors from Neanderthal into a more intelligent and effective slave we call Cro-Magnon man. Based upon the information we have, it appears that one of the reasons these weapons were used, was simply to remove the now unwanted Neanderthal population.

This allows us to easily understand that there must have been many Terrans, especially the ones on Earth, that must have had a moral and ethical problems with using nuclear weapons against such a completely helpless population. As with the Fallen Watchers, it appears that these Terrans on Earth saw our ancient ancestors as more than mere animals to be exploited and exterminated as needed. Although we have next to no information on how this disagreement unfolded, it is an important one that does seem to have influenced later events.

Based on what little information is available, it appears that this first war of the gods was a relatively short-lived affair with a new agreement being reached rather quickly between the warring parties. This agreement appears to have left the original arrangement intact. The only real change seems to be that Neanderthal was to be bred out of existence instead of being exterminated with nuclear weapons. He would also be replaced with two sub-species, again, with one being our immediate ancestor Cro-Magnon man while the other was the mysterious Hairy-Man of legend. It also appears that the Earth Mother or Earth-faction of Terrans was left in control of the human population. Nevertheless, as we will learn in greater detail, there was a second phase to this agreement that the Earth-faction may have been entirely unaware of until it was too late.

This second phase of this agreement took the form of the Terran government assembling a group composed of all the different ethnic and racial groups of humanity organized into numerous tribes. These tribes were focused on the worship and service to a new pantheon of gods. Based upon the available information, it is difficult to know why these tribes were initially placed in Egypt. However, one of the most likely reasons was because the Egyptian civilization could sustain their growing numbers. Once this group had grown large enough, they were then guided out of Egypt and then around the world by the King of the gods, commonly known as the Lord of the waters. The purpose of this great Exodus appears to have been to establish a more uniform society and belief system upon the entire world of humanity. Using our esoteric knowledge, we can understand that the primary purpose of this entire undertaking was simply to take over the entire operation on Earth that was focused primarily on food production and resource extraction.

Shortly before this great Exodus, another war of the gods breaks out between the Terran government and the Terrans on Earth. Unlike the first one, this war was not a short-lived affair, but a prolonged event with many destructive battles that completely reshaped the political, economic, and religious landscape on Earth and possibly their entire civilization. What is remarkable is that although we know a great deal about this war it has always been placed within the wrong part of the story. This is a situation that is exactly the same as the placement of Enoch within the story. Where Enoch has been traditionally been believed to have come at the beginning of the story, wherein the truth is that he came much closer towards the end of the story. In the case of this great war of the gods, it has always been believed to have come at the very beginning of the story, but as we will now begin to learn, its proper place is closer towards the middle.

To begin this part of our journey, we must first fully understand that the polytheistic pantheons of the ancient world like the Greek, Roman, Hindu, and all the other pantheons of the world and the stories associated with them. They all originate from the people who took part in the second phase of the great Exodus out of Egypt under the leadership of the legendary divine twin brothers and the new kingdoms they established. Therefore, all the myths, legends, and folklore associated with this new pantheon of gods also originate just before, during, and shortly after the grand event of the Exodus out of Egypt. Additionally, these ancient Israelites, as they become known, are the people we know historically as the Proto-Indo-Europeans that first settled on the Iranian Plateau and the valleys of the Zagros mountains after leaving the land of Egypt. This brings us to a point where we need to return to the Proto-Indo-European mythology to understand this great war in heaven between the gods.

As we have learned, the earliest known Proto-Indo-European mythology is the mother belief that provides the backbone for all the different pantheons of gods the world over. It is this ancient Proto-Indo-European mythology that is the source material for all the other beliefs that came later. Slowly, over time, the original mythology of the Proto-Indo-Europeans underwent a great change as it fused with other societies, cultures, and traditions. Although the original mythology underwent significant change, there is a small handful of myths with details that have always remained the same no matter the culture or how many centuries had passed since the actual events occurred. Within one of these universal myths of the Proto-Indo-Europeans, which is also believed to be one of the oldest, is where we will find the answers to many of the mysteries we have been exploring.

Within this ancient mythology we find a universal story that speaks of a great war of the gods where the mighty Sky-Father was overthrown by one of his children with the aid of his mother, the Earth Mother. Once this new god defeats the Sky-Father, he then betrays the Earth Mother. Because of this betrayal, the Earth Mother brings forth a terrible monster to fight against this new Supreme god. After a series of horrible battles, this new Supreme god defeats this terrible monster, with the Earth Mother becoming his consort or wife. In all the versions of this myth, this great monster created by the Earth Mother takes the form of a great powerful serpent. Hence, this myth is commonly known as the "*Serpent-Slaying myth.*"

Although the details of this Serpent-Slaying myth often vary from culture to culture, there are several key features that always remain the same. Within all the myths, this great serpent is somehow associated with water and is thought of as being "multiple" in some manner, with it either being multi-headed or it having multiple tails or multiple hand-like weapons protruding from its body. This monstrous serpent is always created by the Earth Mother to do battle with the new Supreme god, her son. A son that she had aided so he could defeat and then replace the great Sky-Father. According to the myths, there were two separate encounters that occur between this new Supreme god and the great serpent that resulted in massively destructive battles. In the first encounter, the great serpent defeats the new Supreme god after an epic battle that lays waste to many lands. In all versions of this myth, the great serpent defeats the new Supreme god in this first battle by making it impossible for him to use his power in some fashion, normally by denying him of his mighty thunderbolt. In many versions, he is also rendered helpless by being immobilized somehow. [1,2,3,4]

After this first epic battle that left the new Supreme god immobilized and powerless, the great serpent and the Earth Mother celebrate their victory. While unbeknownst to them, the other Sky-gods come to the aid of their brother god by healing him in some manner that allows him to use his most powerful weapon once again, the mighty thunderbolt. This is another common feature within the Serpent-Slaying myths that this new Supreme god's primary weapon is always the mighty thunderbolt. Once he is healed and can use his thunderbolt again, he launches a new attack against the great serpent. After another epic battle that shakes the foundations of the Earth and threatens to destroy creation itself, the new Supreme god finally strikes the great serpent down in a hail of mighty thunderbolts that kills the fearsome beast. After this great victory, the new Supreme god then takes his place as the new Sky-Father along with his brother and sister Sky-gods who assume their places of rulership over all of creation. [5,6]

One of the primary reasons this myth is so crucial to the Proto-Indo-Europeans and the later cultures descended from these people is that this story is directly connected to the creation stories of the gods themselves and the earthly society they created for humans. By understanding that this creation story originated from the Proto-Indo-European people and combining it with our esoteric knowledge, we can realize that this creation myth is speaking of a violent political take over. We will also learn that this myth helps provide a wealth of information about the political situation that existed among the Terrans at this distant time.

To help us in understanding this war of the gods, we need to explore one of the most complete versions of this creation myth that we currently have, which is found in Greek mythology. The Greek version of the Serpent-Slaying myth is when the mighty Zeus battles the dreaded monster Typhon. This myth is also the origin story of Zeus's birth and that of his fellow Olympians that resulted in the overthrow of his father Cronus and his fellow Titans.

The Greek myth begins long ago with the Earth Mother, known as Gaea, and Ouranos, known as Father Heaven, also commonly known as Uranus. It is these two ancient gods that are the ones who gave birth to the great and terrible monsters known as the Titans. The first of these monsters that came forth were the three monstrously huge and powerfully strong creatures that each had a hundred hands and fifty heads and were known as the "*Hecatoncheires.*" These horrible monsters were then followed by three Cyclopes who each had an eye like a great wheel in the center of their faces, and then finally the mighty Titans, of which there were several. [7,8]

Although these monsters and the mighty Titans were the children of Father Heaven, the myths tell us that he was a poor father to them. He is said to have hated the Hecatoncheires, even though they were his first-born sons; he imprisoned each one in a secret place deep within the Earth, after each birth. Where they clawed at the Earth day and night, trying to escape their underground prison. Whereas, he left the Cyclopes and the other Titans at large to roam the Earth doing as they pleased. Gaea became enraged at her children's mistreatment by Father Heaven and appealed to all her children to help her. Only one of her children was bold enough, the great Titan Cronus. Cronus lay in wait to ambush his father and wounded him terribly in the attack. Although the Greek myth is vague and does not say that Cronus killed Uranus, it is heavily implied that Uranus died from the wounds he suffered from the ambush. The Giants, the fourth race of monsters, are said to have sprung up from Uranus' blood. From this same blood, the Erinyes, or Furies, were born. Their office was to pursue and punish sinners. They became known as "*those who walk in the darkness,*" they were terrible of aspect, with writhing snakes for hair and eyes that wept tears of blood. In time, the other monsters were finally driven from the Earth or under the control of Cronus, except for the Erinyes. As long as there was sin in the world, they could not be banished. [9]

From that time onward and for untold ages, Cronus, with his sister-queen Rhea, was Lord of the Earth and the universe. Rhea was a Titaness and the older-sister of Cronus. She, like Cronus, was a child of Gaea and Uranus. In the earliest traditions, she was known as *"the mother of gods"* and, therefore, became strongly associated with Gaea and the later Cybele of Roman mythology. Rhea appears to be a slightly different version of Gaea. In classical times, Greeks saw her as the mother of the Olympian gods and goddesses, with her usually taking Gaea's place in the mythology. However, she was not an Olympian goddess in her own right. Depending on the myth, sometimes Rhea is the daughter of Gaea, while in others she takes the place of Gaea. This is another example of the Indo-European people assimilating and fusing with local cultures as they moved around the world. This time of Cronus and Rhea was said to have been a "Golden Age," as the people of this time did not need laws or rules, with everyone doing the right thing, and immorality was absent from the world. Sometime during his rule, Cronus learned that one of his future children would dethrone him, and he thought to go against fate by swallowing them as soon as they were born. [10]

As time goes by, Rhea gave birth to five children, Poseidon, Hades, Hestia, Demeter, and Hera, each of which Cronus quickly swallowed to prevent his overthrow. This enraged Rhea, so she devised a plan to save her children and to eventually get retribution upon Cronus for his acts against his children and for also betraying his father. Rhea then subsequently tricks Cronus by hiding her sixth child Zeus. After hiding Zeus, she then wrapped a stone in swaddling clothes as a substitute. Cronus promptly eats this presentation from Rhea, not suspecting the swap in lieu. Zeus was raised in secret and when he had grown, he, with the help of his grandmother, Gaea, forced Cronus to disgorge his brothers and sisters and the stone. Thereafter followed a terrible war between Cronus, (with the help of his fellow Titans), against Zeus with his five brothers and sisters. It was a war so destructive that it was said to have almost wrecked the universe. [11]

> A dreadful sound troubled the boundless sea.
> The whole earth uttered a great cry.
> Wide Heaven, shaken, groaned.
> From its foundation far Olympus reeled
> Beneath the onrush of the deathless gods,
> And trembling seized upon black Tartarus.

During this war of the gods, which is commonly known as the great *"Titanomachy"* within Greek mythology. Zeus, with the aid of his brothers and sisters, conquered each of the Titans and overthrew Cronus. Zeus was also greatly aided in this war by releasing the powerful Hecatoncheires from their prison, who then fought for him with their irresistible weapons of thunder, lightning, and earthquake. Additionally, the Titan Iapetus, more commonly known as Prometheus and known for his great wisdom, also sided with Zeus. [12]

After untold battles, Zeus was victorious in this destructive war against Cronus and the Titans. After defeating his father, Zeus is said to have punished his conquered enemies terribly; with many of them being imprisoned within the realm of Tartarus. This was a deep abyss that was used as a dungeon for the Titans and to torment the wicked. Even after the Titans were conquered and crushed, Zeus and his fellow Olympians were not wholly victorious. Although the myths do not give a reason, Zeus' grandmother Gaea gave birth to her last and most frightful offspring, a powerful creature that was more terrible than any that come before, the dreaded Typhon. [13]

> *A flaming monster with a hundred heads,*
> *Who rose up against all the gods.*
> *Death whistled from his fearful jaws,*
> *His eyes flashed glaring fire.*

In their first encounter, the dreadful Typhon was victorious by catching Zeus off guard and ripping his tendons from his body, leaving him helpless and useless. Typhon also stripped Zeus of his most potent weapon, his mighty thunderbolt. As Typhon and Gaea were celebrating their victory, Zeus' brothers and sisters secretly helped him regain his tendons, and, more importantly, his ever-famous weapon of thunder and lightning, the thunderbolt, which from this time forward, was used by no other god. Once restored, Zeus sought out another battle with Typhon. In their second encounter and after another epic battle, Zeus finally strikes the terrible beast down in a hail of mighty thunderbolts that shook the whole world. [14]

Although Zeus, with the aid of his fellow Olympians, had finally conquered all that had opposed them, still later, there were at least two more attempts to unseat the mighty Zeus as the new Supreme god. Nevertheless, by the time these attempted rebellions occurred, Zeus had become the strongest of all the gods. The first attempt was by the Giants, who were still loyal to Cronus, but they were quickly defeated and hurled down to Tartarus. From this point forward, Zeus and his brothers and sisters were the undisputed lords of all of creation and Olympus. The second attempt was by his fellow Olympians, who had come to believe Zeus had abused his power, but they too were quickly defeated by Zeus. [15]

With our esoteric knowledge and using the symbolic timeline, we can understand this myth in a way no one has ever imagined before. In the process, we will learn of some of the political events surrounding the Terrans. Additionally, we must always remember that this ancient mythology and the stories that form our folklore originally come from our immediate ancestor Cro-Magnon man. This means that we must always keep in the back of our minds the mental limitations of our Cro-Magnon man ancestors with their general inability to understand advanced technology in any terms but magic or the divine power of the gods.

To begin anew, we must return to the original narrative with our first point of reference and realize that the time of Gaea, the Earth Mother, and Uranus, Father Heaven, are referring to the time that occurred during the Fall of the Watchers. The great overthrow of Uranus by Cronus at the request of Gaea refers to the reconquest of Earth and the time of the Great Deluge. The myth implies that much of the political disagreement was focused on the use of the great Titans and the resources they provided. Although the myth is vague, it hints that some type of agreement existed between the parties during the Fall of the Watchers and much, if not all the conflict was based upon needed resources and the use of these massive machines. Unfortunately, the myth just does not give us enough information to say much else about the situation.

Soon after this overthrow of Uranus, begins the long peaceful Golden Age of Cronus and his sister-wife Rhea. This time refers to the thousands of years between the reconquest of the Earth, that included the event remembered as the Great Deluge through the time of the Exodus out of Egypt. Within the esoteric timeline, this is the time between approximately 72,000 BC to 32,000 BC. It is during this time the simple religious idea of the Sky-Father, Earth Mother, centered around the symbolism of the Bull comes into being. Strangely, and for unknown reasons, the Earth Mother figure appears to be the most important during this time.

With our esoteric knowledge, we can easily recognize that both Father Heaven, Uranus, and his overthrow by his son the Titan Cronus are referring to events that occurred on and around the mighty Heaven floating high above the surface of the Earth. As we will shortly learn, the Titan Cronus as well as the later Zeus represents a smaller craft that was used to attack, defeat, and then take over the Heaven, which then takes on the mantel and becomes the Supreme god or the 'Heaven.'

Rhea, Cronus' sister-wife, is much more mysterious. She is by far the most important of the gods to our ancient ancestors at this distant time. As we will shortly learn, the Earth Mother symbolizes the main manufacturing facilities here on Earth as seen through the eyes of our ancient Cro-Magnon man ancestors. She also represents any transport ships that was used to supply the

156

Heaven, with many of them becoming the various goddesses of the ancient world. That might seem a bit confusing at this moment, but this is where our esoteric understanding that the gods were the technologically advanced craft that the Terrans flew, and not the Terrans themselves which will greatly aid us in understanding the next phase of the story and how these events unfolded. This requires us to properly understand what precisely this Earth Mother was and how it was seen through the eyes of our ancient Cro-Magnon man ancestors.

For us to understand what our Cro-Magnon ancestors were really seeing when they saw the Earth Mother. We must take a moment and imagine a large modern-day industrial manufacturing complex with a large central assembly building. Which is usually a long narrow looking central building. In modern-day industry, this type of building can be up to a dozen city blocks long, surrounded by dozens of outbuildings that prepare material, parts, and other equipment necessary to produce the final product. With this simple idea in mind, we need to imagine what our ancient Cro-Magnon ancestors would think if they saw such a complex.

We also need to consider and remember the limited mental abilities of Cro-Magnon man. By doing this, it is easy to understand and imagine that our ancient Cro-Magnon man ancestors would describe this type of large manufacturing complex in the same manner as they did with all the technology they saw or encountered. They would describe it as a being like a *"living creature,"* but it would be unlike any living creature they knew. From a distance, our Cro-Magnon ancestors would see all kinds of different activities occurring in and around such a complex, with the large central assembly building naturally standing out to them. It is easy to imagine how our Cro-Magnon man ancestors would see this vast industrial complex as if it was truly alive like some great living creature.

To them it would seem to be breathing by taking in vast amounts of air and then expelling toxic waste gases. At night, they would see lights turning on with the building glowing like a fantastic and mysterious beast. They would also hear loud strange sounds as equipment and materials were moved around the site. They would also see it eating, as it took in raw material at one end of the building, and then after a long, strange, mysterious, and unknown process, it would give birth as the finished product came out the other end of the building. This simple understanding allows us to realize that the great Earth Mother was most likely a tremendous industrial manufacturing assembly building within a much larger industrial complex.

This allows us to take the next step to understand that the sister-wife of Cronos, Rhea, must have been a large transport ship that would take the finished product, or 'child,' up to the Heaven, or Cronos as our ancient ancestors would have thought of it. Upon arriving in orbit, this large transport ship would then transfer the product or 'child' to the Heaven for final work or be prepared to be transferred to Mars or other parts of their civilization. For our ancient Cro-Magnon man ancestors looking up from below it would have looked like Cronos was "eating" his children. In this case, the final product or children were six highly advanced craft. However, as we are told in the myth, the sixth one was replaced with a defective or sabotaged copy of that craft, while the real one was constructed in secret and hidden on Earth. This sixth one along with the aid of numerous allies on Earth, was used to force Cronos to "vomit" up his children, all of which then aided the sixth ship in conquering the Heaven and then the operations on Earth.

Although we are still missing many details, this basic information allows us to understand this ancient myth in an entirely new manner. We can now understand that our ancient Cro-Magnon man ancestors were seeing the preparations for war by the Terrans and then the war itself. Nevertheless, they could not see or know of the actual political workings or motivations going on behind the scenes. Although our ancient ancestors were not aware of the broader political factors at work, we can infer several of them if we take a closer look at the *"Enuma Elish."* The Enuma Elish is the Babylonian creation myth; it is commonly known as *"The Seven Tablets of Creation."* Although the myth is not as complete as the Greek version, it is believed to be the oldest version of the Serpent Slaying myth we know of. It is also thought to be the earliest version of the myth, and thereby the closest to the original Proto-Indo-European version.

Since we are aware of how the divine twin brothers led the Indo-European speaking tribes of Israel around the world, which destroyed the Bronze Age civilizations while establishing a new world order of devotion and service to the gods during the second phase of the Exodus. We can understand that there is a direct connection between the Enuma Elish, the oldest and possibly the earliest creation story of these people, and the much later Greek version, which was the last to be established. This knowledge allows us to piece together several parts of the myth that help provide a slightly more precise picture of the Terrans' political situation.

Within the Enuma Elish version of the Serpent Slaying myth the chain of events unfolds in essentially the same manner as the Greek version with one notable difference. In the Enuma Elish, the Earth Mother and the great monster she is said to have spawned for the final battle with the new Supreme god are the same creature and not separate entities as they are within the Greek version. In the Enuma Elish she is a monstrous creature known as *"Tiamat."* Tiamat has normally been viewed as a somewhat ambiguous character. In the beginning of the myth she is depicted as a great mother-like figure. However, later in the myth, she is transformed into the primary antagonist. As with the Greek version, the Sky-Father known as "*Apsu*," which is the Babylonian version of Cronos, created numerous gods with Tiamat, the Earth Mother. However, unlike the Greek version, this creation of the gods took place over several generations. The first gods brought forth by Apsu and Tiamat were the gods known as "*Lahmu*" and "*Lahamu*." These first gods are rather vague deities that do not seem to have played any significant part in subsequent myths. They, in turn, gave birth to the gods "*Anshar*" and "*Kishar*," who are typically thought of as being twins of some type. They are normally viewed as the male and female principles and the twin horizons of sky and Earth. This twin symbolism is another vague reference within the myth to the divine twin brothers that come later. [16,17,18,19]

After two more generations of gods were created, it is said that the younger gods started to become a nuisance to Apsu and Tiamat. They clamored loudly across the surface of the Earth, and Apsu could not quell their voices, nor would they listen to their mother, Tiamat. Despite all the trouble being caused by the younger gods, Tiamat tolerated them, for they were her children. Still, Apsu could not tolerate their destructive behavior any longer and intended to destroy them all. When Tiamat learned of this, she was not pleased and was furious that her lover would plot to destroy their children and confronted him. Nevertheless, Apsu did not listen to his consort Tiamat, but instead listened to his vizier, Mummu, the god of knowledge, and continued to plot the destruction of his children. [20]

However, the other gods learned of Apsu's plan, and one of them, "*Ea*," who is more commonly known by his later Sumerian name, "*Enki*," plotted to destroy Apsu. Enki is the Babylonian-Sumerian version of the Lord of the waters, which we know as the same god the Greeks called Poseidon. This is also the same 'god' of the Bible and that led the Israelites in their great Exodus out of Egypt. Remarkably, this version appears to answer why the later Aryan speaking people originally placed Indra, their name for the Lord of the waters, as the Supreme god, and not Shiva. According to this version of the myth, it was Enki, the Lord of the waters, that originally overthrew Apsu the Supreme god and not the Babylonian version of Zeus, the storm god Marduk. The myth goes on to say that Enki placed a "*sleeping spell*" upon Apsu, rendering him helpless and then killed him. [21]

Soon after these events, it is said that the mighty storm god "*Marduk*" who was born of Enki and the fertility goddess known as "*Sarpanitu*," though in some versions of the myth, his wife is a goddess named "*Nanaya*." After his birth, the great Marduk was given the mighty four-winds of the Earth to play with. Some of the younger gods were greatly disturbed by Enki's actions of him killing Apsu and complained to Tiamat. After endless goading, Tiamat decided to avenge her fallen lover, Apsu, and go to war with her children. She then created an army of chaos to assist her that was made-up of eleven tremendous and terrible monsters. She then appointed her new consort "*Qingu*," also spelled "*Kingu*," as their commander. Tiamat wanted to establish him as the new chief ruler and leader of all the gods. To aid Qingu, Tiamat gave him the "*Tablet of Destiny*," which he wore as a breastplate and was said to have given him great power. [22]

When Enki and his siblings, the other sky gods, learned of Tiamat's plan to destroy them, they formed a council of the gods but they were so filled with despair, they were incapable doing anything. Eventually, the god Marduk stepped forward and offered to the council of gods that he would battle Tiamat and her monstrous offspring. On the condition that if he emerged victorious, he would be given supreme rulership over all the gods and creation. Enki and the council of gods quickly agreed to Marduk's demands. [23]

As with the Greek version of the myth, Marduk, with the help of the other Sky-gods, defeats each of the eleven terrible monstrous offspring of Tiamat led by her consort Qingu. Once the eleven great monsters were defeated, Marduk turned his attention first to Qingu, whom he kills in single combat. Once Qingu was defeated, Marduk then turned his attention to Tiamat, where a mighty battle ensued between the two that was said to have shaken the very foundations of the Earth and threatened all of creation with destruction. After what seemed like an endless series of attacks and counter-attacks between the two, Marduk finally called upon the great four-winds to incapacitate Tiamat by pinning her against a mountain. While the four winds pinned Tiamat, Marduk shot a great arrow, like a mighty thunderbolt, into her belly, which split her down the middle. Then Marduk is said to have used Tiamat's body to make the Earth and the skies. After this great battle and this new creation of the world, Marduk used the blood of the fallen Qingu and mixed it with the clay of the Earth to create humanity, who were then tasked with doing the work of the gods upon the good Earth. [24]

This Babylonian version of the Serpent Slaying myth provides us with slightly more information on the gods' possible political actions than the later Greek version. With one of the more striking points being that the Lord of the waters was the original god to overthrow the Supreme god and who is later replaced by a 'god' he helped create. Although he loses his throne as the Supreme god, the Lord of the waters is made the 'King of the gods' and rules over Earth. We can also see that the earliest version of this myth compared to the Greek version, it changed over time and removed this information. Which, as we have already explored was most likely done to keep the peace of the people the later divine twins conquered. It is also an indication that this event was not a major factor in how the events played out. For us to make sense of these events, we need to combine these two versions of the myth with our esoteric knowledge. Once we do that, then we can at least begin to speculate with some confidence about what might have motivated the Terrans and why these events occurred.

Although it might not be apparent, but both versions of the Serpent-Slaying myth imply that the Heaven was not under the control of the Terran government, nor was it under control of the Terrans on Earth, remembered as the Earth Mother. Based upon the available information we have from the myths; it appears that the Heaven was under the control of an unknown third-party or organization. A party that was powerful enough that it required the combined forces of both the Terran government and the Terran-faction on Earth to dislodge it from power once it had made the decision to remove the great machines.

Remarkably, although we may not know the exact details, all the versions of the Serpent Slaying myth agree that the problems began when the Sky-Father decided to remove all his children from the Earth. These children are the great machines that our Cro-Magnon man ancestors viewed as the mighty Titans; the terribly powerful monsters created by the gods. This decision to remove these machines is the reason that the first uprising or civil war occurred. We can also speculate that this decision must have had a tremendous economic impact on their society, especially for those on Earth. Unfortunately, there does not appear to be any surviving information on why the party in control of the Heaven made this decision.

Although we may not know the reasoning behind this decision to remove the machines, we do know it is why there was a civil war and eventual takeover of the Heaven by what appears to the Terran government with the help of their allies on Earth. One of the more important changes that surround this takeover of the Heaven, is this is the point in time when the mighty Heaven floating up above the clouds ceases to be a 'thing' or 'god' and starts to becomes a 'place' where a mere mortal could go to and return from. In the Enuma Elish, we are told of how after Enki had killed Apsu, he "*entered into Apsu*" and made it his throne and the abode of the Host of Heaven. [25]

Once this first takeover was accomplished, and the Heaven was firmly under the control of the Terran government. There appears to some type of political rearrangement, where the original ruler was quickly replaced with another. Soon after this political change or possibly during it, a second, much more destructive civil war erupts, first against the great machines and then with their Terran allies on Earth. Unfortunately, the ancient stories do not provide us with enough information to precisely explain why this second war erupts between the allies. However, according to the myths, the problem arises when once again, this new Supreme god makes the same decision to remove the great monsters from Earth as the god he just overthrew was planning to do originally. Once again, the myths do not provide us with enough information to why this decision was made. But once it was made, a new and very destructive civil war erupted between the former allies when the Terran government begins destroying the great machines.

While these great machines were being destroyed, the Terrans on Earth and their allies go to war with the new rulers of the Heaven. Within the Babylonian version, it was *"the other gods"* that ultimately convinced Tiamat to turn against her one-time ally. This implies that the entire situation was far more complicated than our Cro-Magnon man ancestors could have possibly understood. With there being numerous economic, political, and social forces at work that were just entirely beyond their understanding or their ability to know about in the first place. Although we may not have many details on the actual inner workings of the Terrans leading up to this war, we can easily begin to see a few of the possible economic and political forces at work behind the scenes.

Using our own modern society as an example, it is easy to understand how removing the great machines would have had a huge economic impact on Earth. Although we do not know how their economy was organized, it makes little difference when an entire section of the economy is removed and thousands of jobs disappear. Even if they had a complete command economy, this type of economic upheaval would still have resulted in many individuals needing to move and start over. This economic upheaval could be the reason why the Terrans on Earth and their allies would have felt betrayed and went to war. It would have simply been because their way of life, that appears to have existed since before the Fall of the Watchers was going to be destroyed. Although this is only one possibility, with the truth being that we may never really know the true motivations of the Terrans for this civil war. Although we are missing a large portion of the details leading up to the out-break of this war of the gods, we do have a great deal of information about this war and its aftermath.

In all versions of the myth, we are told this second civil war was almost the end of everything as the mighty Sky-gods were locked in battle, first with the terrible monsters and then eventually with the Earth Mother and her last horrible offspring. This is the vital clue to understanding that the most extensive and mysterious radioactive spike we explored in our journey through the Dream Vision of Enoch that dates to approximately 32,000 BC is direct evidence of this massive war of the gods. It is also the clue that allows us to realize that this great war of the gods is recorded in the Bible as the Ten Plagues of Egypt. It also allows us to understand that this war of the gods was why the Ten Plagues fell upon Egypt and was the reason behind the Exodus in the first place. [26]

This then allows us to begin understanding what the Terrans were really doing. As the myths tell us, the new Sky-gods under the new Supreme god's leadership were victorious over the monsters and the forces of the Earth Mother. This victory then leads to the next phase of their plan, the great Exodus out of Egypt, and the establishment of a worldwide network of major kingdoms founded by the divine twin brothers after they had settled the Land of Canaan. The primary reason for this was to replace the mighty machines with a new, more environmentally-friendly system to supply them with the resources they needed. It is also equally likely that this fundamental change was due to economic reasons. It is easy to understand that the great machines had just became too costly to operate, while human slaves who took care of themselves were much cheaper and easier to handle.

Additionally, according to the Akkadian epic, the "*Atra-Hasis,*" we are told that there was also some type labor dispute occurring among the gods that may have been a factor in removing the great machines. Within the epic we learn of a group of lower ranking deities known as the "*Igigi*" or "*Igigu,*" who were put to work by a council of Seven Sky-gods, primarily the god Enlil, who is the Akkadian version of Marduk. The Igigi were said to have been tasked with digging a large irrigation channel. The epic implies that the work was brutal and the god Enlil was oppressive to the Igigi. In time, the Igigi rebelled against the Seven Sky-gods by setting fire to the tools and then surrounding Enlil's great house one night in protest. Upon hearing that the toil of the Igigi building the irrigation channel was so great, the council of the Seven decided to create mankind to carry out the agricultural labor of the Igigi. This Akkadian myth, heavily implies that the entire situation was vastly more complex than has been traditionally believed and lends great weight to the idea that the removal of the great machines and replacing them with humans was done primarily for economic reasons. [27,28]

As we have learned, once the great machines were removed, they were replaced by the Indo-European speaking children of Israel under the leadership of the divine twin brothers. In the process, these tribes destroyed all the existing Bronze Age civilizations they encountered while establishing their new kingdoms. All the evidence we have says they established a strictly agricultural society centered around the complete submission, devotion, and service to the whims of the gods that was administered by powerful kings with an equally powerful priesthood. These kings and priests were the descendants of the original leaders of each of the tribes that took part in the great Exodus out of

Egypt, first under Moses and Aaron then later under the divine twin brothers. In time, this entire event becomes known as and is remembered as being a new 'creation' of humanity.

If we take a moment to explore this new creation of humanity with our esoteric knowledge. We will quickly realize that we now have four separate and very different creation stories of humanity. The first creation of humanity was the creation of the First-Men with the species we know as Neanderthal. Based on the latest archeological evidence, this creation of the First-Men may have occurred as far back as 300,000 BC, possibly even earlier. The second creation was during the Fall of the Watchers with the mysterious genetic reset of 90% of the animal life on the planet between 100,000 to 200,000 years ago which is vaguely remembered in the first chapter of the Book of Genesis. The third creation is when the gods broke Neanderthal into two sub-species, with one being Cro-Magnon man, with the other being the mysterious Hairy-man of legend, at approximately 39,000 BC, which is remembered in the Book of Genesis as the birth of Jacob and his brother Esau. Then we have a fourth creation of humanity at around 32,000 BC. However, this event does not appear to be the physical creation of a new species of human like we have seen in the past. However, it is more of a symbolic creation because it was the 'creation' of a new society that was populated by a 'new man and woman' who were utterly devoted to fulfilling the will of the gods. [29]

Based on the historical information and the evidence we have; it is challenging to say just how long this entire process of the second phase of the Exodus under the leadership of the divine twin brothers may have taken. It may have been as short as just a couple of centuries too possibly taking a few thousand years to unfold. The available evidence seems to support the idea that the second phase of the Exodus and the settlement that came with it occurred over thousands of years. Historically we know it usually took many generations for these new Indo-European-speaking settlers to fully take over and be integrated into the local population of the various cultures they encountered, thereby creating entirely new cultures and languages in the process. This supports the original esoteric timeline we explored in the first chapter, with the forty years wandering in the wilderness by the Israelites is also speaking of forty generations with each generation being approximately one-hundred-and-forty years in length, giving us a total of 5,600 years. This allows us to place the events of the great Exodus out of Egypt, the settlement of the Land of Canaan, and the events of the second phase of the Exodus under the leadership of the divine twin brothers with the establishment of an entirely new pantheon of gods between about 32,000 BC to approximately 26,400 BC.

Although we may not know precisely how long this entire process took. We do know that once this new world order had been established, humanity entered a long mysterious Dark-Age that began as the great Bronze Age civilizations collapsed. It was an age where the only reason for the common person's existence was the complete and utter devotion in a never-ending service to the will of the gods. This great Dark-Age was a time of religion, where it was very much like the Middle Ages of Europe, where the Catholic Church, with the aid of local rulers and kings, ruled with an iron fist where heresy was punishable by death.

If we take a few moments and look at this situation with a modern eye. We can easily understand that the entire purpose of the great war of the gods and the Exodus was to establish a worldwide network of similar kingdoms. This was done simply to provide a cheap, steady supply of food and other resources for the Terrans and their civilization. We can also realize that the most likely reason the mighty Titans were removed from service was primarily due to the high cost to use and maintain these machines and numerous labor problems related to their use. It was just vastly simpler and much cheaper to have humans do the work instead of these massive machines that required a costly never-ending maintenance. It is also highly probable that these great machines were thousands upon thousands of years old and had simply outlived their designed lifetime.

This provides us with a small insight into the Terrans' economics and politics by showing us that there was at least one faction of the Terrans, most likely the Terrans on Earth, that opposed using our ancestors in this way. Not only did they oppose it, but it required a highly destructive a war to make it happen. Using our society as an example, this implies that removing the machines must have led to a tremendous economic loss for the Terrans on Earth. Although there appears that there was political and economic opposition to using humanity in this manner, in the end, it was the system that prevailed. This simple agricultural system, with its equally simple religious and political system, appears to have worked for countless generations. That is, until the building of King Solomon's Temple and Citadel, better known as the First Temple.

The building of the First Temple, and its ultimate destruction is the key to understanding the next series of events that were to unfold. The events surrounding this building will also allow us to answer a few of the mysteries that still surround the mysterious Shepherds spoken of in the Dream Vision of Enoch.

As we have learned, before and during the building of the First Temple, a new religious belief was beginning to take hold in the ancient Land of Canaan. This new religion was a radicalized and often violent sect of Zoroastrianism that preached a strict monotheistic doctrine. It was a religious sect that not only openly rejected and mocked the drug fueled mass animal sacrifice to the gods,

165

but it also rejected the very gods that were supposed to be the primary focus of humanity. Remarkably, it also did something that no other religious belief had ever done before, which was to place humans and especially the individual, at the center of its religious doctrine and teachings. As history shows us, these radical humanizing ideas had a significant impact on all levels of ancient society. We also now aware that it was this radical, strict, and often violent sect of this new Zoroastrianism religion that exploded to the forefront once the First Temple was completed.

By understanding the rise of this radical sect of Zoroastrianism, we can speculate with some confidence that this new religion may have been the primary reason why the First Temple was built. It is easy to imagine how the spreading of this new human-centered belief system and doctrine would have been a threat to the existing political, religious, and economic systems that had been established by the Terrans. It is highly probable that the Terrans were hoping that the First Temple would unite the people and return them to the original polytheistic religion they had established. Unfortunately for the Terrans, the building of the First Temple had quite the opposite effect, with it ultimately resulting in the destruction of the First Temple and the entire system they had built. It had other effects that had an even more significant impact on the world they had created. These other impacts will help explain a few of the lingering mysteries of the Shepherds and of the Dream Vision itself.

As we are now aware, one of the most important factors concerning the First Temple was a constant back-and-forth power struggle for control of this building by the followers of the traditional polytheistic religion and the radical and often violent followers of the new humanized monotheistic religion of Zoroastrianism. According to the Bible, it appears that this ongoing power struggle over the First Temple was of little, if any, concern for the Terrans once the First Temple was built. This apparent lack of concern by the Terrans makes sense once we realize that there were at least a dozen or so major kingdoms spread worldwide. With each of these kingdoms being supported by countless smaller kingdoms that were all producing food and resources to be sacrificed to the gods. The disruption from one kingdom must have been a minor affair with any lost resources or food being easily made up from the others. It is even possible that they were generating a large enough surplus that was of no real concern if one or even two of these kingdoms began to faulter.

Although it appears that this power struggle was of little concern to the Terrans, nevertheless, according to the Bible and the Dream Vision, there were at least two separate times that it became enough of a problem that the Terrans sent messengers and prophets to help lead the people back to the original polytheistic belief. The first attempt was by the famous prophet Elijah; the second was the sending of the messengers that included the equally famous scribe known as Enoch. The second time the Terrans sent messengers among the people is by far the more important of the two events. However, the biblical account lacks many details of the events that led up to the sending of these messengers by the Lord. Though the Bible lacks many details on the matter, we can now understand that the primary reason that Enoch and the other messengers were sent was due to this new heretical sect that based on the monotheistic religion of Zoroastrianism.

It is very easy to imagine how this new and dangerous religion was beginning to slowly spread outside the traditional lands of the original six Median tribes into the surrounding lands and nations. As it spread, it appears that this sect of Zoroastrianism had the same corrosive effect upon society as it had in the Land of Canaan. With it leading these other societies and cultures away from the traditional polytheistic religion. The spreading of this radical religious sect of Zoroastrianism with its outright rejection of mass animal sacrifice began to disrupt the food supply and the other resources that the Terrans relied upon for their civilization. This simple realization allows us to quickly understand why this would have been a problem that the Terrans could not easily ignore. A problem that would eventually require the Terrans to directly interfere in human affairs.

By understanding that it was these radical and often violent followers of Zoroastrianism that had taken over the First Temple. We can also easily recognize that they are also the people that rejected the message that was brought by Enoch and the other messengers of the Lord. First by mocking them and then by murdering all of them, except for one that had somehow managed to escape this slaying of the messengers, the one remembered as Enoch. Which according to the Dream Vision, Enoch was eventually rescued by the *"three that came and looked like white men."* The slaying of these messengers is the event that leads to the Terrans to directly interfere with human affairs. With one of the first results of this direct interfering was the destruction of the First Temple and the Babylonian captivity of the chosen people who had been corrupted by a radical human-centered sect of the monotheistic religion of Zoroastrianism, a people who will become known as the Jews.

There was another remarkable unforeseen effect of this spreading of Zoroastrianism and the destruction of the First Temple. This unforeseen effect was that within one or two generations of the First Temple's destruction, the great Dark-Age that had befallen humanity ended abruptly. Not only did it come to an end, but it appears that the native populations violently overthrew their leaders and priesthoods. Soon after this overthrow, we see an incredible explosion of culture, government, trade, building, the arts, and writing worldwide along with all the wonderful things that will become known as the Classical Age of the ancient world. Not only do we see a great cultural and economic revolution, we also see that many of these new cultures and civilizations were much more human-focused. With many of them questioning the gods themselves and whether humans should have anything to do with them.

This allows us to realize that once the First Temple was destroyed and the followers of this radical sect of Zoroastrianism were led away to the city of Babylon by King Nebuchadnezzar. It would have significantly weakened the political claims to power for all the earthly rulers and priesthoods of the other kingdoms spread around the world. This general weakening of the political power of the kingdoms combined with this new human-centered monotheistic religion of Zoroastrianism provided an opportunity for the common people to rise-up and overthrow their overlords.

After these kings, priests, and their supporters had been removed from power. The local people appointed new kings and leaders from their ranks based upon their own ancient traditions and lines of power. In turn, they quickly set about restoring their societies to the way they were before the coming of the divine twin brothers. They also set upon the task of removing the very memory of these former rulers and this Dark Age in general by destroying everything that was connected to them. Once this was accomplished, these new kingdoms and nations quickly grew into the mighty civilizations of the Classical Age of the ancient world, with many of them giving birth to the western tradition.

Within in a generation or two after the First Temple was destroyed, the entire political, economic, and religious system the Terrans had established for humanity quickly fell apart. Not only did it fall apart, but in the process, it also disrupted the flow of food and resources that the Terrans depended upon to feed their population and support their civilization.

Given later events, it appears that the entire supply network for food and resources completely collapsed. Understanding this collapse allows us to answer one of the greatest mysteries of the Dream Vision of Enoch and why the equally mysterious Shepherds were set upon their task of slaying those who had been marked and delivered onto them. It will also answer the greater mystery of why the Lord *"remained unmoved"* and even *"rejoiced that they were devoured."*

"But He remained unmoved, though He saw it, and rejoiced that they were devoured and swallowed and robbed, and left them to be devoured in the hand of all the beasts. And He called seventy shepherds, and cast those

sheep to them that they might pasture them, and He spake [spoke] to the shepherds and their companions: 'Let each individual of you pasture the sheep henceforward, and everything that I shall command you that ye. And I will deliver them over unto you duly numbered, and tell you which of them are to be destroyed and them destroy ye.' And He gave over unto them those sheep."
(Book of Enoch; 89: 58-60)

By understanding that their entire supply line of food and other resources from Earth had collapsed. We can quickly realize that the Terran's entire political and economic situation would have been radically changed in a very short amount of time. We can now also understand that there were two primary reasons why the mysterious Shepherds were sent. The first was to help reestablish some form of direct control over humanity to supply the needed food and other resources for their civilization. The second was to remove the humans that were following this new human-centered monotheistic religion of Zoroastrianism and corrupting the others.

There is also a possible third reason that does not become apparent until the next set of verses of the Dream Vision of Enoch. This third reason also appears to be directly related to the quickening food crisis the Terrans had now found themselves in. Within the Dream Vision, we learned that the next events to unfold was that the Shepherds, with the aid of numerous humans, began to "*eat and devoured the greater part of those sheep*." We are also told that the Shepherds slay and destroy many more than they were commanded. Which, if we consider the worsening food crisis, these references of the sheep being "*devoured*" take on an entirely new meaning and could be referring to literally 'eating' these sheep or people after they were killed.

"And I saw till those shepherds pastured in their season, and they began to slay and to destroy more than they were bidden, and the delivered those sheep into the hand of the lions. And the lions and tigers eat [ate] and devoured the greater part of those sheep, and the wild boars eat along with them; and they burnt that tower and demolished that house."
(Book of Enoch; 89: 64-66.)

This idea at first may seem rather gruesome, but when we consider that historically, at about the same time, we have the development of the highly detailed mythologies of a multi-level Hell-like Underworld. Within these mythologies, we find an Underworld that sounds eerily like a modern-day industrial slaughter-house that is processing animals for their meat.

If we take a few moments and return to the Underworld's mythology while keeping in mind that an acute food crisis was developing for the Terrans. We will discover that these ancient myths of the Underworld take on an entirely new and sinister meaning that may be more frightening than traditionally believed. Because within all the ancient myths, legends, and folklore of the dreaded Underworld, they all describe what appears to be the same physical place with the same horrible things happening to those wretched damned souls who were unlucky enough to be taken inside its gates.

All the ancient myths of the Underworld begin with the same description of a large cave-like entrance that takes the damned through a long dark passageway that leads deep underground into the very bowels of the Earth. In Meso-America mythology, this journey could take up to four days. In some Eastern traditions, it was a journey that could last months, while in a few, largely forgotten traditions, the journey could take years. However, in all the versions, sooner or later, the damned individual would come to a large cavern with a river they must cross. To the ancient Greeks and Romans, this was the river "*Styx*" with the dead's ferryman, "*Charon*," who demanded payment of a gold coin to transport the unlucky soul to the other side. In Mesopotamian mythology, this was "*Urshanabi*," the ferryman of the river of the dead, known as the "*Hubur*." In eastern traditions, it is common for the wretched soul to have to build a boat or raft to cross the river of the dead. In other eastern traditions, there was a great bridge the damned must cross, while still, in others, the unfortunate souls are picked up by the spirits of their dead ancestors that had suffered the same fate. In all the myths, there is always this same frightful river of the dead that the damned had to cross in some manner. [30,31,32,33,34]

After crossing the river of the dead, the damned soul would then approach the Underworld's mighty gates, which were always protected by a fearsome guardian beast that kept the dammed from escaping. In Greek and Roman mythology, this was "*Cerberus*," the "*hound of Hades*" that was a fearsome three-headed dog that guarded the gates of the Underworld to prevent the dead from leaving. To the Egyptians, this was "*Aker*," depicted as two recumbent lion torsos merged into one, with their heads looking away from one other. In Norse mythology, this guardian was "*Garmr*" or "*Garm*," who was described as a fearsome blood-stained wolf that guarded Hel's gate. This great beast was also associated with Ragnarök, the end of the world. As with the river of the dead, there was always some type of fearsome guardian that kept the damned souls confined behind the gates of the Underworld, preventing their escape. After passing the guardian, the unfortunate soul would pass through the mighty gates that led deeper into the Underworld and then finally to the point of no return. [35]

Once they had passed the guardian and through the gates of the Underworld, the damned would then come to a large central area so they could be judged. Depending upon the tradition, this judgment was done by any number of the many gods, lords, or kings and queens of the Underworld. This judgment would decide which level of the Underworld the damned soul would be sent for punishment that fit their transgression or sin. This is the next point where all the ancient traditions of the Underworld fully agree upon, that there were numerous different levels to the Underworld. The two most common number of levels that is remembered for this dreadful place is seven or nine. However, several ancient religious traditions and mythologies put the number of levels as being higher or lower than seven or nine. For example, in Buddhist belief, there are up to eighteen different levels, while in ancient Chinese Daoist and folk traditions it is believed there were ten fearsome courts of Hell. In Greek and Roman belief, they traditionally believed in only three or four levels to the Underworld, but it was not uncommon for the Greeks and Romans to think there were more. [36,37,38]

All these ancient ideas of the Underworld are best perservered in Dante Alighieri's vivid description of the "*Inferno of Hell*" in his famous masterpiece, "*The Divine Comedy.*" Although it is not an ancient text, with it being completed in 1320 AD, we do find within its pages what is possibly the single best description of this ancient idea of a multi-level Hell-like Underworld. It also provides us with a small insight into the motivation behind the "*The Divine Comedy*" and why the Catholic Church of the Medieval Age helped promote it. It was primarily done because the Catholic Church of Medieval Europe was simply trying to "Christianize" this ancient traditional belief of the Underworld as it spread across the lands of Europe.

By understanding this, we can then strip away all the "Christian symbolism," and the "Christianized thought" from Dante's Inferno. Once we do this, we will find that we are left with a list of the most common ancient beliefs of what was claimed to have occurred on each level of the Underworld. Once we have stripped away the Christian symbolism from Dante's Inferno, we are left with a multi-level Underworld that is composed of nine primary levels with fifteen sublevels, making a total of twenty-four different levels for the Underworld, as seen below. [39]

#1 – Limbo/darkness
#2 – Strong winds
#3 – Icy rain

#4 – Crushing weight

#5 – Drowning, water

#6 – Fire

#7 – Boiling, transformed into trees or hanging from thorny limbs,

#8 – Ten Levels – Torture, excrement, placed in tube-like holes with fire and heat, with the bodies distorted, torn to pieces with the claws of the demon Malebranche ("Evil Claws") and grappling hooks, repetitive tasks, biting by reptiles that bind their hands, pillars of flame, hacked & mutilated, disease, starvation.

#9 – Five levels, all related to ice or freezing, with the center being the realm of Satan that ruled over all the other levels of Hell.

Not only are we left with a detailed description of the Underworld, it also incorporates enough information that allows us to understand that almost all the ancient beliefs and mythology about the Underworld are speaking of these individual levels or sub-levels of this multi-level Underworld. For example, within the Daoist belief that there are *"ten courts of Hell"* that appear to be speaking of the ten sub-levels of the eighth level of Hell found in Dante's description. Within Buddhist belief, the Underworld has up to eighteen levels, which could be a combination of the last three levels of Dante's Inferno. It also appears to have been very common for the first seven levels to be combined into just one or two levels. In comparison, the only notable difference is that in Dante's idea the lowest levels of the Underworld were icy, cold, freezing places of endless ice, and not the fiery Hell of the damned that is traditionally believed within modern western Christian thought. This is because of the Medieval Christian belief that Hell was a cold frozen place because it was a place that was as far as one could get from the light and love of God. [40]

If we take this information and combine it with our esoteric knowledge of the symbolism and the secret history of creation that it holds. We can begin understanding several of the mysteries surrounding the Underworld that helps bring it out of the realm of mythology.

Our first step is the realization that the Underworld was like the mighty Heaven was thousands of years ago and that it was a real physical place that a mere mortal could go to and return from. Not only was it a real physical place, but in all the mythologies, it was a place were only the evilest and most destructive elements of human society were sent to be punished for their sins and transgressions by the gods. Typically, this event would occur just after the individual had been exiled or banished from their community for their crimes, sins, or transgressions. Once this individual had been banished from the community, the rest of the community would view them as if they had undergone an actual physical death. Once the exiled or banished individual had left their community, they would be picked up and taken to the Underworld entrance by one of the Underworld's gods or one of their many servants.

Unfortunately, we do not know where this physical entrance of the Underworld was located. Based on the mythology and folklore, there may have been numerous entrances across the world that all led to the same Underworld. This would explain why it appears it took different people from different parts of the world longer to reach the gates of the Underworld than it did others. But, unfortunately, the actual location of this terrible place appears to have been truly lost to history, or if it has been found, it has never been disclosed to the public in any manner. According to numerous ancient myths, sometimes an individual would be lucky enough to escape from the Underworld or be saved by some powerful god that took pity upon them from time to time. Once they had escaped this hell, they would tell the tales of the unimaginable horrors which happened there and thereby becoming the basis of the numerous stories of the Underworld we know of today.

Understanding that this ancient place of horrors remembered as the Underworld, ruled over by the terrible lords of death, was a real physical place. We can begin to understand that the gruesome activities that were said to have occurred there, must also be true in some fashion. If we take a closer examination of the ancient myths of the Underworld, we will discover that there are two different but equally gruesome activities that were occurring within this multi-level chamber of horrors.

The first appears to be some type of medical or possibly genetic experimentation that was being performed upon the unfortunate human victims. Within the mythology, there are numerous accounts that sound more horrific than any human experimentation under the Nazi regime during World War II. It does not take much imagination to realize that the almost unspeakable horrors of human medical experimentation that occurred during World War II would be viewed in much the same manner as we read in the ancient mythologies of the Underworld. Within many of the myths, we see the same horrific elements that seem eerily like the horrors of human medical experimentation. The myths tell us stories of the damned soul being subjected to freezing or high temperatures. In others, their bodies appear to be injected with strange substances or of having items surgically implanted within them. It is possibly even more horrifying because many myths imply that much of this is done by some type of automation while the victims were still very much alive.

The mythologies are also filled with incredible imaginary and striking icons of individuals being physically transformed into hideous monsters that possessed the elements of both humans and animals. When placed into a modern context, these nightmarish stories indicate that some form of real-time genetic engineering was being undertaken in this hellish place. Additionally, there are numerous myths of the Underworld that are filled with stories of people having to perform the same repetitive task or be subjected to the same horrific treatment in an endless cycle. This also supports the conclusion that some type of frightful medical or even possible genetic experimentation was being undertaken in this place of unspeakable suffering.

With our new understanding that the Terrans were having a critical food crisis that was putting massive strains on all levels of their society. We can speculate with confidence that these ancient stories could be related to human experimentation being done by the Terrans in order to try and regain control over their human workforce. Although this might seem horrific to us, we have seen time and time again that these Terrans normally had little to no moral or ethical problem with using genetic engineering to create a slave-race to fulfill their needs. Nor did they have any problem with having this slave-race view and worship them as gods. We have also seen that the Terrans viewed our ancestors and ourselves as little more than cattle or sheep and treated us as such.

The other activity that is said to have occurred in this Underworld could be even more gruesome than any medical or genetic experimentation that the Terrans may have performed upon our ancient ancestors. This horror appears to have been using our ancient Cro-Magnon man ancestors as a food source. Although this might be a rather gruesome subject, it is one of the oldest ideas that is associated with the multi-leveled Underworld of the Classical Age. There are numerous mythologies and folklore that speak of the many creatures and monsters of the Underworld using the damned souls as food. This idea that human beings were being used as a food source to feed the many different dark lords, horrible creatures, and evil monsters that were said have inhabited the Underworld is found in every mythology, culture, and religious tradition worldwide, including Christianity. If we look at these ancient mythologies of the Underworld with this idea in mind. We can easily imagine how this terrible world of horrors seems very much like a modern-day automated slaughter-house for processing animals.

In all the myths, once the damned soul had gone beyond the gates of the Underworld, they were judged in some manner by one or more of the various lords of the dead. We can now realize that this 'judging' of the individual may have been a type of selection process that selected or assigned grades to each individual for slaughter, much like we do with cattle or other livestock. Soon after this selection process, the damned individual would then be sent to a certain level of the Underworld to be prepared for slaughter and processed into food for shipment.

By realizing that these poor souls may have been used as a food source, we can understand that the description of the multiple level Underworld given by Dante is a step-by-step process outlining the required steps to prepare an animal corpse for food. Once the individual had been killed within the mythology, their bodies would then be skinned, gutted, and hung to bleed them out. Once the corpse had been bled out, they would then place the corpse into a cold environment to preserve it until it was needed for processing. Once they were needed, the corpse would then be removed for processing. The corpse would be butchered, possibly cooked, or persevered in some other manner, packaged, and then frozen for long-term storage or shipment. Additionally, many of the myths tell us that the numerous inhabitants of the Underworld ate them. Finally, any of the biological waste or unused body parts from either food production or medical experimentation would need to be disposed of. Which according to the myths, this biological material was burned in a massive furnace-like structure.

Although this type of scenario may seem gruesome, but when we combined these mythologies of the Underworld with our esoteric knowledge that a critical food crisis was underway. We can easily begin to understand that the Terran civilization must have been under an incredible amount of social, political, and economic stress that was tearing their civilization apart. If we also consider the added factor that there was a political faction of Terrans on Earth that opposed this massive exploitation of humans as slaves. We can easily understand how the entire political situation could quickly get out of hand once the food situation became so critical that the Terrans began using our ancient ancestors, who they viewed as little more than animals, as a food source.

Based upon on our history and first-hand experience, we know that once a government begins having trouble supplying enough food for its people, it does not take much time until it reaches a point where the entire situation begins to take on a political, economic, and social life of its own. We also know how such situations can quickly spiral out of control for all the parties involved. We also know that once this type of situation begins to unfold, it can easily lead to complete and total war. A war that can just as easily reach a point of no return that eventually destroys everything.

In this incredibly sad case, we know that the 'point-of-no-return' was when the Terrans on Earth, with the help of a small group of humans, attacked the mighty Heaven. Thereby damaging it beyond repair and dooming it and their entire civilization to certain destruction. We can also realize that trying to stop this food process may have been the real reason behind the attack on the Heaven in the first place. This then allows us to begin understanding the chain of events that led this ancient civilization, who had ruled over the Earth and their human slaves as if they were the gods themselves, to destroying itself so long ago. It also allows us to begin placing all these events into their proper order, thereby providing us with our first real look at our forgotten history.

As we know from our esoteric knowledge, our story begins with the Terrans creating the First-Men or Neanderthal. Which based upon new finds, it appears that Neanderthal may have first appeared closer to 300,000 years ago, and not 225,000 years ago which has been the accepted time of their appearance in the fossil record. This would mean that the horrible slavery of the First-men experienced may have gone on for almost a hundred thousand years longer than was originally presented. [41,42]

The next major event to occur was the legendary Fall of the Watchers and the freedom of the First-Men. Which we estimated to have occurred around 155,000 BC ($\pm$10,000 years). We also explored the evidence of the tremendous genetic reset that occurred sometime between 100,000 to 200,000 years ago. Where 90% of all animal life on Earth was genetically reset back to zero. We also discovered that the 'creation' of the world as it is recorded in the Book of Genesis is most likely speaking of this mysterious genetic reset. The next significant event to occur was the reconquest of the Earth by the Terran government and the defeat of the Fallen Watchers. An event that eventually resulted in the Great Deluge and the destruction of the world the Fallen Watchers had built around 72,000 BC ($\pm$5,000 years).

As we have touched upon during our journey, the time of the Fallen Watchers and the Lord-of-Light, came to an end once the Terrans had reestablished control. It appears that the great Lord-of-Light was replaced entirely with the mighty Heaven taking his place among our Neanderthal ancestors. We also learned that once the Terrans defeated the Fallen Watchers with the help of allies on Earth, they established a new Supreme god. This political change was recorded within ancient mythology as the first great war in Heaven with the overthrow of the First gods. To the Greeks, this was when the Titan Cronus overthrew his father, Uranus, Father Heaven, with the help of the Earth Mother.

Within the ancient mythology of this political change among the gods, we get a small glimpse of the fundamental disagreement among the different factions of Terrans. Just as with the overthrow of Cronus by Zeus, the overthrow of Uranus by Cronus was because of the way Uranus poorly treated his and Gaea's children, the Titans. By realizing that the Titans were great earthmoving and mining machines, we can understand that there was some form of political, economic, and labor disagreement about using these machines and how to exploit humanity to supply the food and other resources they needed for their civilization. With it rather apparent that one side wanted to continue using the great machines, while in contrast, the other side wanted to use our ancient ancestors.

Within the mythologies, it is implied that some type of agreement was reached between the parties after the Great Deluge. It is made clear that the great machines or Titans would still be used and that our ancient Neanderthal ancestors would also be exploited, but not at the same level as before the Fall of the Watchers. The primary reason for this agreement appears to be the simple fact that the Neanderthal population was almost wiped out by the reconquest of Earth and the Great Deluge.

The exploitation and slavery of our Neanderthal ancestors after the Great Deluge appears to have been much more humane during this time. According to the mythology, this time is remembered as a great Golden Age when everybody, including the gods, knew their place in the grand order of creation. It was a time of a simple and straightforward religious belief system for Neanderthal that was primarily focused on the worship of Earth Mother, with the great Sky-Father being of lesser importance, built around the symbolism of the Bull or First-men.

The next significant development was the creation of Cro-Magnon man and the mysterious Hairy Man of legend. This event occurred roughly around 39,000 BC with it resulting in a short war that is remembered in the Bible as the destruction of the cities of the plains known as Sodom and Gomorrah. This short war is also recorded as the first radioactive spike we explored in our journey through the Dream Vision of Enoch.

Although the information is vague, we can once again clearly see that the Terrans were broken into at least two separate political groups or factions with an unknown number of other special interest groups. It appears rather apparent that the Terran government wanted to exploit and use our ancient ancestors as slaves. Whilst in comparison, the Terrans that were situated on Earth and remembered as the Earth Mother had some type of moral or ethical problem with this exploitation and slavery of our ancestors with numerous economic and political factors contributing towards their opposition. This allows us to speculate with some confidence that one of the primary political drivers in their society was this basic economic argument about using our ancient ancestors as slaves instead of using their technology and machinery to supply the food and resources they needed.

If we also consider that the Terrans and ourselves are very closely related with similar thinking and behavior. We can understand that these massive machines, the great Titans, must have been costly to operate and maintain from an economic point of view. While simple humans, whom they viewed as little more than animals and who were also a product of their genetic engineering, must have been seen as an incredibly cheap, low maintenance, and easy to control resource. Which given their overwhelming need to supply food and resources for their entire civilization, it was, to put it bluntly, a no brainer for them. It was simple economics with the added plus that they viewed us as nothing more than stupid animals to be used as they needed or wanted.

The coming of Cro-Magnon man and the general replacement of Neanderthal appears to have been a critical part of this transition. One of the more remarkable changes to occur during this transition period to our Cro-Magnon man ancestors was the coming of what we call the Bronze Age. Amazingly, although our Cro-Magnon man ancestors were starting to use metal on a large scale at this early point in time. The *"gods of the forge"* commonly known as the *"Smith gods"* and traditionally associated with metalworking do not appear until after the Exodus and the new pantheon of gods it brought to the world. Although this might seem strange at first, it does give us a unique insight that shows us that human society changed very little with the coming of Cro-Magnon man. With the great change not occurring for thousands of years until the great war of the gods and the great Exodus out of Egypt at around 32,000 BC. It also shows us that it was around this time that the Terrans began requiring our ancestors to supply metal to them, thereby completely replacing the need for the great machines.

As we have learned throughout our journey, the great Exodus out of Egypt by the Israelites was a much more complex and vital event than almost all have ever even suspected. It was essentially a complete and total takeover of all the operations on Earth that replaced the Terrans' massive machinery and the labor needed to maintain it with a human labor force. Not only did the Terrans once again enslave humanity on a grand scale as they had done with the First-Men. But they also introduced a new worldwide rigid religious, social, economic, and political system to control their new human workforce. This massive worldwide undertaking is remembered as the great Exodus out of Egypt by the tribes of Israel, first under Moses and Aaron's leadership and then through a later second phase with their journey around the world under the leadership of the legendary divine twin brothers.

This understanding once again allows us to answer the great mystery of why all the different ancient cultures worldwide all have the same architecture style, gods, iconography, mythology, and the same polytheistic religious structure built around the complete devotion and sacrifice to the gods. It is simply because every single ancient Bronze Age culture and civilization was either taken over or completely wiped out by the second phase of the Exodus under the leadership of the divine twin brothers. It was the establishment of this new worldwide system of exploitation and slavery that led humanity into a great Dark Age. A time of religion that was ruled over by an elite class who were the descendants of those men who saw God and were appointed to their places of power and given their right to rule by the divine twin brothers during their great trek around the world. This great Dark Age lasted until the destruction of the First Temple, which resulted from the corruption of the original polytheistic religion by the followers of a radically violent sect of the monotheistic human-centered religion of Zoroastrianism.

Although it is challenging to place exact dates on these ancient events, we do know that the events surrounding Enoch being taken from the generations of the Earth and the destruction of the First Temple occurred sometime around 14,415 BC. (±50 years). With this date in hand and our esoteric knowledge that the great Exodus out of Egypt began around 32,000 BC with it taking approximately 5,600 years to fully complete and establish this new system of control over humanity. We can realize that this great Dark Age of religion and slavery to the gods may have lasted approximately 11,985 years.

At some point during this great Dark Age, a new human-centered monotheistic belief arose, Zoroastrianism. A religion and way of thinking that began to challenge the system imposed upon humanity by the gods. As we have discovered, as this new religion spread and began to take hold, it eventually led to the destruction of the First Temple, which in turn, collapsed the entire food and resource system that the Terrans relied upon to support their civilization. As this system fell apart, it led to incredible social, political, and economic chaos that ultimately led to a war that in the end, completely destroyed their civilization and everything they had built.

With this new esoteric knowledge, we almost have a complete picture of what occurred all those thousands of years ago that ultimately led to the destruction of their civilization on Earth and Mars. In the next chapter, we will begin our final leg of our journey into the secret history of creation and answer one of the most enigmatic mysteries of the ancient world and how the Terrans ruled their human subjects during the long Dark Age.

Chapter 10

One final mystery

As we have discovered on our journey through the Exodus and beyond, the mystery behind the great Dark Age that befell humanity that started with the collapse of Bronze Age civilizations was due to the second phase of the Exodus under the leadership of the divine twin brothers. Over time the once-great Bronze Age civilizations were slowly replaced with a simple agriculturally based society ruled over by a small group of primarily illiterate tribal elites.

These new elite rulers were broken into two different but equally powerful classes. With one being a warrior class led by a King, while the other was a priesthood led by the High-priest. Both classes of rulers claimed to be the direct descendants of the original leaders of their tribes during the time of the Exodus. These rulers also imposed a new religion with a new pantheon of gods upon the local populations they conquered. A religion that preached a strict belief of absolute devotion to the will of the gods that was based upon on a new polytheistic religion that was often fused with the existing local traditions, customs, and rituals so much so that it created entirely new cultures.

We have learned a great deal about how these new societies of this Dark Age were structured and why the art of writing was lost, amongst other things. Yet, we still have an abysmal understanding of the people who composed this new elite class that ruled over a mostly rural population of agricultural workers.

Although there is scant knowledge about these elite rulers, there are numerous clues that can be found when we realize that this time was not a complete "Dark Age" as it is so often depicted within the history books. It was a time akin to when the Catholic Church, with the aid of local rulers had complete and total domination over all phases of Medieval European society, often ruling with an iron fist. It was a time when religion dominated all levels of government, economics, and society from birth to the grave.

As with Medieval Europe, even though it was a time deeply influenced and controlled by religion, it was also a time where we see the flowering and the building of vast temple complexes dedicated to the gods. These massive religious complexes were infused with incredible artwork that recounted the extraordinary story of the Exodus and the founding of their societies written in stone. These sites tended to become the new centers of social interaction for the native populations. In time, these sites also became the de facto power centers from which the new elites would rule.

Within these ancient temple complexes, we find our first clues that help us to identify these new elites and their claims to rule. In all of them, we find the same story. A story of how their right to rule comes directly from the gods, commonly known in the western world as the *Divine Right of Kings."* We also find that these elites are connected in some manner to the divine twin brothers within the various mythologies. It appears very common for the twin brothers to slowly transform into gods or semi-divine beings directly connected to the gods as the centuries went by. Incredibly, as the twin brothers slowly transformed into legend, the original land claims that are remembered in the Bible that were the reason for the second phase of the Exodus, seem to have disappeared in the process. It is unknown why these original land claims were lost, but this missing information is crucial to understanding how all the various ancient civilizations were at one time, all connected through culture, religious belief, mythology, symbolism, and architecture.

While much of the information from this period has been all but lost, destroyed, obscured, or in most cases-just not recorded, there is an essential clue from a most unlikely source that will provide us with a small glimpse into this lost time period and the mysterious men and women who ruled over it. Not only will this clue help us identify who these elite rulers were, but it will also allow us to answer one of the greatest mysteries and enigmas of the ancient world. The worldwide phenomena of individuals with elongated skulls and why modern scholars go to such great lengths to ignore or debunk them.

At first, it might seem a bit strange that these oddly shaped skulls could have anything to do with our journey into the Exodus or the legendary divine twin

182

brothers. Nevertheless, we will soon learn how these mysterious people with their strangely shaped skulls are far more important than any have imagined. We will also discover how they are the key to understanding who the elite rulers of the great Dark Age really were. To understand how these elongated skull people fit into the story, we must first explore what little we know about these people from modern science.

According to modern scholars and archeologists, all elongated skulls are always rationalized as a form of head-binding or artificial cranial deformation. This practice of identifying all elongated skulls as the result of intentional artificial cranial deformation began in the first half of the 19th century to explain the unusual skulls discovered in Peru, South America and in Southeastern Europe in the Crimea. Since the early 19th century to this day, individuals with elongated skulls have been found worldwide. [1]

Remarkably, there is ample evidence that destroys the scientific paradigm that all elongated skulls are exclusively the product of artificial cranial deformation through head-binding. This is simply because since 1852 there have been numerous fetuses with elongated skulls found in-utero. This strongly suggests that these individuals were not fully 'human,' i.e., of Homo sapiens. Besides, there are numerous elongated skulls of young infants under the age of one year of age that indicate no extraneous artificial pressure was induced. Remarkably, such knowledge was readily available to European researchers as early as 1838. There have also been numerous mummies found in Peru that contain fetuses with an elongated skull in-utero since the two original specimens were found during the mid-1800s. Furthermore, there appears to have been hundreds of infants and very young children with elongated skulls that are far too young for such a suggested head-binding to have an effect, with no signs of external pressure ever being applied to the skulls that have been found all over the world. [2,3,4,5,6,7]

Much more recently, Brien Forester of Hidden Inca Tours has been able to obtain and test DNA taken from several different elongated skulls from Paracas and Nazca, in Peru, South America. In the first round of testing, Mitochondrial DNA or 'mDNA' was recovered from one of the skulls, with the results that were obtained being highly controversial. The mDNA results showed that the individual was a hybrid of some type; with its mother being human, while its father is unidentified. [8]

A significant number of people concluded that the unknown father was of extraterrestrial origin. However, it is more likely that the father is not of extraterrestrial origin but rather one of the unidentified, closely related hominids we know that existed at the time. The next controversial finding was that it appeared highly unlikely that this individual would have been able to interbred with humans and could only breed with other hybrids like itself. Even then, it appears that mating may have proven difficult and highly dangerous for the mother. In addition to these results, it was discovered that several of the skulls from Paracas region of South America had genetic markers that have only been found in Middle Eastern populations and not in South American ones. [9]

At first glance, these results may appear to be initially of lesser importance and attributed to various additional factors that are easily dismissed. Nevertheless, as we will now begin to learn, these controversial results are pivotal towards understanding who these people were and why they are ignored. To better understand who these unidentified hominids were, we must first turn to what may seem like an unusual but familiar place of folklore and fairy tales.

The critical narrative that interweaves such folklore is that regardless of the story being told, 'persons of royalty' were always distinctively recognizable to the everyday person, even if they were in disguise. This common belief is almost universally known and is still widely used within modern storytelling. What is truly remarkable is the fact that not one of these ancient myths, legends, folklore, or fairy tales tells us why 'royalty' was always so recognizable to the commoner. We tend to fill in these little blanks with the idea that perhaps it is their behavior and being waited on hand and foot without the need to correlate it with their physical appearance.

If we assume that it was because of their "appearance" and not their "behavior," as has been traditionally done. It becomes incredibly easy to understand that an individual with an elongated skull would find it next to impossible to hide and would be instantly recognizable to a commoner. Almost every individual with an elongated skull found outside of Paracas, Peru, tends to be a royal burial. The few that are not royalty are clearly high-ranking elites who appear to be some type of religious leader or a great warrior who had somehow earned the right to be buried with royal trappings. When we combine this idea of it being their appearance with the traditional ideas and customs regarding royalty along with the controversial DNA testing, we can figure out for the first time who these elongated skull people were and how they fit into this story.

Our first step is to realize these elongated skull people were 'royalty.' Once we understand this, we can then understand many of the ancient customs that are still applied to royalty to this day. The first being the universal tradition that royalty can only marry other royals. It has been traditionally believed that the primary reason for this was because of the family lines of inheritance for wealth and political power. However, when we consider the mDNA from the elongated skulls and that these people could not breed with normal humans or any other closely related hominids alive at the time. We can quickly understand that this ancient custom of royalty only marrying other royalty was simply because they could not breed successfully with commoners and produce children that could inherit their power and standing.

With understanding that the ruling class of these ancient societies was composed of these elongated skull people with their limited ability to mate and produce offspring. We can begin explaining the mystery of why the original members of the *"tribes of Israel"* under Moses and Aaron were forbidden to marry foreign wives or husbands. In chapter seven of the Book of Deuteronomy, we are told that not only are the Israelites forbidden to marry outside of the tribes, but we are also told that these tribes of Israel were *"the fewest of all people."* This entire mystery quickly melts away with realizing that the elites, if not all the members of the tribes of Israel were primarily composed of these elongated skull people. They would have been a distinct class of people that formed the backbone of the government and religious class of rulers that could only mate with others like themselves. These 'Chosen Ones' became the new Kings and priests of the societies they took over during the second phase of the Exodus. Their elongated skulls are what singled them out as being 'different' from the commoner.

According to the Bible, not only were the Israelites the *"fewest of all the people,"* but they were also supposed to be the *"chosen ones"* that were a *"holy people."* If we consider that in the ancient world, government and religion tended to be the same thing. We can easily imagine how a small group of people with elongated skulls that initially formed the upper leadership of the tribes would, in time, come to dominate all the elite classes of society. Since it is the general rule that ancient texts only recorded the actions of society's elites and very seldom the lower classes. We can then understand that these people would view themselves as the *"chosen ones"* ordained by the gods to be a *"holy people,"* leading the great unwashed masses to the proper service and devotion to the gods.

Unfortunately, we have next to no evidence or records of how these 'chosen leaders' actually ruled. Nevertheless, based on biblical tradition, mythology, and ancient folklore, we can speculate with some confidence that it was a harsh and often brutal rule where their word was unquestionable law. A time when any member of the lower classes could be killed as punishment for the smallest of infractions. We are also provided an important clue that their rule was unkind once the First Temple was destroyed, when the lower classes began to overthrow them. Because not only did the common people overthrow these elites, but they also went to great lengths to erase all traces and memory of these leaders.

The best-known example of this erasing of these rulers is the ever-famous heretic Pharaoh Amenhotep IV, better known as Akhenaten. Once Akhenaten had died, the ancient Egyptians went to great lengths to remove all traces of him from existence. His temples were destroyed, with the material being used to construct new temples to the old gods. All records that contained his name were changed or completely rewritten to remove any reference to him with all engravings, carvings, or statues of him destroyed—thereby erasing him from memory and history as if he never existed, while also denying him an afterlife in the process.

As seen in the few surviving statues and carvings, Akhenaten, along with his wife and children, had an elongated skull. This allows us to realize that it is highly likely that Akhenaten was a first attempt to place a 'chosen one' in power in Egypt. However, as we all know, the Egyptians ultimately rejected Akhenaten's rule and his religious teachings. Although the Egyptians rejected Akhenaten, it is evident that many of the events surrounding the second phase of the Exodus and the divine twin brothers' stories do become incorporated into Egyptian thought, society, and religious belief.

It is unknown how this happened, but it is highly probable that it occurred after the 'Sea Peoples' arrived and conquered the other Bronze Age civilizations around the Mediterranean as these invaders established new civilizations and societies. The Egyptians had to deal with these new societies through trade. Eventually, as the centuries went along, the Egyptians just naturally began to incorporate these new people's stories into their society and culture. During this long process, they changed the stories into something uniquely Egyptian, very similar to what happened to the stories, customs, and rituals in China and Japan.

By understanding who these elongated skull people were, we can very easily understand why modern scholars and archeologists go to such great lengths to either ignore or debunk these people. It is merely because sooner or later, the connection would be made to the legendary divine twin brothers and the second phase of the great Exodus out of Egypt by the Indo-European speaking children of Israel. Once this connection is made, the next step is to realize that these people are the elite ruling class of ancient people known as the Hebrews, and later as the Israelites. This realization also helps explain why these people were hated and looked upon with such disdain in the Classical ancient world. They were a reminder of the great Dark Age when the average person was little more than a slave, always at their divine mercy. Additionally, we can also realize that the later followers of Judaism, commonly known as the Jews, had little to no connection to the original Israelites and were primarily viewed as heretics by most people.

This then brings us to the next logical question. Which is, of course, did these elongated skull people have any special powers? Unfortunately, according to the ancient stories, these people do not appear to have extraordinary mental powers. The only thing that appears to make these people different than the average human is that they seem to have the ability to communicate directly with the gods through dreams and visions. The myths also refer to many of these individuals as having some unique healing ability. Nevertheless, it should be noted that these stories tend to be so vague, it is just as equally possible that they did not have any "healing powers," but they were just slightly more intelligent than the average person of the time and just applied basic medical care, so it appeared they had healing abilities. Additionally, numerous of these individuals came to be known as Soothsayers, Seers, magicians, prophets, and Shaman, who filled the royal courts and were the advisers of kings and queens. There are numerous stories within the Bible that speak of these individuals' importance in consulting or advising the king or queen of different kingdoms. According to the Bible, and historically with the Medes, these individuals normally came from one tribe of people.

One of the best known of these ancient biblical stories related to Soothsayers and Seers is the story of Joseph being sold into slavery by his eleven brothers and later becoming an adviser to Pharaoh through his ability to interpret the meaning of dreams as told in the Book of Genesis. As we already know, the entire Jacob and Esau story is related to the creation of first Cro-Magnon men and the legendary Hairy Man. As we will now learn, the story of Joseph is much like his father's story and that it is the creation story of this new class of elite rulers that have elongated skulls. One of the greatest mysteries of this story is why Joseph stands out from his eleven brothers and why his father Jacob cared for him more than his brothers. The reason that is given in Genesis is:

"Now Israel (Jacob) loved Joseph more than all his children, because he was the son of his old age: and he made him a coat of many colours. And when his brethren saw that their father loved him more than all his brethren, they hated him, and could not speak peaceably unto him."
(Genesis 37: 3,4)

Although the true meaning of this *"coat of many colours"* is unknown. It has traditionally been viewed as a unique tunic or robe representing a special relationship or favor. It is also commonly believed by many that it was a robe that extended to the feet with long-sleeves that was richly-ornamented with gold threading and possibly with gemstones sewn into it. [10]

These ideas of what the *"coat of many colours"* is a remarkably good description of the common idea of the traditional robe believed to have been worn by wizards or magicians in modern pop-culture. As we already know, modern day wizards are also known by many names, with mage, warlock, witch, sorcerers, or spellcaster being some of the more common ones. They are commonly based upon and thought of as 'wise old men' who practice magic, who typically acts as a mentor, with Merlin from the King Arthur saga being a prime example.

Although in our modern world, wizards, or magicians as they were known to the ancients, are thought of being primarily in the world of fantasy with them being either good or evil. Nevertheless, the magicians that appear in myth, folklore, and even the Bible are not always so clearly labeled as good or evil. In most traditions, they tend to be unpredictable and of uncertain character, with them being neither good nor evil with their treatment of other people, usually depending on how they are treated. One of the most common examples of this is the tales that speak of a person meeting an old woman or man and not realizing that they are dealing with a witch or magician. In most cases, the witch or magician will reward kindness and punish rudeness. Although these ancient magicians tended neither to be good or evil, they were commonly believed to have possessed the unique skill of interpreting the meaning of dreams in the hope to foretell future events. [11]

According to the Bible, all these qualities were possessed by Joseph. In the story of Joseph, we are told that Pharaoh had two disturbing dreams; in the first, he saw that seven fat cows that devoured seven lean cows. In his second dream, he saw seven withered ears of corn devour seven fat ears of corn. When all of Pharaoh's magicians, wise men, soothsayers, seers, and prophets had failed in their attempts to interpret his dreams. Pharaoh's chief butler who had been imprisoned with Joseph told him of Joseph's ability to interpret dreams. Pharaoh then summoned Joseph, who then interpreted his dreams as meaning that in the land of Egypt there would be seven years of abundance that would be followed by seven years of famine. Joseph then advised Pharaoh to store surplus corn during the years of abundance to weather the years of famine and save the people of Egypt. Pharaoh takes Joseph's advice, and, after these events unfold, Joseph is given great political power in Pharaoh's court.

With our esoteric knowledge, it is not much of a leap to realize that it is probable that Joseph, along with his full brother, Benjamin, were the first of these elongated skull people. Whereas the tribe of Benjamin would provide Israel's first King, there was no tribe named for Joseph. In this ancient setting, and although the Bible provides a slightly different chain of events, strongly supports that Joseph was the first Head-priest of these people. It was also very common at this ancient time the priesthood normally would not be allowed to own land or wealth and would not have been given a title, or tribal name. Hence, this could explain why no tribe was named for Joseph. It also explains why an imprisoned slave would have been allowed to interpret Pharaoh's dreams. It is also easy to imagine that if Joseph had an elongated skull, the Egyptians and his brothers would have looked upon him as being different and possibly even touched by the gods themselves.

In time, Joseph's brothers and his father Jacob join him in Egypt after he attained a high standing within Pharaoh's court. In time and primarily because of Joseph, his brothers become the elite class of rulers and religious leaders of tribes of Israel. Although there is little evidence, it is easy to imagine how their physical appearance with an elongated skull would set them apart from the average Egyptian. It also helps explain the mystery as to why the Egyptians would have allowed foreigners to settle in their lands and why these Israelites were viewed as being so 'different' from the Egyptian people.

This knowledge also helps explain why and how the heretic Pharaoh Akhenaten came to power, even though he was not the firstborn of Pharaoh. It may have been because of his physical appearance of being like Joseph and the other elite rulers of the tribes of Israel, whose God had devastated the land of Egypt and led them on their great Exodus, as spoken of in the Bible and the Dream Vision of Enoch. This again brings us back to the idea that their rule was brutal and cruel for the average person and why they were wiped from history once their grip on power began failing.

Remarkably, this information destroys the currently accepted mythology and historical timeline put forward by scholars and archeologists. However, it also provides another critical connection back to the mighty gods that our ancient ancestors worshipped and modern-day UFO lore.

As we learned with Esau being the legendary Hairy-Man that is now commonly known as Bigfoot or Sasquatch. Modern UFO lore is filled with stories of 'aliens' that appear to be human in appearance but with large elongated skulls. This allows us to understand that these elongated skull people also survived the great destruction and the transformation and must still be in service to the gods. This is another example of the deception that these so-called gods perpetuate upon humanity to make people think they are "aliens" from another planetary system and not originally from the Earth. This also obscures the fact that these creatures utterly destroyed their civilization over twelve thousand years ago.

We must also consider another critical connection when thinking about modern UFO lore and the ancient world. This connection is the modern-day idea of Deep Underground Military Bases, commonly referred to as D.U.M.B.s. According to the claims, an unknown number of alleged underground bases have been built by and are currently occupied by 'aliens.' It is also claimed that a small group of human allies is aiding them. Unfortunately, outside of the many claims, there is little to no available evidence that such bases exist, and many believe them to hoaxes or misinformation. Although that may or may not be true, there is no denying that numerous governments of the world have built an unknown number of underground military bases, with the United States Air Force's Cheyenne Mountain Complex located under Cheyenne Mountain in Colorado near the city of Colorado Springs, possibly being the most famous of these underground bases.

What is truly remarkable is that within this modern-day UFO lore, there are numerous claims that the same horrific things that our ancient ancestors described as happening in the Underworld are still occurring to this very day on these bases. Many of these accounts claim that gruesome human medical and genetic experiments are being performed by non-human hands. If we take these claims and combine this with the general idea that these creatures may have used humans as a food source. Then, these claims become eerily similar to the ancient accounts of a Hell-like Underworld. All of which leaves us to wonder if there is not more truth to these claims and that some remnant of the Underworld may still exist somewhere within the bowels of the Earth.

Bibliography and References

Chapter 1

1. von-Bruening, R.J.; "UNLOCKING THE DREAM VISION: The secret history of creation." R.J. VON-BRUENING, USA. 2018. ISBN: 978-1-7329096-1-8. Chapter 18, pp. 301.
2. Roberts, J.M., "History of the World." Oxford University Press, New York. 1993. ISBN: 0-19-521043-3. pp. 242-243.
3. Perry, Marvin. Chase, Myrna. Jacob, James. Jacob, Margaret. Von-Laue, Theodore.; "Western Civilization: Ideas, Politics & Society." Houghton Mifflin Company, Boston, New York. 2007. ISBN: 978-0-618-61300-7. Chapter 9, pp. 196-197.
4. von-Bruening, R.J.; "UNLOCKING THE DREAM VISION: The secret history of creation." R.J. VON-BRUENING, USA. 2018. ISBN: 978-1-7329096-1-8. Chapter 7, pp. 98-99.
5. Roberts, J.M., "History of the World." Oxford University Press, New York. 1993. ISBN: 0-19-521043-3. pp. 52-55.

Chapter 2

1. Mark, Joshua J. "Hyksos." Ancient History Encyclopedia. Last modified February 15, 2017. Accessed May 20, 2020. https://www.ancient.eu/Hyksos/.
2. Manetho's account as recorded by Josephus, Flavius. "Against Apion" Whiston, M.A., William. "The Genuine Works of Flavius Josephus, The Jewish Historian." University of Cambridge, London. 1737. 1:86-90.

3. Finkelstein, Israel.; Silberman, Neil Asher. "The Bible Unearthed: Archaeology's New Vision of Ancient Israel and the Origin of Its Sacred Texts." The Free Press, New York City. 2001. pp. 54.

4. Manetho's account as recorded by Josephus, Flavius. "Against Apion" Whiston, M.A., William. "The Genuine Works of Flavius Josephus, The Jewish Historian." University of Cambridge, London. 1737. 1:234-250.

5. Ibid.

6. Safrai, Shmuel. "The Jewish People in the First Century: Historical Geography, Political History, Social, Cultural and Religious Life and Institutions, Second Printing." Van Gorcum, Assen/Maastricht, Fortress Press, Philadelphia. 1987. ISBN: 90-232-1436-6 (Van Gorcum), ISBN: 0-8006-0602-7 (Fortress Press). pp. 1,113.

7. Manetho's account as recorded by Josephus, Flavius. "Against Apion". Whiston, M.A., William. "The Genuine Works of Flavius Josephus, The Jewish Historian." University of Cambridge, London. 1737. 1:234-250.

8. Finkelstein, Israel.; Silberman, Neil Asher. "The Bible Unearthed: Archaeology's New Vision of Ancient Israel and the Origin of Its Sacred Texts." The Free Press, New York City. 2001. pp. 54.

9. Blenkinsopp, Joseph. "Judaism, The First Phase: The Place of Ezra and Nehemiah in the Origins of Judaism." Willian B. Edrdmans Publishing Company, Grand Rapids, Michigan. 2009. ISBN: 978-0-8028645-0-5.

10. Freedman, David Noel.; Myers, Allen C.; Beck, Astrid B. "Dictionary of the Bible." Willian B. Edrdmans Publishing Company, Grand Rapids, Michigan. 2000. ISBN: 0-8028-2400-5. Heading: Hapiru, Apiru. pp. 549-550.

11. Collins, John J. "A Short Introduction to the Hebrew Bible." Fortress Press, Philadelphia. 2014. ISBN: 978-1-4514843-5-9.

12. Finkelstein, Israel.; Siblerman, Neil Asher. "David and Solomon: In Search of the Bible's Sacred Kings and the Roots of the Western Tradition." Free Press of Simon and Schuster, New York, NY. 2006. ISBN: 978-0-7432-4362-9.

13. Hamblin, William J. "Warfare in the Ancient Near East to 1,600 BC." Routledge, New York, NY. 2006. ISBN: 978-0-415-25588-2.

14. Redford, Donald B. "Egypt, Canaan and Israel in Ancient Times." Princeton University Press, Princeton, New Jersey. 1992. ISBN: 0-691-03606-3.

15. Roberts, Scott Alan.; Ward, John Richard. "The Exodus Reality: Unearthing the Real History of Moses, Identifying the Pharaohs, and Examining the Exodus from Egypt." New Page Books, A Division of Career Press, Inc., Pompton Plains, New Jersey. 2014. ISBN: 978-16016329-1-3. Chapter five.

16. Redford, Donald B. "Egypt, Canaan and Israel in Ancient Times." Princeton University Press, Princeton, New Jersey. 1992. ISBN: 0-691-03606-3.
17. Miller, Robert D. "Chieftains of the Highland Clans: A History of Israel in the 12th and 11th Centuries BC." Wipf and Stock Publishers, Eugene, Oregon. 2012. ISBN: 978-1-62032-208-6.
18. Levy, Thomas E.; Adams, Russell B.; Muniz, Adolfo. "Archaeology and the Shasu Nomads." In Richard Elliott Friedman. "Le-David Maskil: A Birthday Tribute for David Noel Freedman." Published for Biblical and Judaic Studies, The University of California, San Diego, California. 2004. 1-57506-084-1.
19. Ibid.
20. Miller, Robert D. "Chieftains of the Highland Clans: A History of Israel in the 12th and 11th Centuries BC." Wipf and Stock Publishers, Eugene, Oregon. 2012. ISBN: 978-1-62032-208-6.
21. Breasted, Hames Henry. "History of Egypt from the Earliest Time to the Persian Conquest." Literary Licensing, LLC., Whitefish, Montana. 2014. ISBN: 978-1-1981332-5-8. pp. 216.
22. Manetho's account as recorded by Josephus, Flavius, "Against Apion". Whiston, M.A., William. "The Genuine Works of Flavius Josephus, The Jewish Historian." University of Cambridge, London, England. 2009. 1737. 1:75-77.
23. Winlock, Herbert E. "The Rise and Fall of the Middle Kingdom in Thebes, First Edition." Macmillan Publishing, New York, NY. 1947. ISBN: 978-1-1355443-5-5.
24. Ibid.
25. Miller, Robert D. "Chieftains of the Highland Clans: A History of Israel in the 12th and 11th Centuries BC." Wipf and Stock Publishers, Eugene, Oregon. 2012. ISBN: 978-1-62032-208-6.
26. Hamblin, William J. "Warfare in the Ancient Near East to 1,600 BC." Routledge, New York, NY. 2006. ISBN: 978-0-415-25588-2.
27. Johnston, Sarah Iles. "Religions of the Ancient World: A Guide." The Belknap Press of Harvard University Press, Cambridge, Massachusetts, and London, England. 2004. ISBN: 0-674-01517-7. pp. 173-176.
28. Allen, Spencer L. "The Splintered Divine: A Study of Istar, Baal, and Yahweh Divine Names and Divine Multiplicity in the Ancient Near East." DeGruyter, Hubert & Co. GmbH & Co. KG, Gottingen. 2015. pp. 10-11.
29. Clay, Albert T. "The Origin of Biblical Traditions: Hebrew Legends in Babylonia and Israel." Wipf and Stock Publishers, Eugene, Oregon. 2006. ISBN: 978-1-59752-718-7. pp. 38-40.

30. Pinches, Theophilus G. "The Religion of Babylonia and Assyria." Published by the Library of Alexandria, 1908. ISBN: 978-1-4655467-0-8. pp. 15-16.

31. Fontenrose, Joseph. "Python: A Study of Delphic Myth and Its Origins." University of California Press, Berkeley, Los Angeles, London. 1980. First published 1959. ISBN: 0-520-04091-0. pp. 157-158.

32. Green, Alberto R. W.; "The Storm-god in the Ancient Near East, Volume 8 of Biblical and Judaic studies of University of California, San Diego," Eisenbrauns. 2003. ISBN: 978-1-5750606-9-9. pp. 166.

33. Armstrong, Karen. "A History of God, The 4000-Year Quest of Judaism, Christianity and Islam." Alfred A. Knopf, Inc., New York, NY. 1993. pp. 11-12.

34. Green, Alberto R. W.; "The Storm-god in the Ancient Near East, Volume 8 of Biblical and Judaic studies of University of California, San Diego." Eisenbrauns, Penn State University Press, Ann Arbor, Michigan. 2003. ISBN: 978-1-5750606-9-9. pp. 51-52, 54.

35. Armstrong, Karen. "A History of God, The 4000-Year Quest of Judaism, Christianity and Islam." Alfred A. Knopf, Inc., New York, NY. 1993. pp. 19.

36. Green, Alberto R. W.; "The Storm-god in the Ancient Near East, Volume 8 of Biblical and Judaic studies of University of California, San Diego," Eisenbrauns, Penn State University Press, Ann Arbor, Michigan. 2003. ISBN: 978-1-5750606-9-9. pp. 18-24, 59-60.

37. Ibid.

38. Ibid.

39. Redford, Donald B. "Egypt, Canaan and Israel in ancient times; New Ed edition." Princeton University Press. Princeton, New Jersey. 1993. ISBN: 978-06910008-6-2.

40. Ryholt, K.S.B.; Bulow-Jacodsen, Adam.; "The Political Situation in Egypt During the Second Intermediate Period, C. 1800-1550 BC." Carsten Niebuhr Institute of Near Eastern Studies, University of Copenhagen, Copenhagen, Denmark. 1997. ISBN: 978-8-7728942-1-8.

41. Bietak, Manfred. "Egypt and Canaan During the Middle Bronze Age." Bulletin of the American Schools of Oriental Research. The University of Chicago Press. No. 281, Egypt and Canaan in the Bronze Age. DOI: 10.2307/1357163. Feb., 1991. pp. 27-72.

42. Shubert, Steven Blake. "Encyclopedia of the Archaeology of Ancient Egypt." Routledge, Abingdon-on-Thames, United Kingdom. ISBN: 978-0-4151858-9-9. "Second Intermediated Period, overview," pp. 57.

43. Ryholt, K.S.B.; Bulow-Jacodsen, Adam. "The Political Situation in Egypt During the Second Intermediate Period, C. 1800-1550 BC." Carsten Niebuhr Institute of Near Eastern Studies, University of Copenhagen, Copenhagen, Denmark. 1997. ISBN: 978-8-7728942-1-8.

44. Oren, Eliezer D. "The Hyksos: New Historical and Archaeological Perspectives; First Edition." Symposium Series 8, University Museum Monograph, Book 96. University of Pennsylvania Museum of Archaeology and Anthropology, Philadelphia, Pennsylvania. 1997. ISBN: 978-0-9241714-6-8.

45. Booth, Charlotte. "The Hyksos Period in Egypt." Shire Egyptology, Book 27. Shire Books, Bloomsbury Publishing, London, England. 2008. ISBN: 978-0-7478063-8-7. pp. 15-18.

46. Ibid. pp. 29-31.

47. Shaw, Ian. Editor. "The Oxford History of Ancient Egypt; 1st Edition." Oxford Illustrated Histories. Oxford University, Oxford, England. 2000. ISBN: 978-0-1981503-4-3.

48. Wilson, John Albert. "The Culture of Ancient Egypt." Kessinger Legacy Reprints, Kessinger Publishing, LLC. Whitefish, Montana. 2010. ISBN: 978-1-1661369-4-9. pp. 160.

49. Booth, Charlotte. "The Hyksos Period in Egypt." Shire Egyptology, Book 27. Shire Books, Bloomsbury Publishing, London, England. 2008. ISBN: 978-0-7478063-8-7. pp. 15-18, 29-31.

50. Ibid.

51. Redford, Donald B. "The Oxford Essential Guide to Egyptian Mythology." Berkley Publishing Group of Penguin Random House. New York, NY. 2003. ISBN: 978-0-4251909-6-8. pp. 20-21.

52. Ibid.

53. Shaw, Ian. Editor. "The Oxford History of Ancient Egypt; 1st Edition." Oxford Illustrated Histories. Oxford University, Oxford, England. 2000. ISBN: 978-0-1981503-4-3. pp. 203.

54. Ryholt, K.S.B.; Bulow-Jacodsen, Adam.; "The Political Situation in Egypt During the Second Intermediate Period, C. 1800-1550 BC." Carsten Niebuhr Institute of Near Eastern Studies, University of Copenhagen, Copenhagen, Denmark. 1997. ISBN: 978-8-7728942-1-8.

55. Ibid.

56. Ibid.

57. Manetho's account as recorded by Josephus, Flavius, "Against Apion" Whiston, M.A., William. "The Genuine Works of Flavius Josephus, The

Jewish Historian." University of Cambridge, London, England. 2009. 1737. 1:75-77, 1:86-90, 1:234-250.

58. Ibid.

59. Ibid.

60. Charlesworth, James H. "The Old Testament Pseudepigrapha: Expansions of the "Old Testament" and legends, wisdom and philosophical literature, prayers, psalms and odes, and fragments of lost Judeo-Hellenistic works, Vol. II." Darton Longman & Todd. London, United Kingdom. 1984. ISBN: 978-0-2325162-7-2. pp. 703.

61. Schreiber, Mordecai.; Klenicki, Leon.; Schiff, Alvin I.; "The Shengold Jewish Encyclopedia." Schreiber Publishing, Inc., Rockville, Maryland. 2003. ISBN: 978-1-8875637-7-2. pp. 141.

62. Mills, Watson E.; Bullard, Roger Aubrey.; "Mercer Dictionary of the Bible." Mercer University Press, Macon, Georgia. 1990. ISBN: 978-0-8655437-3-7. pp. 466-467, 928.

Chapter 3

1. von-Bruening, R.J.; "UNLOCKING THE DREAM VISION: The secret history of creation." R.J. VON-BRUENING, USA. 2018. ISBN: 978-1-7329096-1-8. Chapter 8, 101-119.

2. Ibid. Chapter 9, pp. 121-137.

3. Agnes, Michael. "Webster's New World College Dictionary, Fourth Edition." IDG Books Worldwide, Foster City, California. 2001.

4. Wallis Budge, E. A.; "An Egyptian Hieroglyphic Dictionary, Volume I." Harrison And Sons, London, England. 1920.

5. Denoon, Steven. "Yan Suph: The Sea of Reeds." Faithful Life Publishers, North Fort Myers, Florida. 2013. ISBN: 978-1-93712953-8.

6. Wick, Alexis. "The Red Sea: In Search of Lost Space." University of California Press, Oakland, California. 2016. ISBN: 978-0-52028592-7.

7. Fritz, Glen A.; "The Lost Sea of the Exodus: A modern Geographical Analysis." UMI Publishing, Pennsylvania State University, State College, Pennsylvania. 2006. ISBN: 978-1-59872745-6.

8. Seiglie, Mario. "The Bible and Archaeology: The Red Sea or the Reed Sea?" June 3, 1997. Beyond Today. Accessed July 15, 2020. https://www.ucg.org/the-good-news/the-bible-and-archaeology-the-red-sea-or-the-reed-sea.

9. Karabell, Zachary. "Parting the Desert: The Creation of the Suez Canal." Vintage Books, New York, NY. 2004. ISBN: 978-0-37570812-1.

10. Burchell, S.C.; "Building the Suez Canal." HarperCollins Publishers, LLC. New York, NY. 1966. ISBN: 978-0-06020916-2.

11. Lindquist, Sandra J.; "The Red Sea Basin Province: Sudr-Nubia(!) and Maqna(!) Petroleum Systems." U.S> Department of the Interior, U.S. Geological Survey. Denver, Colorado. 1998. USGS Open-File Report OF99-50-A. Accessed July 21, 2020. https://pubs.usgs.gov/of/1999/ofr-99-0050/OF99-50A/OF99-50A.pdf.

12. Ibid.

13. Lambeck, Kurt. Rouby, Helene. Purcell, Anthony. Sun, Yiying. Sambridge, Malcolm. "Sea Level and Ice Volume since the Glacial Maximum." Proceedings of the National Academy of Sciences Oct 2014, 111 (43) 15296-15303; DOI: 10.1073/pnas.1411762111. Accessed July 25, 2020. https://www.pnas.org/content/111/43/15296.

14. Egal, Florent. "The Saudi Arabia Tourism Guide." Accessed July 25, 2020. http://www.saudiarabiatourismguide.com/jebel-al-lawz/.

15. Jabal Maqla. "Mount Sinai's Distinct Blackened Peak" June 4, 2018. Last Modified July 5, 2019. Accessed July 25, 2020. https://jabalmaqla.com/blackened-peak/.

16. Bible Archaeology, Search & Exploration (BASE) Institute. "Mt. Sinai." Bible Archeology Search and Exploration Foundation. Monument, Colorado. Accessed July 25, 2020. https://baseinstitute.org/pages/mt-sinai

17. Richardson, Joel. "Mount Sinai in Arabia." WinePress Media, Enumclaw, Washington. 2019. ISBN: 978-1-94972904-7.

18. "Finding the Mountain of Moses." Documentary by Doubting Thomas Research Foundation. Last Modified October 29, 2020. Accessed November 18, 2020. https://doubtingthomasresearch.com/.

19. Ibid.

20. Ibid.

21. Jabal Maqla. "Mount Sinai's Distinct Blackened Peak" June 4, 2018. Last Modified July 5, 2019. Accessed July 25, 2020. https://jabalmaqla.com/blackened-peak/.

22. Bible Archaeology, Search & Exploration (BASE) Institute. "Mt. Sinai." Bible Archeology Search and Exploration Foundation. Monument, Colorado. Accessed July 25, 2020. https://baseinstitute.org/pages/mt-sinai

23. Richardson, Joel. "Mount Sinai in Arabia." WinePress Media, Enumclaw, Washington. 2019. ISBN: 978-1-94972904-7.

24. Schreiber, Mordecai.; Klenicki, Leon.; Schiff, Alvin I.; "The Shengold Jewish Encyclopedia." Schreiber Publishing, Inc., Rockville, Maryland. 2003. ISBN: 978-1-8875637-7-2. pp. 141.

25. Mills, Watson E.; Bullard, Roger Aubrey.; "Mercer Dictionary of the Bible." Mercer University Press, Macon, Georgia. 1990. ISBN: 978-0-8655437-3-7. pp. 466-467, 928.

26. Encyclopaedia Britannica's editors. "Al-Hajar Mountains, Arabia." Encyclopaedia Britannica. Accessed November 18, 2020. https://www.britannica.com/place/Al-Hajar.

Chapter 4

1. Anthony, David W. "The Horse, The Wheel And Language. How Bronze-Age Riders From the Eurasian Steppes Shaped The Modern World." Princeton University Press, Princeton, New Jersey. 2007. ISBN: 978-0-691-05887-0. pp. 132,135,138,145,147,155-157,164.

2. Ibid.

3. Adams, Douglas Q.; Mallory, J.P., "Encyclopedia of Indo-European Culture." Fitzroy Dearborn Publishing, Chicago, Illinois. 1997. ISBN: 978-1-8849649-8-5. pp. 4,6,13,16,243,127-128,653.

4. Ibid.

5. Adam, Douglas Q.; Mallory, J.P.; "The Oxford Introduction to Proto-Indo-European and the Proto-Indo-European World." Oxford University Press, Oxford, New York. 2006. ISBN: 978-0-1992879-1-8. pp. 442.

6. Roberts, J.M., "History of the World." Oxford University Press, New York, NY. 1993. ISBN: 0-19-521043-3. pp. 95-104.

7. Ibid.

8. Ibid.

9. Ibid.

10. Ibid.

11. Ibid.

12. Ibid.

13. Ibid.

14. Ibid.

15. Ibid.

16. Neubecker, Ottfied.; Brooke-Little, John Philip.; Tobler, Robert. "Heraldry: Sources, Symbols, and Meaning." McGraw-Hill, New York, NY. 1976. ISBN: 978-0-0704630-8-0. pp. 120.

17. Rao, T.A. Gopinatha. "Elements of Hindu Iconography, Vol II, Part I." Law Printing House, Madras (Chennai), India. 1914. pp. 65.

18. Littlewood, R. Joy. "A Commentary on Ovid: Fasti Book 6." Oxford University Press, Oxford, New York, NY. 2006. ISBN: 978-0-19-927134-4. pp. 73.

19. Wiseman, Timothy Peter. "Remus: A Roman Myth." Press Syndicate of Cambridge University Press, New York, NY. 1995. ISBN: 0-521-48366-2. pp. 61.

20. Rykwert, Joseph. "The Idea of a Town: The Anthropology of Urban Form in Rome, Italy, and the Ancient World." The MIT Press, Cambridge, Massachusetts. ISBN: 979-0-26268056-1. pp. 101, 159.

21. Berry, Thomas. "Religions of India: Hinduism, Yoga, Buddhism." Columbia University Press, New York, NY. ISBN: 978-0-23110781-5. pp. 20-21.

22. Griswold, Hervey De Witt. "The Religion of the Rigveda." Motilal Banarsidass Publishers Private Limited, Delhi, India. Firist Edition 1971, Reprint 1999. ISBN: 81-208-0745-6. pp. 177-180.

23. Murray, Alexander Stuart. "Manual of Mythology: Greek and Roman, Norse, and Old German, Hindoo and Egyptian Mythology, 2nd Edition." First Published by C. Scribner's Sons. 1891. Reprint by Kessinger Publishing, LLC., Whitefish, Montana. 2004. ISBN: 978-0-76618976-8. pp. 329-331.

24. Max Müller, Friedrich. "Contributions to the Science of Mythology." Longmans, Green and Company, London, New York, Bombay. 1897. pp. 744-749.

25. Griswold, Hervey De Witt. "The Religion of the Rigveda." Motilal Banarsidass Publishers Private Limited, Delhi, India. First Edition 1971, Reprint 1999. ISBN: 81-208-0745-6. pp. 180-183, & footnotes.

26. Macdonell, Arthur Anthony. "Vedic Mythology." First Published Oxford University Press, 1897. Reprint: Motilal Banarsidass Publishers Private Limited, Delhi, India. 1995. ISBN: 978-81-208-1113-3. pp. 15-16, 92-93.

27. Bodewitz, H.W.; "The Daily Evening and Morning Offering (Agnihotra) According to the Brahmanas." First Published by E.J. Bril, Leiden, The Netherlands. 1976. Reprint: Motilal Banarsidass Publishers Private Limited, Delhi, India. 2003. ISBN: 81-208-1951-9. pp. 14-19.

28. Lochtefeld, James G.; "The Illustrated Encyclopedia of Hinduism: A-M." The Rosen Publishing Group, New York, NY. 2002. ISBN: 0-8239-3179-X. pp. 14-15.

29. Cavendish, Richard. "Mythology, An Illustrated Encyclopedia of the Principal Myths and Religions of the World." Tiger Book International, London, England. 1998. ISBN: 978-18-4056070-1.

30. Jansen, Eva Rudy. "The Book of Hindu Imagery: Gods, Manifestations and Their Meaning." RedWheel/Weiser, LLC., Newburyport, Massachusetts. 1993. ISBN: 978-9-07459710-4. pp. 65.

31. Roshen, Dalal. "Hinduism: An Alphabetical Guide." Penguin Books, London, England. 2010. ISBN: 978-0-14-341421-6. pp. 5, 39, 247, 343, 399-401.

32. Flood, Gavin. "An Introduction to Hinduism." Cambridge University Press, Cambridge, United Kingdom. 1996. ISBN: 0-521-43304-5. pp. 113.

33. Kinsley, David. "Hindu Goddesses: Vision of the Divine Feminine in the Hindu Religious Traditions." University of California Press, Berkley, California. 1986. ISBN: 0-520-06339-2.

34. Flood, Gavin. "An Introduction to Hinduism." Cambridge University Press, Cambridge, United Kingdom. 1996. ISBN: 978-0-521-43878-0. pp. 17.

35. McDaniel, June. "Offering Flowers, Feeding Skulls: Popular Goddess Worship in West Bengal." Oxford University Press, Oxford, England. 2004. ISBN: 978-0-19-534713-5. pp. 90.

36. Possehl, Gregory L.; "The Indus Civilization: A Contemporary Perspective." Rowman and Littlefield Publishing Inc., Walnut Creek, California. 2003. ISBN 0-7591-0172-8. pp. 238.

37. Bryant, Edwin. "The Quest for the Origins of Vedic Culture: The Indo-Aryan Migration Debate." Oxford University Press, Oxford, England. 2001. ISBN: 0-1951-3777-9. pp. 203, 306.

38. Kochhar, Rajesh. "The Vedic People: Their History and Geography." First published by Orient Longman. 2000. Reprint: Orient Blackswan Private Limited, Himayatnagar, Hyderabad, India. 2009. ISBN: 978-8125013846. pp. 185-186.

39. Puhvel, Joan. "Comparative Mythology." Johns Hopkins University Press, Baltimore, Maryland. 1989. ISBN: 0-8018-3938-6. pp. 285-286.

40. "Effectuation of Shani Adoration." Saturn Publication, Lvt, Ltd. New Delhi, India. 2006. ISBN: 978-81-9063327-1-3. pp. 10-15.

41. Wilson, H.H.; "The Vishnu Purana, Volume 1." Read Books, Vancouver, BC. 2006. ISBN: 978-1-406-71541-5. pp. 384.

42. Macdonell, Arthur Anthony. "Vedic Mythology." Motilal Banarsidass Publishers Private Limited, Delhi, India. 1995. ISBN: 978-81-2081113-3. pp. 172.

43. Roberts, J.M., "History of the World." Oxford University Press, New York, NY. 1993. ISBN: 0-19-521043-3. pp. 27, 40, 45, 72, 80, 85, 102, 107, 117, 128, 354, 369.

44. Ibid.

45. Ibid.

46. Ibid.

Chapter 5

1. Hays, Jeffrey. "Early History of Cambodia and the Khmers. Last modified April 2014. Accessed June 1, 2020. http://factsanddetails.com/southeast-asia/Cambodia/sub5_2a/entry-2838.html.

2. Ibid.

3. "Hindu Mythology, Naga." Encyclopaedia Britannica. Accessed June 15, 2020. https://www.britannica.com/topic/naga-Hindu-mythology.

4. Apte, Vaman Shivram. "The Student's English-Sanskrit Dictionary." Motilal Banarsidass Publishers Private Limited, Delhi, India. 1960. ISBN: 81-208-0299-3. pp. 423, 539.

5. Flood, Gavin. "An Introduction to Hinduism." Cambridge University Press, Cambridge, United Kingdom. 1996. ISBN: 978-0-521-43878-0. pp. 151.

6. Elgood, Heather. "Hinduism and the Religious Arts." Cassell, London, New York. 1999. ISBN: 0-304-33820-6. pp. 234.

7. Plubins, Rodrigo Q. "Khmer Empire." Ancient History Encyclopedia. Last modified March 12, 2013. Accessed June 1, 2020 https://www.ancient.eu/Khmer_Empire/.

8. Ibid.

9. Ibid.

10. Radcliffe-Brown, A. R. "The Rainbow-Serpent Myth of Australia." The Journal of the Royal Anthropological Institute of Great Britain and Ireland 56 (1926): 19-25. doi:10.2307/2843596.

11. Roberts, J.M., "History of the World." Oxford University Press, New York, NY. 1993. ISBN: 0-19-521043-3. pp. 105-117.

12. Ibid.

13. Ibid.

14. Ibid.

15. Ibid.
16. Ibid.
17. Ibid.
18. Ibid.
19. Ibid.
20. Ibid.
21. Ibid.
22. Ibid.
23. Ibid.
24. Roberts, J.M., "History of the World." Oxford University Press, New York, NY. 1993. ISBN: 0-19-521043-3. pp. 369-378.
25. Ibid.
26. Ibid.
27. Ibid.
28. Ibid.
29. Ibid.

Chapter 6

1. Whelan, Ed. "First Americans Arrived by Sea Over 15,000 Years Ago, Surprise Finding Suggests." August 30, 2019. Ancient Origins, Dublin, Ireland. Last modified June 24, 2019. Accessed June 15, 2020. https://www.ancient-origins.net/news-history-archaeology/first-americans-0012508?fbclid=IwAR2YxAOnGtHDVCZH15fbpondjRzmgp36lfATKybz vYtTadi3ZCtRZcu9nIA.

2. McDermott, Alicia. "By Land or Sea? The Heated Debate on the Peopling of the Americas Continues." August 13, 2017. Ancient Origins, Dublin, Ireland. Last modified June 24, 2019. Accessed June 15, 2020. https://www.ancient-origins.net/news-science-space/land-or-sea-heated-debate-peopling-americas-continues-008593.

3. Diehl, Richard A. "The Olmecs: America's First Civilization." Thames & Hudson, New York, NY. 2004. ISBN: 978-0-5000211-9-4. pp. 11-12, 46, 96-97, 111, 182.

4. Pool, Christopher A. "Olmec Archaeology and Early Mesoamerica." Cambridge University Press, Cambridge, United Kingdom. 2007. ISBN: 978-0-5217888-2-3. pp. 5, 110, 251.

5. Ibid. pp. 7, 105-106, 117-118.

6. Diehl, Richard A. "The Olmecs: America's First Civilization." Thames & Hudson, New York, NY. 2004. ISBN: 978-0-5000211-9-4. pp. 108-109, 111-112, 146, 164.
7. Adams, Richard E.W.; MacLeod, Murdo J. "The Cambridge History of the Native Peoples of the Americas: Volume II, Mesoamerica, Part 1." Cambridge University Press, Cambridge, United Kingdom. 2000. ISBN: 0-521-35165-0. pp. 193-194.
8. Coe, Michael D. "Mexico: From the Olmecs to the Aztecs, 5th edition, revised & enlarged." Thames & Hudson, London, United Kingdom. 2002. ISBN: 978-0-5002834-6-2. pp. 4, 7, 9.
9. Diehl, Richard A. "The Olmecs: America's First Civilization." Thames & Hudson, New York, NY. 2004. ISBN: 978-0-5000211-9-4. pp. 11-12, 46, 96-97, 111, 182.
10. Hancock, Graham. "Finger-Prints of the Gods." Three Rivers Press, New York, NY. 1995. ISBN: 0-517-88729-0. pp. 121-139.
11. von-Bruening, R.J.; "UNLOCKING THE DREAM VISION: The secret history of creation." R.J. VON-BRUENING, USA. 2018. ISBN: 978-1-7329096-1-8.
12. Pauketat, Timothy R. "The Oxford Handbook of North American Archaeology." Oxford University Press, Oxford, United Kingdom. 2012. ISBN: 978-0-19-538011-8. pp. 86.
13. Cordell, Linda S.; Lightfoot, Kent.; McManamon, Francis.; Milner, George. "Archaeology in America: An Encyclopedia, Volumes 1, 2, 3, 4." ABC-CLIO, LLC., Santa Barbara, CA. 2008. pp. 3
14. Wells, Spencer.; Read, Mark. "The Journey of Man – A Genetic Odyssey. Random House Books, New York, NY. 2009. ISBN: 978-0-8129-7146-0. pp. 138-140.
15. Jones, Peter N. "American Indian MtDNA, Y Chromosome Genetic Data, and the Peopling of North America." Bauu Institute, Boulder, Colorado. 2002. ISBN: 978-0-9721349-1-0. pp. 4.
16. Zakharov, I.A.; "Mitochondrial DNA variation in the aboriginal populustion of the Altai-Baikal region: implication for the genetic history of North Asia and America." Annals of the New York Academy of Sciences, vol. 1011, issue 1, pp. 21-35 Bibcode: 2004NYASA1011...21Z. doi:10.1196/annals.1293.003. PMID 15126280.
17. Schurr, Theodore G. (2000). "Mitochondrial DNA and the Peopling of the New World" American Scientist. American Scientist Online May–June 2000 (3): 246. Bibcode: 2000AmSci..88..246S. doi:10.1511/2000.3.246.

18. Starikovskaya, Elena B., Sukernik, Rem I., Derbeneva, Olga A., Volodko, Natalia A., Ruiz-Pesini, Eduardo, Torroni, Antonio, Brown, Michael D., Lott, Marie T., Hosseini, Seyed H., Huoponen, Kirsi, and Wallace, Douglas C. (January 2005). "Mitochondrial DNA diversity in indigenous populations of the southern extent of Siberia, and the origins of Native American haplogroups". Ann. Hum. Genet. 69 (Pt 1): 67–89. doi:10.1046/j.1529-8817.2003.00127.x. PMC 3905771. PMID 15638829.

19. Pohl, Mary; Kevin O. Pope; Christopher von Nagy (2002). "Olmec Origins of Mesoamerican Writing". Science. 298 (5600): 1984–1987. Bibcode:2002Sci...298.1984P. doi:10.1126/science.1078474. PMID 12471256.

20. Pool, Christopher A. "Olmec Archaeology and Early Mesoamerica. Cambridge World Archaeology." Cambridge University Press, Cambridge, United Kingdom. 2007. ISBN 978-0-521-78882-3. pp. 26-27, 135, 150-151, 157, 161-162.

21. Diehl, Richard A. "The Olmecs: America's First Civilization." Thames & Hudson, New York, NY. 2004. ISBN: 978-0-5000211-9-4. Pp. 9-25, 27, 58-89, 82.

22. Roberts, J.M., "History of the World." Oxford University Press, New York, NY. 1993. ISBN: 0-19-521043-3. pp. 71-75, 85-88.

23. Ibid. pp. 32, 76-85.

24. Ibid. pp. 71-75.

25. Ibid. pp. 76-85.

26. Ibid. pp. 71-88.

27. Ibid. pp. 85-88.

28. Ibid. pp. 76-85.

29. Ibid.

30. Ibid.

31. Smith, William. "Dictionary of Greek and Roman Biography and Mythology, Volume I." Little, Brown and Company, Boston, Massachusetts. 1867.

32. Ibid.

33. Fortenrose, Joseph. "Python. A Study of Delphic Myth and Its Origins." Biblo &Tannen, New York, NY. 1974. ISBN: 0-8196-0285-X.

34. Roberts, J.M., "History of the World." Oxford University Press, New York, NY. 1993. ISBN: 0-19-521043-3. pp. 76-88.

35. Ibid.

36. Ibid.

37. Ibid.

38. Ibid.

39. Ibid. pp. 71-75.

40. Garcia, Brittany. "Romulus and Remus." Ancient History Encyclopedia. Last modified April 18, 2018. Accessed June 20, 2020. https://www.ancient.eu/Romulus_and_Remus/.

41. Ibid.

42. "Romulus and Remus; Roman Mythology." Encyclopaedia Britannica. Accessed June 20, 2020. https://www.britannica.com/biography/Romulus-and-Remus.

43. Dhwty. "The Lupercal Cave: A Refuge for Romulus and Remus and the Roman Festival of Lupercalia." Ancient Origins. Last modified on November 14, 2015. Accessed June 20, 2020. https://www.ancient-origins.net/myths-legends/lupercal-cave-refuge-romulus-and-remus-and-roman-festival-lupercalia-004538.

44. Whelan, Ed. "Experts May Have Identified the Long-Lost Tome of Romulus, Founder of Rome." Ancient Origins. Last modified February 5, 2019. Accessed June 20, 2020. https://www.ancient-origins.net/news-history-archaeology/romulus-tomb-0011485.

45. Garcia, Brittany. "Romulus and Remus." Ancient History Encyclopedia. Last modified April 18, 2018. Accessed June 20, 2020. https://www.ancient.eu/Romulus_and_Remus/.

46. Ibid.

47. Childs, M.L.; "Romulus and Remus, Osiris and Moses: Are the Storytelling Similarities a Mere Coincidence?" Ancient Origins. Last modified on September 5, 2018. Accessed June 20, 2020. https://www.ancient-origins.net/history-important-events/romulus-remus-story-0010653.

48. Wiseman, Timothy Peter. "Remus, A Roman Myth." Cambridge University Press, Cambridge, United Kingdom. 1995. ISBN: 0-521-48366-2.

49. Kock, John. "Celtic Culture: A Historical Encyclopedia. Volume I, A-Celti." ABC-CLIO, LLC., Santa Barbara, CA. 2006. ISBN: 1-85109-440-7. pp. 396.

50. Maier, Bernard. "Dictionary of Celtic Religion and Culture." Illustrated, reprint by Boydell & Brewer, Woodbridge, United Kingdom. 1997. ISBN: 0-851-15660-6. pp. 69.

51. Roberts, J.M., "History of the World." Oxford University Press, New York, NY. 1993. ISBN: 0-19-521043-3. pp. 43-44.

52. Hamilton, Edith. "Mythology, Timeless Tales of Gods and Heroes." Grand Central Publishing, New York, NY. 1999. (Originally published by Little, Brown, and Company, 1942). pp. 313-318.

53. Ibid. pp. 18, 48.
54. Roberts, J.M., "History of the World." Oxford University Press, New York, NY. 1993. ISBN: 0-19-521043-3. pp. 42-43.
55. Patterson, Don. "Journey to Xibalba: A Life in Archaeology." University of New Mexico Press, Albuquerque, New Mexico. 2007. ISBN: 978-0-8263429-2-8. pp. 75.
56. Christenson, Allen J. "Popol Vuh: The Sacred Book of the Maya. The Great Classic of Central American Spirituality, Translated from the Original Maya Text." University of Oklahoma Press, Norman, Oklahoma. 1950. ISBN: 978-0806138398.
57. Recinos, Adrian; Goetz, Delia; Morley, S.G.; "Popol Vuh: Sacred Book of the Ancient Quiche Maya. Civilization of American Indian. 13th Printing edition. Book 29." University of Oklahoma Press, Norman, Oklahoma. 1991. ISBN: 0-8061-2266-8.
58. Ibid.
59. Ibid.
60. Ibid.
61. Anthony, David W. "The Horse, the Wheel, and Language: How Bronze-Age Riders from the Eurasian Steppes Shaped the Modern World." Princeton University Press, Princeton, New Jersey. 2007. ISBN 978-1-40-083110-4. pp. 78-79.
62. West, Martin L. (2007). "Indo-European Poetry and Myth." Oxford University Press, Oxford, England. 2007. ISBN 978-0-19-928075-9. pp. 274, 279.
63. Anthony, David W. "The Horse, the Wheel, and Language: How Bronze-Age Riders from the Eurasian Steppes Shaped the Modern World." Princeton University Press, Princeton, New Jersey. 2007. ISBN 978-1-40-083110-4. pp. 78-79.
64. Mallory, James P.; Adams, Douglas Q. (2006). "The Oxford Introduction to Proto-Indo-European and the Proto-Indo-European World." Oxford University Press, Oxford, England. 2006. ISBN 978-0-19-929668-2. pp. 129, 408-410, 431.
65. Ibid. pp. 203.
66. West, Martin L. (2007). "Indo-European Poetry and Myth." Oxford University Press, Oxford, England. 2007. ISBN 978-0-19-928075-9. pp. 266, 269.
67. Hamilton, Edith. "Mythology: Timeless Tales of Gods and Heroes." Grand Central Publishing, New York, NY. 1999. (Originally published by Little, Brown, and Company, 1942). pp. 18, 48.

Chapter 7

1. Book of Judges, 21:25.
2. Parpola, Asko. "The Roots of Hinduism: The Early Aryans and The Indus Civilization." Oxford University Press, Oxford, New York, NY. 2015. ISBN: 978-0-19022693-0.
3. Gombrich, Richard. "Theravada Buddhism: A Social History from Ancient Benares to Modern Colombo." Routledge Kegan Paul Ltd., New York, NY. 2006. ISBN: 978-1-134-90352-8. pp. 24-25.
4. Liverani, Mario. "The Ancient Near East: History, Society and Economy." Taylor & Francis Group, Milton Park, England. 2013. ISBN 978-1-134-75091-7. Pp. 170-171.
5. Mallory, J.P.; Adams, D.Q.; "The Oxford Introduction to Proto-Indo-European and Proto-Indo-European World." Oxford University Press, New York, NY. 2006. ISBN: 0-19-928791-0.
6. Anthony, David W. "The Horse, The Wheel and Language. How Bronze-Age Riders From the Eurasian Steppes Shaped The Modern World." Princeton University Press, Princeton, New Jersey. 2007. ISBN: 978-0-691-05887-0. pp. 336.
7. Adams, Douglas, Q.; Mallory, J.P.; "The Oxford Introduction to Proto-Indo-European and the Proto-Indo-European World." Oxford University Press, New York, NY. 2006. ISBN: 978-0-19-929668-2. Pp. 284-285.
8. Fortson, Benjamin W. "Indo-European Language and Culture." Blackwell Publishing, Hoboken, New Jersey. 2004. ISBN 1-4051-0316-7. pp. 17-19.
9. Anthony, David W. "The Horse, The Wheel and Language: How Bronze-Age Riders From the Eurasian Steppes Shaped The Modern World." Princeton University Press, Princeton, New Jersey. 2007. ISBN: 978-0-691-05887-0. pp. 134-136.
10. Adams, Douglas Q.; Mallory, J.P., "Encyclopedia of Indo-European Culture." Fitzroy Dearborn Publishing, Chicago, Illinois. 1997. ISBN: 978-1-8849649-8-5. pp. 452-453.
11. Fortson, Benjamin W. "Indo-European Language and Culture." Blackwell Publishing, Hoboken, New Jersey. 2004. ISBN 1-4051-0316-7. pp. 25-26.
12. Adams, Douglas, Q.; Mallory, J.P.; "The Oxford Introduction to Proto-Indo-European and the Proto-Indo-European World." Oxford University Press, New York, NY. 2006. ISBN: 978-0-19-929668-2. pp. 437.

13. Anthony, David W. "The Horse, The Wheel and Language: How Bronze-Age Riders From the Eurasian Steppes Shaped The Modern World." Princeton University Press, Princeton, New Jersey. 2007. ISBN: 978-0-691-05887-0. pp. 134-136.

14. Adams, Douglas Q.; Mallory, J.P., "Encyclopedia of Indo-European Culture." Fitzroy Dearborn Publishing, Chicago, Illinois. 1997. ISBN: 978-1-8849649-8-5. pp. 452-453.

15. Fortson, Benjamin W. "Indo-European Language and Culture." Blackwell Publishing, Hoboken, New Jersey. 2004. ISBN 1-4051-0316-7. pp. 25-26.

16. Adams, Douglas, Q.; Mallory, J.P.; "The Oxford Introduction to Proto-Indo-European and the Proto-Indo-European World." Oxford University Press, New York, NY. 2006. ISBN: 978-0-19-929668-2. pp. 437.

17. Anthony, David W. "The Horse, The Wheel and Language. How Bronze-Age Riders From the Eurasian Steppes Shaped The Modern World." Princeton University Press, Princeton, New Jersey. 2007. ISBN: 978-0-691-05887-0.

18. Lincoln, Bruce. "The Indo-European Cattle-Raiding Myth." History of Religions. University of Chicago Press, Chicago, Illinois. 1976. 16 (1): 42–65. doi:10.1086/462755. ISSN: 0018-2710. JSTOR: 1062296.

19. Adams, Douglas, Q.; Mallory, J.P.; "The Oxford Introduction to Proto-Indo-European and the Proto-Indo-European World." Oxford University Press, New York, NY. 2006. ISBN: 978-0-19-929668-2. pp. 432.

20. West, Martin L. "Indo-European Poetry and Myth." Oxford, England: Oxford University Press, Oxford, England. 2007. ISBN 978-0-19-928075-9. pp. 279.

21. Adams, Douglas Q.; Mallory, J.P., "Encyclopedia of Indo-European Culture." Fitzroy Dearborn Publishing, Chicago, Illinois. 1997. ISBN: 978-1-8849649-8-5. pp. 432.

22. West, Martin L. "Indo-European Poetry and Myth." Oxford, England: Oxford University Press, Oxford, England. 2007. ISBN 978-0-19-928075-9. pp. 185-191.

23. Ibid. pp. 166-168, 171.

24. Adams, Douglas, Q.; Mallory, J.P.; "The Oxford Introduction to Proto-Indo-European and the Proto-Indo-European World." Oxford University Press, New York, NY. 2006. ISBN: 978-0-19-929668-2. pp. 410, 427, 432.

25. West, Martin L. "Indo-European Poetry and Myth." Oxford, England: Oxford University Press, Oxford, England. 2007. ISBN 978-0-19-928075-9. pp. 217-227.

26. Adams, Douglas Q.; Mallory, J.P., "Encyclopedia of Indo-European Culture." Fitzroy Dearborn Publishing, Chicago, Illinois. 1997. ISBN: 978-1-8849649-8-5. pp. 230-231.
27. Fortson, Benjamin W. "Indo-European Language and Culture." Blackwell Publishing, Hoboken, New Jersey. 2004. ISBN 1-4051-0316-7. pp. 23.
28. Adams, Douglas, Q.; Mallory, J.P.; "The Oxford Introduction to Proto-Indo-European and the Proto-Indo-European World." Oxford University Press, New York, NY. 2006. ISBN: 978-0-19-929668-2. pp. 409, 431-432.
29. Burkert, Walter. "Greek Religion.": Harvard University Press. Cambridge, Massachusetts. 1985. ISBN 0-674-36281-0. pp. 17.
30. West, Martin L. "Indo-European Poetry and Myth." Oxford, England: Oxford University Press, Oxford, England. 2007. ISBN 978-0-19-928075-9. pp. 178-182, 191.
31. Ibid.
32. Adams, Douglas Q.; Mallory, J.P., "Encyclopedia of Indo-European Culture." Fitzroy Dearborn Publishing, Chicago, Illinois. 1997. ISBN: 978-1-8849649-8-5. pp. 174.
33. Roberts, J.M., "History of the World." Oxford University Press, New York, NY. 1993. ISBN: 0-19-521043-3. pp. 38, 48-49, 51, 92-93.
34. Gershevitch, I.; "The Cambridge History of Iran." Cambridge University Press, Cambridge, United Kingdom. 1985. ISBN: 978-0-521-20091-2. pp. 75.
35. Alice-Mary Maffry Talbot, Denis F. Sullivan. "The History of Leo the Deacon: Byzantine Military Expansion in the Tenth Century." Dumbarton Oaks Research Library and Collection, Washington D.C.; 2005. ISBN: 9780884023241. pp, 204.
36. Boyce, Mary (1982). "A History of Zoroastrianism: Volume II." E.J. Brill, Leiden, The Netherlands. 1982. ISBN: 90-04-06506-7.
37. Media, ancient region, Iran; Encyclopaedia Britannica Online. Accessed June 18, 2020. https://www.britannica.com/biography/Harpagus.
38. Herodotus. "The Histories: Book 1." Chapter. 95-130. 1.101. A.D. Godley, Ed.
39. Ellis, Edward Sylvester; Horne, Charles F. "The story of the greatest nations; a comprehensive history, extending from the earliest times to the present, founded on the most modern authorities, and including chronological summaries and pronouncing vocabularies for each nation; and the world's famous events, told in a series of brief sketches forming a single continuous story of history and illumined by a complete series of notable illustrations

from the great historic paintings of all lands." Francis R. Niglutsch, New York, NY. 1913. Republished by University of California Libraries.

40. Cameron, George G. "The History of Early Iran." University of Chicago Press, Chicago, Illinois. 1938.

41. Edwards, Stephen. Iorwerth, Eiddon. "The Cambridge Ancient History, Volume 4." Cambridge University Press, Cambridge, England. 1970. ISBN: 0-521-22804-2.

42. Kent, Ronald Grubb. "Old Persian: Grammar, Text, Glossary (in Persian). translated into Persian by S. Oryan." 2005. ISBN 964-421-045-X. pp. 406.

43. "Phraortes: king of Media." Encyclopaedia Britannica. Accessed July 4,2020, https://www.britannica.com/biography/Phraortes.

44. Herodotus (425 BC). "The Histories." [Histories 1.103]; (2008 ed.). Oxford University Press.

45. Ibid.

46. Gershevitch, I.; Fisher, William Bayne; Avery, Peter; Boyle, John Andrew; Frye, Richard Nelson; Yarshater, Ehsan; Jackson, Peter; Melville, Charles Peter; Lockhart, Laurence; Hambly, Gavin. "The Cambridge History of Iran." Cambridge University Press, Cambridge, England. 1985. ISBN: 9780521200912. pp. 139.

47. Herodotus (425 BC). "The Histories." [Histories 1.73-74]; (2008 ed.). Oxford University Press.

48. Dalley, Stephanie. "The Mystery of the Hanging Garden of Babylon: an elusive World Wonder traced." Oxford University Press, New York, NY. 2013. ISBN: 978-0-19-966226-5.

49. Herodotus (425 BC). "The Histories." [Histories 1.103]; (2008 ed.). Oxford University Press.

50. Roberts, J.M., "History of the World." Oxford University Press, New York, NY. 1993. ISBN: 0-19-521043-3. pp. 93, 129.

51. Grousset, Rene. "The Empire of the Steppes: A History of Central Asia." Rutgers University Press, New Brunswick, New Jersey. 1970. ISBN 0-8135-1304-9. pp. 8-9.

52. Gershevitch, Ilya. "The Cambridge history of Iran: The Median and Achaemenian period." Cambridge University Press, Cambridge, England. 1985. ISBN: 0-521-20091-1.

53. "Takht-e Soleyman." UNESCO: World Heritage Center. Last modified June 15, 2020. http://whc.unesco.org/en/list/1077.

54. Herodotus (425 BC). The Histories [Histories i.110]; (2008 ed.). Oxford University Press.

55. Roberts, J.M., "History of the World." Oxford University Press, New York, NY. 1993. ISBN: 0-19-521043-3. pp. 93, 129.

56. Ibid.

57. "Cyropaedia: The Education of Cyrus." by Xenophon.

58. Kuhrt, Amélie. "Babylonia from Cyrus to Xerxes: The Cambridge Ancient History: Persia, Greece, and the Western Mediterranean, C. 525-479 B.C." pp. 112-138. Cambridge University Press, Cambridge, England. 1988. ISBN: 0-521-22804-2. pp. 112-138.

59. Ibid.

60. Huff, Dietrich. "TAKT-e SOLAYMĀN." Encyclopædia Iranica Foundation, Inc. Last modified July 20, 2002. Accessed June 15, 2020. http://www.iranicaonline.org/articles/takt-e-solayman.

61. "Takht-e Soleyman." UNESCO: World Heritage Center. Accessed June 15, 2020. http://whc.unesco.org/en/list/1077.

62. dhwty "The Ancient Site of Takht-e Soleyman: Iran's Throne of King Solomon." Ancient Origins. Last modified May 24, 2015. Accessed June 15, 2020. https://www.ancient-origins.net/ancient-places-asia/ancient-site-takht-e-soleyman-iran-s-throne-king-solomon-003115.

63. Ibid.

64. Huff, Dietrich. "The Ilkhanid Palace at Takht-I Suleyman: Excavation Results". Edited by Linda Komaroff, in "Beyond the Legacy of Genghis Khan." BRILL Publishing, Leiden, Netherlands. 2006. ISBN: 978-90-04-15083-6. pp. 94-110.

65. Huff, Dietrich. "TAKT-e SOLAYMĀN." Encyclopædia Iranica Foundation, Inc. Last modified July 20, 2002. Accessed June 15, 2020. http://www.iranicaonline.org/articles/takt-e-solayman.

66. Ibid.

67. dhwty "The Ancient Site of Takht-e Soleyman: Iran's Throne of King Solomon." Ancient Origins. Last modified May 24, 2015. Accessed June 15, 2020. https://www.ancient-origins.net/ancient-places-asia/ancient-site-takht-e-soleyman-iran-s-throne-king-solomon-003115.

68. Boyce, Mary. "A History of Zoroastrianism: Volume I: The Early Period." E.J. BRILL, Leiden, Netherlands. 1975, reprint 1996. ISBN: 90-04-10474-7. pp. 2-26.

69. West, Martin Litchfield. "The Hymns of Zoroaster: A New Translation of the Most Ancient Sacred Texts of Iran." I.B. Tauris, London, United Kingdom. 2010. ISBN: 978-0-85773-156-2. pp. 4-10.

70. Boyce, Mary. Grenet, Frantz. Beck, Roger. "A History of Zoroastrianism, Zoroastrianism under Macedonian and Roman Rule. Series: Handbook of

Oriental Studies. Section 1 The Near and Middle East, Volume: 8/3." E.J. BRILL, Leiden, Netherlands. 1991. ISBN: 978-90-04-29391-5. pp. 491-565.

71. Ibid.

72. Boyce, Mary. "A History of Zoroastrianism: Volume I: The Early Period." E.J. BRILL, Leiden, Netherlands. 1975, reprint 1996. ISBN: 90-04-10474-7. pp. 2-26.

73. Boyce, Mary. Grenet, Frantz. Beck, Roger. "A History of Zoroastrianism, Zoroastrianism under Macedonian and Roman Rule. Series: Handbook of Oriental Studies. Section 1 The Near and Middle East, Volume: 8/3." E.J. BRILL, Leiden, Netherlands. 1991. ISBN: 978-90-04-29391-5. pp. 491-565.

74. Boyce, Mary. "A History of Zoroastrianism: Volume I: The Early Period." E.J. BRILL, Leiden, Netherlands. 1975, reprint 1996. ISBN: 90-04-10474-7. pp. 2-26, 68, 182-184, 187, 190–192, 621.

75. Ibid.

76. Mallory, J. P.; Adams, Douglas Q. "Encyclopedia of Indo-European Culture." Fitzroy Dearborn Publishers, Chicago, Illinois. 1997. ISBN 978-1-884964-98-5 pp. 310–311, 653.

77. West, Martin Litchfield. "The Hymns of Zoroaster: A New Translation of the Most Ancient Sacred Texts of Iran." I.B.Tauris, London, United Kingdom. 2010. ISBN: 978-0-85773-156-2. pp. 4-10, 17-20, 29, 31.

78. Boyce, Mary. Grenet, Frantz. Beck, Roger. "A History of Zoroastrianism, Zoroastrianism under Macedonian and Roman Rule. Series: Handbook of Oriental Studies. Section 1 The Near and Middle East, Volume: 8/3." E.J. BRILL, Leiden, Netherlands. 1991. ISBN: 978-90-04-29391-5. pp. 491-565.

79. Boyce, Mary. "A History of Zoroastrianism: Volume I: The Early Period." E.J. BRILL, Leiden, Netherlands. 1975, reprint 1996. ISBN: 90-04-10474-7. pp. 2-26, 68, 182-184, 187, 190–192, 621.

80. Ibid.

81. Jackson, A. V. Williams (1899), "Zoroaster, the prophet of ancient Iran." Published for the Columbia University Press by the Macmillan Co., New York, NY. 1899 p. 162.

82. Mallory, J. P.; Adams, Douglas Q. "Encyclopedia of Indo-European Culture." Fitzroy Dearborn Publishers, Chicago, Illinois. 1997. ISBN 978-1-884964-98-5 pp. 310–311, 653.

83. Boyce, Mary (1982), "A History of Zoroastrianism: Volume II: Under the Achaemenians." E.J. BRILL, Leiden, Netherlands. 1982. ISBN: 90-04-06506-7 pp. 68, 261.

84. Boyce, Mary. Grenet, Frantz. Beck, Roger. "A History of Zoroastrianism, Zoroastrianism under Macedonian and Roman Rule. Series: Handbook of Oriental Studies. Section 1 The Near and Middle East, Volume: 8/3." E.J. BRILL, Leiden, Netherlands. 1991. ISBN: 978-90-04-29391-5. pp. 491-565.

Chapter 8

1. Boyce, Mary. Journal Article "On the Zoroastrian Temple Cult of Fire." Journal of the American Oriental Society, Journal of the American Oriental Society, Vol. 95, No. 3. July-September 1975. pp. 454-465. DOI: 10.2307/599356. JSTOR: 599356, https://www.jstor.org/stable/599356.

2. Woodard, Roger D. "The Ancient Languages of Asia and the Americas." Cambridge University Press, Cambridge, United Kingdom. 2008, ISBN 0-521-68494-3, p. 123.

3. Herodotus. "The Histories." [Histories 131, Vol. I]; (2008 ed.). Oxford University Press.

4. Boyce, Mary. "Zoroastrians: Their Religious Beliefs and Practices." Routledge, Taylor & Francis Group, Milton Park, United Kingdom. 2001. ISBN 978-0-415-23902-8.

5. Drower, Elizabeth S. Journal Article "The Role of Fire in Parsi Ritual." Journal of the Royal Anthropological Institute of Great Britain and Ireland., Royal Anthropological Institute. Vol 74, No. 1/2: 1944. Pp. 75–89, DOI: 10.2307/2844296. https://www.jstor.org/stable/2844296.

6. Boyce, Mary. "Zoroastrians: Their Religious Beliefs and Practices." Routledge, Taylor & Francis Group, Milton Park, United Kingdom. 2001. ISBN 978-0-415-23902-8.

7. Jackson, A. V. Williams. "The Location of the Farnbāg Fire, the Most Ancient of the Zoroastrian Fires". Journal of the American Oriental Society. Vol. 41. 1921. pp. 81–106. doi:10.2307/593711. ISSN 0003-0279. JSTOR 593711. https://www.jstor.org/stable/593711.

8. Drower, Elizabeth S. Journal Article "The Role of Fire in Parsi Ritual." Journal of the Royal Anthropological Institute of Great Britain and Ireland., Royal Anthropological Institute. Vol 74, No. 1/2: 1944. Pp. 75–89, DOI: 10.2307/2844296. https://www.jstor.org/stable/2844296.

9. Boyce, Mary. "A History of Zoroastrianism: Volume I: The Early Period." E.J. BRILL, Leiden, Netherlands. 1975, reprint 1996. ISBN: 90-04-10474-7. pp. 2-26, 68, 182-184, 187, 190–192, 621.

10. Boyce, Mary (1982), "A History of Zoroastrianism: Volume II: Under the Achaemenians." E.J. BRILL, Leiden, Netherlands. 1982. ISBN: 90-04-06506-7.

11. Roberts, J.M., "History of the World." Oxford University Press, New York. 1993. ISBN: 0-19-521043-3. pp. 105-117.

12. Khanbolouki, Mahbod. "Emergence of Zoroastrianism and The Legacy of Zarathustra." Ancient Origins. Last modified May 18, 2015. Accessed June 12, 2020. https://www.ancient-origins.net/history-famous-people/emergence-zoroastrianism-and-legacy-zarathushtra-003078.

13. Huff, Dietrich. "TAḴT-e SOLAYMĀN." Encyclopædia Iranica Foundation, Inc. Last modified July 20, 2002. Accessed June 22, 2020. http://www.iranicaonline.org/articles/takt-e-solayman.

14. Jackson, A. V. Williams. "The Location of the Farnbāg Fire, the Most Ancient of the Zoroastrian Fires". Journal of the American Oriental Society. Vol. 41. 1921. pp. 81–106. doi:10.2307/593711. ISSN 0003-0279. JSTOR 593711. https://www.jstor.org/stable/593711.

15. Drower, Elizabeth S. Journal Article "The Role of Fire in Parsi Ritual." Journal of the Royal Anthropological Institute of Great Britain and Ireland., Royal Anthropological Institute. Vol 74, No. 1/2: 1944. Pp. 75–89, DOI: 10.2307/2844296. https://www.jstor.org/stable/2844296.

16. Boyce, Mary. Journal Article "On the Zoroastrian Temple Cult of Fire." Journal of the American Oriental Society, Journal of the American Oriental Society, Vol. 95, No. 3. July-September 1975. pp. 454-465. DOI: 10.2307/599356. JSTOR: 599356, https://www.jstor.org/stable/599356.

17. Boyce, Mary. "Zoroastrians: Their Religious Beliefs and Practices." Routledge, Taylor & Francis Group, Milton Park, United Kingdom. 2001. ISBN 978-0-415-23902-8.

18. Brandon, S.G.F.; "Dictionary of Comparative Religion" Weidenfeld & Nicolson London, United Kingdom. 1970. ISBN: 0-29-700044-6. pp. 573: "Shekhinah."

19. Dan, Joseph. "Kabbalah: A Very Short Introduction; First Edition." Oxford University Press, Oxford, United Kingdom. 2006. ISBN: 978-0-19530034-5. pp. 46.

20. Kohler, Kaufmann. Blau, Ludwig. "SHEKINAH (lit. "the dwelling")." The unedited full-text of the 1906 Jewish Encyclopedia.

JewishEncyclopedia.com. Last modified June 15, 2020. http://www.jewishencyclopedia.com/articles/13537-shekinah.

21. Roberts, J.M., "History of the World." Oxford University Press, New York. 1993. ISBN: 0-19-521043-3. pp. 94, 129-131.

22. Ibid.

Chapter 9

1. Adams, Douglas, Q.; Mallory, J.P.; "The Oxford Introduction to Proto-Indo-European and the Proto-Indo-European World." Oxford University Press, New York, NY. 2006. ISBN: 978-0-19-929668-2. pp. 436-437.

2. Fortson, Benjamin W. "Indo-European Language and Culture." Blackwell Publishing, Hoboken, New Jersey. 2004. ISBN 1-4051-0316-7. pp. 26-27.

3. West, Martin L. "Indo-European Poetry and Myth." Oxford, England: Oxford University Press, Oxford, England. 2007. ISBN 978-0-19-928075-9. pp. 255-259, 460.

4. Watkins, Calvert. "How to Kill a Dragon: Aspects of Indo-European Poetics." London: Oxford University Press, London, England. 1995. ISBN: 978-0-19-514413-0. pp. 297-301, 324-330, 374-383, 414-441, 460-464.

5. Ibid.

6. West, Martin L. "Indo-European Poetry and Myth." Oxford, England: Oxford University Press, Oxford, England. 2007. ISBN 978-0-19-928075-9. pp. 255-259, 460.

7. von-Bruening, R.J.; "UNLOCKING THE DREAM VISION: The secret history of creation." R.J. VON-BRUENING, USA. 2018. ISBN: 978-1-7329096-1-8. pp. 29-36.

8. Hamilton, Edith. "Mythology: Timeless Tales of Gods and Heroes." Grand Central Publishing, New York, NY. 1999. (Originally published by Little, Brown, and Company, 1942). pp. 76-87.

9. Ibid.

10. Ibid.

11. Ibid.

12. Ibid.

13. Ibid.

14. Ibid.

15. Ibid.

16. Pritchard, James, B.; "Ancient Near Eastern texts relating to the Old Testament: Third edition with supplement." Princeton University Press, Princeton, New Jersey. 1969. ISBN: 978-0-691-03503-1.

17. Heidel, Alexander. "The Babylonian Genesis; 2nd ed." University of Chicago Press, Chicago, Illinois. 1951. (Originally published in 1942). ISBN: 0-226-32399-4. pp. 1-3, 61–81.

18. Mark, Joshua J. "Enuma Elish - The Babylonian Epic of Creation - Full Text." Ancient History Encyclopedia. Last modified May 04, 2018. Accessed July 15, 2020. https://www.ancient.eu/article/225/.

19. King, L. W.; "The Seven Tablets of Creation: The Babylonian and Assyrian Legends concerning the creation of the world and of mankind. Luzac's Semitic Text and Translation Series; English Translations." Luzac and Company, London, England. 1902. Introduction, v.1, preface; pp. 116-155, 219, XXVI–XXX, XLIX, LIV, CXIII, LXVII, LXIII, Appendix IV.

20. Ibid.

21. Ibid.

22. Ibid.

23. Ibid.

24. Ibid.

25. Ibid.

26. von-Bruening, R.J.; "UNLOCKING THE DREAM VISION: The secret history of creation." R.J. VON-BRUENING, USA. 2018. ISBN: 978-1-7329096-1-8. pp. 105-108.

27. Brown, Willian P.; "The Ethos of the Cosmos: The Genesis of Moral Imagination in the Bible." Willian B. Eerdmans Publishing, Grand Rapids, Michigan. Cambridge, United Kingdom. 1999. ISBN: 0-8028-4539-8. pp. 140.

28. Millard, A.R.; "New Babylonian 'Genesis' Story." The Tyndale Biblical Archeology Lecture. Tyndale Bulletin 18 (1967) 3-8, Cambridge, England. pp. 8.

29. von-Bruening, R.J.; "UNLOCKING THE DREAM VISION: The secret history of creation." R.J. VON-BRUENING, USA. 2018. ISBN: 978-1-7329096-1-8. pp. 29-119.

30. Hamilton, Edith. "Mythology: Timeless Tales of Gods and Heroes." Grand Central Publishing, New York, NY. 1999. (Originally published by Little, Brown, and Company, 1942). pp. 40, 132, 332.

31. Edmonds III, Radcliffe G. "Myths of the Underworld Journey: Plato, Aristophanes, and the 'Orphic' Gold Tablets" Cambridge University Press, Cambridge, United Kingdom. 2004. ISBN: 978-1-13945600-5. p. 9.

32. Mills, Jon. "Underworlds: Philosophies of the Unconscious from Psychoanalysis to Metaphysics." Taylor & Francis, Park Drive, United Kingdom. 2014. ISBN: 978-13-1774905-9. pp. 1.

33. Smith, Evans Lansing. "The Descent to the Underworld in Literature, Painting, and Film, 1895-1950." Edwin Mellen Press, New York, NY. 2001. ISBN: 978-0-7734749-2-5. pp. 7, 257.

34. Wallace, Isabelle L; Hirsh, Jennie. "Contemporary Art and Classical Myth" Ashgate Publishing, Ltd., Farnham, United Kingdom. 2011. ISBN: 978-0-7546697-4-6. pp. 295.

35. Hamilton, Edith. "Mythology: Timeless Tales of Gods and Heroes." Grand Central Publishing, New York, NY. 1999. (Originally published by Little, Brown, and Company, 1942). pp. 39, 309, 456-457, 461.

36. Ibid.

37. Edmonds III, Radcliffe G. "Myths of the Underworld Journey: Plato, Aristophanes, and the 'Orphic' Gold Tablets" Cambridge University Press, Cambridge, United Kingdom. 2004. ISBN: 978-1-13945600-5. p. 9-10.

38. Smith, Evans Lansing. "The Descent to the Underworld in Literature, Painting, and Film, 1895-1950." Edwin Mellen Press, New York, NY. 2001. ISBN: 978-0-7734749-2-5. pp. 7, 257.

39. Mandelbaum, Allen. "The Divine Comedy: By Dante Alighieri. Bantam Classic education edition." Bantam Books, New York, NY. 1982. ISBN: 978-0553213393.

40. Ibid.

41. Stringer, Chris. "The status of Homo heidelbergensis (Schoetensack 1908)". Evolutionary Anthropology. 2012. 21 (3): 101–107. doi:10.1002/evan.21311. PMID 22718477. https://pubmed.ncbi.nlm.nih.gov/22718477/.

42. McDermott, Alicia. "DNA Study Suggest Early Neanderthals Had Europe As Their Homebase." Ancient Origins. Last modified June 27, 2019. Accessed July 15, 2020. https://www.ancient-origins.net/news-history-archaeology/neanderthal-dna-0012200.

Chapter 10

1. Rivero, M.E., Tschudi, J.D. "Antigüedades peruanas." Vienna, 1851. (Spanish). Rivero, M.E., von Tschudi, J.J. "Peruvian antiquities." New York, NY. 1853. (English).

2. Ibid.

3. Gontcharov, Igor. "Elongated Skulls in Utero: A Farewell to the Artificial Cranial Deformation Paradigm." Ancient Origins. Last modified January 3, 2015. Accessed August 5, 2020. https://www.ancient-origins.net/unexplained-phenomena/elongated-skulls-utero-farewell-artificial-cranial-deformation-paradigm-002526?nopaging=1.

4. Morton, Samuel George. "Crania Americana; or, A Comparative View of the Skulls of Various Aboriginal Nations of North and South America. To which is Prefixed an Essay on the Varieties of the Human Species." London, England. 1839.

5. Graves, Robert J. "Remarkable Skulls Found in Peru. No.15 of the Dublin Journal of Medical and Chemical Sciences." 1835.

6. Bellamy, P. F. "A brief Account of two Peruvian Mummies in the Museum of the Devon and Cornwall Natural History Society." in 'Annals and Magazine of Natural History'. Vol. X. October 1842.

7. Meigs, J. Aitken. "Catalogue of Human Crania in the Collection of the Academie of Natural Sciences of Philadelphia: Based Upon the Third Edition of Dr. Morton's " Catalogue of Skulls". Philadelphia. 1857.

8. Foerster, Brien. "Hidden Inca Tours: Explore Mankind's Hidden History." Hidden Inca Tours. Accessed August 6, 2020. https://hiddenincatours.com/.

9. Ibid.

10. Swanson, James. "Dictionary of Biblical Languages With Semantic Domains: Hebrew (Old Testament)." Faithlife, LLC., Bellingham, Washington. First edition 1997. Second edition. 2001.

11. Encyclopedia of World Mythology. "Witches and Wizards." Encyclopedia.com. Accessed August 11, 2020. https://www.encyclopedia.com/history/encyclopedias-almanacs-transcripts-and-maps/witches-and-wizards.

www.ingramcontent.com/pod-product-compliance
Lightning Source LLC
LaVergne TN
LVHW051115080426
835510LV00018B/2050